Letters to a Buddhist Jew

Akiva Tatz
David Gottlieb

TARGUM PRESS

Hard cover edition first published 2004
Soft cover edition first published 2005

Copyright © 2004 by A. Tatz and D. Gottlieb
ISBN 1-56871-356-8

Published by:
TARGUM PRESS, INC.
22700 W. Eleven Mile Rd.
Southfield, MI 48034
E-mail: targum@netvision.net.il
Fax: 888-298-9992
www.targum.com

Printing plates by Frank, Jerusalem
Printed in Israel by Chish

Dedicated in memory of

Faige, daughter of **C**haim **I**srael

A Woman of Noble and Selfless Spirit

"King David instructed his son Solomon: 'Know the God of your father.' That lesson is important in our times especially for Jews who have been attracted by foreign cultures while having little acquaintance with their own. It is my hope that this book will correct that lack of knowledge and help restore Jews to their heritage."

The Bostoner Rebbe, Grand Rabbi Levi Y. Horowitz

Contents

Preface

The writing of this book was a spiritual journey unto itself. It was unpredictable, often difficult and sometimes exhilarating. The journey was everything – all inquiry and no destination; and then, there was a book.

Zen Buddhism is leading people to great awakenings and realizations. It led me to a Torah scholar. I could not have predicted any of the events that led to this book, least of all that I would have the honor of sharing authorship with Akiva Tatz. I must thank him for being generous with his time and his wisdom and for being understanding of, and easily able to bridge, the distances and differences between us.

Steve Yastrow and Karyn Kedar are writing companions whose presence and advice has helped me surmount the obstacles I keep throwing in front of myself.

Teachers appear to those who need them, I guess. The Buddhist mentors with whom I've been in contact have been, without exception, generous with their time. These include Liz Hulshizer, Kaaren Wiken, and Diane Martin, my first and most influential teacher.

My Jewish teachers have had the formidable task of awakening me to my Jewish identity. These individuals – Rachel Rosenberg and Rabbis Yehoshua Karsh, Zev Kahn and Sam Fraint – are true teachers in everything they do.

Alan Morinis, through his *mussar* work, has shown me the many ways in which the Jewish character building discipline is intertwined with the study of Torah and with Jewish literacy. His teaching and mentoring are invaluable to me. My *chavruta* partner, Gary Grad, has been endlessly patient and has taught by the example of his discipline and his joy in Jewish learning.

My children Danielle, Rebecca and Gabriel have all taught me well, but my wife Galit is my greatest teacher. To her I owe everything, including, on average, one apology per day. I hope this will suffice for today.

David Gottlieb
Northbrook, Illinois
November, 2004

I am always behind in my correspondence; sometimes far behind. But when I received a letter from a Jew in Chicago asking: *"Do I commit myself fully to Judaism and abandon Zen altogether – the Zen that helped me to awaken spiritually for the first time in my adult life?"* I replied immediately. And when he asked: *"Where can I find the vibrancy, the wisdom and the source of spiritual connection which, for me, Judaism has never held?"* I kept writing.

This book is a record of that correspondence. It is also the record of a relationship – getting to know David over the two years that our writing spans has been a joy. Preparing a book for publication is as good an exercise as any to bring out the rough edges in anyone's character, and he has been a gentleman throughout. All smooth edges, as far as I can tell.

Most modern Jews who have been attracted to Buddhism have no experience of genuine Torah. It is certain that if they had been exposed to its depth, many would have investigated their home territory before emigrating. In writing to David I have tried to explore some of that territory; in publishing our exchange, I hope we shall reveal some of the Torah's depth to her children wandering Eastern roads, or at least those who may find themselves casting an occasional glance over their shoulders.

This book is not a debate between Buddhism and Judaism. It is not even a comparison, although inevitably some comparison has crept in. It is a book about Judaism, written to an honest Jewish searcher, well versed in Buddhist thought and practice, who is seeking his way back. It does not pretend to present Buddhism or critique it; I am not qualified for that kind of exercise, and it is not my interest. My sole aim is to explore Torah and share its fascination with anyone who asks; in this particular instance Buddhism formed the context that framed the questions.

In preparing our correspondence for publication, I invited comment from an Israeli friend. I knew that he had studied Buddhism deeply during and after his studies at Oxford, that he had spent time in the East before embarking on his investment banking career, and that he was currently engrossed in Talmudic study in Jerusalem. In response, he related the following personal incident, which I quote for those who may find it relevant.

"In February 2001, I was invited to attend teachings of the Dalai Lama on suffering and compassion in Bodh Gaya – the place where Gautama was enlightened under the Bodhi tree some 2,500 years ago. There, a close friend of mine, an internationally acclaimed Buddhist activist, arranged for me to have an audience with the Dalai Lama.

I entered his room at sunset following nine hours of intensive teaching. He was sitting cross-legged on a pillow and signalled me to sit beside him. He greeted me with his warm, loving smile and asked me if I was Israeli.

'Yes,' I immediately answered.

'Are you Jewish?' he continued.

'Indeed,' I replied.

He was silent for a couple of minutes and then said: 'You come from the most ancient wisdom... the source... You do not need to travel all the way here to seek the truth... You should return to your country and learn your religion well. Return here if you feel the need, but only after you have done so...'

At the time I was deeply disappointed and kept thinking: 'Have I ventured all the way to Bihar to discover that I should learn the Torah?'"

Everything in these letters derives from classic Torah sources, either directly or through my great teachers. Nothing I have said here is original except the errors.

Without Rabbi Moshe Shapira, who has opened a world of insight to this generation and from whom I have been privileged to learn, I would have very little understanding of Torah indeed. For me and many others, he is the immediate source.

My thanks are due to my wife Suzanne, who makes everything possible with grace and ease; my mother, Mrs Minde Tatz for her meticulous proofing, Annie Gottlieb whose editing added immeasurably, and all who contributed essential components along the way:

Rabbi Danny Kirsch, Director of the Jewish Learning Exchange of London, Rabbi Marcel Bordon, Rabbi Professor David Gottlieb, Rabbi Aubrey Hersh, Simon Blomfield, Rivka Cohen, Bracha Erlanger, Rabbi Danny Fluss, Jake Greenberg, Ilan and Ruth Halberstadt, Karen Joelson, Laurence Kirschel, Stuart Roden, Ariel Kor, Paul Simons, Avron Smith, Tamar Tatz and the staff of Targum Press.

Akiva Tatz
London
November, 2004

Questions

Dear Rabbi Tatz,
I am a Zen Jew struggling to resolve these two identities.

Two Orthodox rabbis here in Chicago, Yehoshua Karsh and Zev Kahn, suggested that you might be able to provide me with some counsel and direction, and after listening to recordings of some of your lectures that Rabbi Kahn has been kind enough to give me, I think they may be right. My wife, my daughters and I have studied with these warm and wise rabbis and they have helped my wife maintain perspective and patience with me and my Zen practice; but her visceral discomfort has now reached the point of the unbearable ("David, your practising Buddhism is a knife in my heart").

It is I who have brought her to this point, and I must make a significant decision: do I commit myself fully to Judaism and abandon Zen altogether – the Zen that helped me to awaken spiritually for the first time in my adult life? And if I do commit to Jewish study and practice, where can I find the vibrancy, the wisdom and the source of spiritual connection which, for me, Judaism has never held?

My wife and I belong to a Conservative synagogue in Chicago's northern suburbs, but for some years I studied meditation at a Zen Buddhist center in nearby Evanston, Illinois. My involvement in the practice became rather intense and I underwent "lay ordination," meaning that I formally accepted the basic Buddhist precepts (quite similar to the Ten Commandments) as a code for living.

My wife was raised with a strong Jewish identity and education; I was not. Consequently, my ability to learn and adapt to the strictures of Conservative Judaism and to learn its language and liturgy initially proved a barrier in my spiritual awareness and religious practice. It was in this context, being drawn to meditation and believing that there really was no such thing as Jewish meditation, that I immersed myself in the study of Buddhism.

However, my Zen practice caused increasing discomfort and friction, not only within myself but between me and my wife. In time, I came to see certain elements of Buddhist meditation as extremely helpful to me personally, but the adoption of Buddhism as a religion to be a source of internal and external division.

I have resumed studying Hebrew and begun to learn to read the Torah in the hope of doing an "adult Bar Mitzva," and am steadily increasing my Jewish literacy.

If you agree, I would like to pose some of the questions that bother me and others who have walked this path. Some of these questions are sharp for me now, others have been sharper in the past, but they all need resolving. I will give you some further personal background if that will be helpful; I shall also suggest some basic Buddhist texts that will help frame these issues more clearly. For a start, I am attaching a reference to a basic work on "The Noble Eightfold Path," and a book by Shunryu Suzuki. Suzuki was a Japanese Buddhist monk who came to San Francisco in the late 1950's; he started the San Francisco Zen Center, now the nation's largest, and was largely responsible for the surge of popularity of Zen Buddhism in America. This book contains excerpts from his lectures (called "dharma talks" in Zen lingo) to his students about approaching Zen, and life, with the clear and open mind of a beginner. These two books would, I think, give you a clear picture of what captivates Westerners, and especially Western Jews, about Buddhist thought and practice.

Wishing you peace and good health,
David Gottlieb.

Dear David,

I am not sure you have come to the right address, but go ahead and send your questions; I shall do my best to answer.

Best wishes,
Akiva Tatz.

Dear Rabbi Tatz,

Thank you for your willingness to help me navigate towards the answers to these questions. As you'll see, they are complaints or objections due partly to my experience and partly to my ignorance.

Here, then, are some 15 questions and observations about Buddhism's "advantages" over Judaism that concern me and often trouble Jews who are involved in the practice of Zen Buddhism.

A JEWISH BUDDHIST'S COMPLAINTS ABOUT JUDAISM AND COMPARISONS OF JUDAISM WITH ZEN

1. GOD

Although Zen Buddhism does not deny the existence of a Divine force at work in the Universe, it does not focus on a God who must be obeyed or, more importantly, believed in. Buddhism focuses on what can be experienced, and although many believe they can experience God... can they, really? The whole concept of building a worship system around a Supreme Being who cares at all about what we do and don't do, and all the "myths" attendant on that belief, is like building a castle to live in and expecting it to float in mid-air.

2. ACCESSIBILITY

Although Buddhism can get very ornate and very intricate, its basic tenets are extremely simple, and it is therefore not only extremely accessible, it's also portable: *that is, it does not conflict with the practice of other religions. You can practise Buddhism and still be a Jew. After all, I'm merely cultivating mindfulness, watching my breath, realizing the interconnectedness of all things and beings, and striving to recognize and uproot the causes of suffering.*

Judaism, on the other hand, is confoundingly inaccessible, and the deeper one tries to go, the denser the thicket of laws, and texts, and beliefs, and practices gets.

3. CHOSENNESS vs. UNIVERSALITY

Buddhism recognizes and focuses on the interconnectedness of all things and beings. In fact, in meditation one can concretely experience this, and it is extremely liberating. Contrast this with the concept of chosenness, which is a fundamental cause of the Jewish people's deliberate separation of themselves from the rest of society – a cause, one might even say, of resentment leading to anti-Semitism and its horrifying consequences. To be a practising Jew, you really have to believe that you are part of a covenant in which you have been selected for a special task or role in life. This fundamentally sets you apart, and obstructs you from experiencing the true nature of the Universe.

4. SELF-KNOWLEDGE

Buddhism helps one to see that there is no such thing as the "self," with a small "s". Sure, there's a body, and an agglomeration of personality traits within it. But all our "selves" are interconnected like bicycle spokes. This perspective frees us from grasping and clinging to ideas and desires – the ultimate causes of suffering.

Judaism, on the other hand, upholds the notion of self, and from the get-go, puts burdens on it: 613 commandments; and sets for one goals that lead to grasping, clinging and the endlessness of the cycle of suffering. One could say, then, that in focusing on the true nature of "Big Self," that is, the interconnectedness of larger Universal identity, in which we all repose, Buddhism gives a deeper, more accurate, less agonizing self-knowledge than Judaism could, and after all, it is with self-knowledge that we begin to ready ourselves to serve the larger world and avoid inflicting suffering on others.

5. BELIEF

Now, Buddhism in some forms does entertain certain ideas that might be called belief, but if we're talking here about Buddhism in its sparest and most common Western form – specifically, Soto Zen – then one of its great strengths would be that you don't have to believe. You experience for yourself. This is what made Shakyamuni Buddha such a revolutionary spiritual leader. He saw belief systems as forms of enslavement, either to political systems or to mirages that inflamed suffering. In Zen, you simply experience. Belief is a kind of smokescreen that obscures reality.

6. TORAH FROM SINAI

This is connected to my previous question concerning belief, of course. If one does not believe in the revelation at Mt. Sinai, how can one call oneself Jewish? One may hear many distinguished Jewish scholars, yourself included, note that there is no revelation in history like that of the Jews at Sinai. Hundreds of thousands, if not millions, blown backwards by the voice of God Himself, and the numerous experiences of God by the desert wanderers thereafter.

But a Buddhist might say that this is little more than an excellent myth, and if you can't fully believe this myth, are you really Jewish? And if you do believe it, are you not suffering from delusion, one of the Three Poisons? In contrast, a Buddhist might say, the Buddha was, we're sure, an historical figure, whose movements were tracked, sermons documented, whose life and death are historically known. He was utterly human, and transformed himself through inquiry. No hocus-pocus.

7. LEGALISM

The preservation of arcane traditions, and the inability of Judaism to adapt itself to the different times and cultures in which Jews have found themselves, can account for a lot of Jewish seeking, and finding, in Buddhism. How can a spiritual tradition with a close connection to a vibrant, present One God maintain that connection in the mind-numbing tracts of legislation and commentary through which Jews approach their relationship with God?

8. SPIRITUAL VACUITY

Many see Judaism as so engulfed in procedure and law that it, and its adherents, are utterly lacking in spiritual identity. A Buddhist almost invariably puts openness and awareness and compassion front and center, and is a spiritually enlivened being. Many Jews seem utterly unconcerned with spiritual life and development, but still proud to call themselves Jews, and it is the sons and daughters of these people who join other religions or fall away from all spiritual practice, who intermarry, who lose any connection to Jewish identity.

9. CULTURAL PERCEPTIONS OF JUDAISM IN THE WORLD

Buddhists in the West are compassionate and caring, socially active and humble people. It may be an overgeneralization verging on anti-Semitism, but some Buddhists who are Jews might say that they are turned away from Judaism in no small measure by the way they see Jews living: in self-selected enclaves of, largely, wealth and privilege. How can a vibrant spiritual tradition lead to this kind of self-imposed spiritual apartheid?

10. EMPTINESS

This is a Buddhist concept that I'll have to recommend a text for. But essentially, it is that all things, all beings, are creating themselves from moment to moment, and have no inherent quality or personality. Rather, it is the overlay of our perceptions, born of our own misconceptions and our chemical and psychological interplay, that lead us to mistakenly endow things and people with qualities that, in the whole, they do not have

This radical view, arrived at by great Buddhist philosophers of roughly the 10th century, unravels more traditional views of personality, personal experience, and of course, God.

11. TRADITIONS AND STORIES RENDERED MEANINGLESS OR TERRIBLE BY TIME

Shaking the Lulav and Etrog, dwelling in booths; the dedicated reading of Torah portions about brutal savagery in war, sacrifice, plagues and torment visited upon enemies: some aspects of Jewish life and observance, and the stories by which we guide ourselves, seem to modern sensibilities arrogant, bizarre, war-like. Although it is beyond argument that the Jewish people endowed the Western world with much, if not all, of its moral code, it is nonetheless strange that we adhere to the customs and tell the stories of an ancient agrarian conglomerate of nomadic tribes when the world has changed so much.

Much of Judaism appears impenetrable and archaic, so that it becomes the last place many Jews would look for a vital connection to the Divine. A book that recently received a lot of attention here in the States makes the claim that Judaism is dying because rituals have frozen the spiritual truth of the religion in inaccessible amber, and what's left has been expropriated by Jewish agencies using the Israeli/Palestinian crisis as an excuse to raise money to perpetuate themselves. This view is not entirely unrepresentative of much of my generation's take on contemporary Judaism.

12. THE CULT OF JEWISH VICTIMHOOD

Some feel that Judaism as a whole perversely revels in its victimhood on the one hand, and that the current version of Zionism is imposing this very kind of victimhood on others. In contrast, Buddhism espouses detachment from forms of identity, from all places or things, that would lead to this kind of suffering. Many Buddhists (and particularly ex-Jews) might point to relentless reminders of the Holocaust on one hand, and the current strife in Israel on the other, and simply say: "You see? This is what comes of a religion that clings to ancient ideas, to myths and to lands. Show me a country torn apart by Buddhist strife." (One might respond that Buddhist priests in WW II Japan advocated mindfulness while killing the enemy, but that's another story.)

13. JOY

When one experiences emptiness, when one frees oneself from delusions and attachments, one experiences a profound upwelling of compassion for all sentient beings. This egalitarian openness is a major avenue leading to the elimination of suffering. Even if you aren't enlightened, this is a joyful experience. Joy is not the major aim of Buddhism. Understanding is. But the two are closely related.

Where is the joy in Judaism?

14. MEDITATION

Most Jews are drawn to Buddhism because it is, by its very nature, quiet, deliberate, even solitary. It is inwardly focused, calm, serene. No minyans, no noisy shuls, no scolding rabbis. Is there such a thing as Jewish meditation?

15. SUFFERING

Buddhism aims to eliminate suffering. Judaism seems to see suffering as integral to growth. Yom Kippur, one could say, positively enshrines suffering – ennobling the very thing Buddhism seeks to extirpate! There is a fundamental gap here.

Rabbi Tatz, I look forward to hearing from you.

Rabbi Kahn tells me that you will be coming to Chicago later this month, perhaps we could meet? My wife and I would be honored to host an informal dinner for you Sunday evening in our home; others would be interested in joining us and hearing you speak.

David Gottlieb.

Source

Dear David,

I have looked carefully through your points; I shall try to demonstrate an authentic Jewish approach to these questions as far as I am able. I would like first to explore the issues raised by Buddhist thinking and practice. Many of your complaints spring from the modern and particularly American perception of Judaism; I will deal with these, but I would prefer to begin with the elements *that draw Jews to Buddhism*, not the elements that may drive them *away from Judaism*. Under the former we may discover some fascinating similarity and perhaps even more fascinating difference; under the latter we will engage in some contemporary soul-searching and enter an entirely different arena. If I can contribute anything it will be a fresh insight into Torah and its power, rather than speculation concerning the assimilation of today's Jews.

I shall answer your questions briefly and definitively where I can; however, I shall deal at greater length with those areas that are pervasively misunderstood by modern Jews who lack a Torah background. I would like to show how a better understanding of these issues clears up the difficulty in most cases. I would contend that many Jews have gone to Buddhism in their spiritual search because they are unaware that Judaism contains the elements that they have found so appealing in Buddhism. Although I cannot claim to be an expert on Buddhism, I shall try to show that what you have demonstrated of its ideas is basic in Judaism.

A disclaimer: it is my experience that the quality of what a person says decreases in inverse proportion to the frequency with which the words "I" and "me" appear in his communication (I suspect that a Buddhist might agree with me on this point). That frequency is very often an index of ego at the expense of content. But because this is a personal correspondence those words will frequently creep in; I hope you will not judge me unfairly on that account.

Thanks for the invitation to meet you and speak to your friends. It will be my pleasure.

For now, I am attaching some initial thoughts in response to your first point. I shall try to answer the others as time allows.

Best regards,
Akiva Tatz.

GOD

"Although Zen Buddhism does not deny the existence of a Divine force at work in the Universe, it does not focus on a God who must be obeyed or, more importantly, believed in. Buddhism focuses on what can be experienced, and although many believe they can experience God... can they, really? The whole concept of building a worship system around a Supreme Being who cares at all about what we do and don't do, and all the "myths" attendant on that belief, is like building a castle to live in and expecting it to float in mid-air."

I see there is something we agree on already – that this must be the place to begin.

"...Zen Buddhism does not deny the existence of a Divine force at work in the Universe..."

David, what exactly is the meaning of "does not deny"? If that means *accepts* the existence of God, then not to go on to investigate what God is, says and does would be either madness or willfully evil. (It is a principle of Jewish intellectual analysis to exclude both of those categories from our universe of discourse – you *cannot* debate with those beyond logic, and you do *not want* to debate with those who question in order to destroy, unless you are forced to. Torah learning begins and thrives by asking the most penetrating questions, but they must be questions that aim to discover, not to destroy.)

If, however, "does not deny" means simply "has no interest in," we are faced with a logical problem. There cannot conceivably be anything more important than the existence of God. In the light of God's existence literally everything takes on vastly greater proportions; not only do moral obligations, for example, take on meaning in the deepest sense, but the very notion of meaning itself comes to life. In a godless Universe, does anything really matter? Surely this is the first point to clarify; nothing could possibly change the shape of all other issues more. This is not a matter for simply "not denying." If one comes to the conclusion that the Universe has a conscious Creator and Master, all one's investigations and subsequent conclusions will be radically different in the deepest way. And if one comes to the opposite conclusion, then quite frankly, for me on a personal level the discussion loses most of its flavor. If nothing transcends the world of our finite experience there can be nothing *really* worth striving for. Certainly, strive if you wish, work if you will, but compared to the Absolute alternative any other project tastes flat to me.

"Buddhism... does not focus on a God who must be obeyed or... believed in. Buddhism focuses on what can be experienced."

You raise the issues of obedience, belief and experience. (Since you raise the question of belief again in another of your points, I shall deal with it there.)

What is meant by Buddhism's focus on experience? If the idea is to deny the reality of all that cannot be experienced directly, that approach is neither logical nor wise. To define out of existence all that I do not personally experience would be intolerably egocentric, even downright arrogant, and it would seriously limit growth. I would be forever locked into the limited world of my own perception. No matter how broad my consciousness may become, if I never approach those dimensions beyond my conscious apprehension I may be excluding the major part of reality from my worldview and my world-work.

And if the idea is that things beyond experience are not reliably true and therefore not worth engaging, that too is problematic. Inference is a perfectly valid tool. You question whether anyone can experience God. Even if you were right about that, inference is a valid objective tool for relating to that which cannot be experienced directly. Much that wisdom teaches as real lives in our knowledge only by inference. If you insist on relating only to direct experience you are severely limiting the scope of knowledge. If at least part of our aim is transcendence, then by definition we are seeking to come to know that which at any given point on the path can only be inferred. If it turns out that God's existence cannot be experienced directly but known only by inference, this would in no way detract from its reality or its importance.

(Does Judaism assert that God can be known or only that His existence can be inferred? And if we assume the latter, what is the strength of that inference? In fact, we say that God-consciousness goes far beyond inference; but inference is perfectly acceptable as a starting point. When we discuss belief I shall try to say more about this process and the nature and strength of the inferences involved.)

I must assume that the Buddhist intention here is more subtle. I would guess that the intention is not to deny or disparage those aspects of wisdom and reality that are inferential at all, but rather that the proper focus of the mind should be simply to connect with reality directly.

If that is the case, and such a program of development leads to perfection of mind and character, what could be wrong with it? If it is not constrained by immediate experience, if it leads to ever larger dimensions of awareness, dimensions that are beyond the self initially and attained later, then this would seem a valid path – it will lead eventually to the broadest apprehension possible. But if it aims to deal only with those aspects of mind and world that are naturally grasped, those things that are always in the arena of human knowledge, then it will not be possible to pass into the utterly transcendent by this method.

If Buddhist life and thought relate only to the empirically known and immediately experienced, we must differ. That would place the world of spirit and wisdom no higher than the physical and material objects of its contemplation. However, if Buddhist thinking demands a basis in fact and experience for its development, but soars beyond immediate fact into the transcendent while *never relinquishing an umbilical connection* to the world of fact, we and they would be at one.

Now if Buddhism "does not focus on God" because its agenda is not more than correctly and deeply training the mind, and such a mind will go on to discover God in due course, from a Jewish perspective that would be close to our notion of *derech eretz*, loosely and broadly understood as mind and character training, the necessary precursors to God-consciousness.

But if Buddhism posits *no more* to its view of human development than the training of mind and the refining of experience to the *exclusion* of a relationship with God; if it sees awareness of the Universe without awareness of its Source as *sufficient*, that would not be valid for Jews (what it would mean for non-Jews I am not going to discuss here). We define our existence in our relationship with God, that is where we live. In essence we live at Mount Sinai; we visit elsewhere, we travel through space and time, but there our camp is pitched. To be sure, as I have pointed out, discipline of mind and character are absolutely necessary on the Jewish path, they are worth a lifetime of effort and represent a great achievement in themselves, but they are only tools for the real purpose of life. We would have a sense of tragedy at the idea of a lifetime's work honing and perfecting tools of unfathomable and exquisite beauty and never putting those tools to their proper use.

Imagine, if you find the analogy useful, a king who sends his faraway son a perfect vehicle in which to travel back to his father, and must watch his son pay minute attention to the vehicle itself, appreciating, exploring and mastering its every angle and using it to travel the length and breadth of the kingdom, never realising that it was sent for him to come home.

And if you are going to relate to God at all, there can be only one way to do so: on His terms, not yours. The issue then becomes not what Buddhism (or anyone else, for that matter) says about Him, but what He says. So we must go to revelation, one way or another.

"Buddhism...does not focus on a God who must be obeyed"

With regard to obedience: David, I think the way forward here is for me to ask you some questions, if I may. If Buddhism has no conception of God, or at least no conception of a God who obligates, what is the source of the Buddhist obligations of right view, right intentions and so forth? What obligates? Why must I develop these refined sensitivities and patterns of self-control and action? If the largest of all possible circles in Buddhist thought is the oneness of the Universe, how does that oblige me any more than any one of its parts? How does reality itself *obligate*? Why must I become one with it? That may be a highly esthetic notion, truly beautiful and resonating within me, but why *must* I?

What is the ultimate origin of Buddhism's precepts or the steps on the eightfold path? If these are the correct steps to generate deep and pervasive harmony in the Universe, and they are obvious to the developed mind, still, why do they obligate? More deeply, why do they matter? Why does harmony in the Universe *matter*? The deep motivation here seems to be the termination of all suffering, the ending of suffering for all sentient beings, if I follow your elegant exposition correctly. But why does that matter at a deep level? Of course it matters to me; of course any sensitive human *feels* the imperative here, but is that enough?

If the source of obligation is the Divine, however, that infinite source generates obligation in the deepest sense possible. These things would matter because He says so; there can be no deeper obligation than that, and no greater meaning. If that is the source of obligation, such obligation is real in the most profound sense.

I am not pretending that this is a simple point: the nature of obligation emanating from the Divine as opposed to a sense of obligation welling up from within human consciousness and the consequences of these alternatives have been addressed in philosophy for centuries. (See, for example, *Morality,* by Bernard Williams, Cambridge, 1993, on the absolute underpinnings of morality.) I do not mean to enter the debate about whether an absolute source of moral principles is necessary for morality to exist; I am simply pointing out *the difference it makes.* Even if we agree that a sense of moral obligation exists without reference to an absolute source, the question I mean to ask here is what is the deep meaning of that sense, how deep is the obligation, without an absolute frame of reference?

Perhaps the Buddhist position is that there is in fact no obligation at all: the desire to end suffering is simply an awareness that I come to in my meditation; just as I do not want to suffer, I come to see that it is right and good to extend that awareness to other beings who feel the same aversion to suffering. I am thereby motivated to work and to serve so that no sentient being suffers. (I have seen this line of thought followed in some of the writings you refer to.)

But I do not think we can get away from the question of obligation that way: surely the meaning here is that I become *obligated* to work and to serve? What is happening within me is that I perceive my *obligation* to relieve and prevent suffering; I certainly feel obliged, and deeply. Look at it this way: what is the meaning of a desire to end suffering that I do not perceive as obliging me? Simply something optional that I feel I would *like*? Do we mean "like" in the sense that it will gratify me on a personal level? Surely Buddhism is not teaching that the ultimate mover of my working and serving to reduce suffering is my own personal gratification; if I understand you correctly,

Buddhism is clear that we should not be attached to personal needs or desires in the first place.

No; the drive here is very clearly a sense of obligation. There is no other honest way to describe what I experience when I relate deeply to the problem of suffering. Genuine compassion must oblige. One who does not perceive an obligation in the face of suffering that he can do something about is missing an essential human faculty. If he feels nothing at all he manifests one of the diagnostic criteria of psychopathy; if he feels no more than an opportunity for personal gratification he is dangerously immature at best; but if he feels what we would both agree is the appropriate response, he is feeling obligation. There is no other word for it.

Judaism sees obligation as a major theme, perhaps even *the* major theme, in the developed human psyche. Torah thinkers indicate that this was the primary element that Abraham discerned and clarified in his approach to discovering the Source. (I will say more about this when we talk about honoring parents.) For now, consider this: does the truth not oblige? Who can perceive truth, shake off its fetters, and claim to be honest? And like all major themes in the world of spirit, this leads to paradox: only a slave to the truth is free.

There are other issues here too. How reliable is the human sense of right and good? Can we be sure that the agenda any human sets up for the world is not colored by vested interests, even an agenda perceived in the relative clarity of detached meditation? After all, it must take many stages of meditative refinement before absolute clarity – enlightenment – is attained. Without an appeal to the absolute, how can we posit a life program on relatively unclear stages of human perception? How can we be sure that any imperative arises in the mind in complete objectivity? No; to posit an absolute obligation we need an absolute obligator. (Note that this is not the reason we attach ourselves to God; we do that because it is true, not because it is necessary. But it is necessary too.)

To put this more bluntly: if my sense of obligation derives from my own intuition and from no point of reference outside of myself, it cannot guarantee a constant standard. It is likely to wax or wane with the quality of my own conscience. With no point of fixity external to the self, no anchor locked to an immovable bedrock, the ship of my consciousness and conscience is adrift. Of course that does not mean that it *will* drift, but the fact that it *may* changes everything. If I am my own judge, if there is no standard outside of myself other than an inanimate and non-sentient Universe, we have pitifully shrunken the world of the moral.

An anchor cast deep into the deck of its own ship is a dangerous illusion. An anchor cast securely onto another, larger ship's deck may be better, but not by much. Even a whole fleet, though they be lashed together and trail the deepest of sea anchors, will drift with the ocean. Nothing less than attachment to a separate frame of reference will do.

I have not missed the point that Buddhism itself teaches the need to detach and to escape the trap of self-referential illusion, the trap of personal desire and the delusions that result from false notions of self. But I am making a larger point here. I am suggesting that even detachment from the "small self" and expanding to the scope and scale of the Universe in all its vast and objective reality is not enough. I am suggesting to you that the entire Universe is only a larger ship than the ship of "small self," that all of reality is no more than a ship sailing an infinitely larger ocean. We are seeking to anchor ourselves not to the largest ship that there is, that should not satisfy us; we are seeking to discover a point of attachment that is outside entirely, a truly separate frame of reference. What you refer to as Big Self, though it may swell to the proportions of the Universe, is a very small self indeed in these terms.

Our mystical sources indicate that this is the deep understanding of one of the Divine Names: "*HaMakom* – the Place." The idea is that the Universe is not His place; He is the place of the Universe.

Freedom and Obligation

Dear Rabbi Tatz,
Firstly, thank you again for coming to our home upon your arrival in
Chicago. It was an honor to meet you and hear you speak, both in our
home and at the larger event at the North Shore Center.

Thank you for your stimulating response to my first question. Before I
turn to that, I will try to put down in writing some of my experience; to
detail what led me into Buddhist study and practice and to identify
what attracted me and others like me to that path.

(A recent poll here in America revealed that 75% of Americans
consider themselves to be engaged in a spiritual search. While this
may simply reflect our ability to extend our talent for shopping into
every corner of life, even the spiritual, it also shows that people need
and want spiritual knowledge and grounding. American Jews are
especially hungry for this, I believe.

It's interesting to note that many of the most prominent American Zen
practitioners and scholars are Jewish by birth, and that more than
one-fifth of all American Buddhists are Jewish.)

In this instance – the instance of a Jew seeking spiritual grounding,
having first found spiritual resonance in Buddhism but recognizing
himself to be first, last and foremost a Jew – many questions must be
addressed and many methods employed, but they will lead me in
circles without some expert guidance from the Jewish perspective.

The Zen Buddhism that I have studied and practised requires almost a scientist's rigorous eye for empirical truth, to which belief is an obstacle, and what we call knowledge, unless constantly re-examined, can be a smokescreen. Buddhist thought defies belief and it constantly, gently removes the tentacles that attach us to beliefs, desires, or characteristics that we think of as "me." If you practice Zen meditation regularly and study with a good teacher, you may be able, in time, to experience the radically and constantly changing everpresence of existence. It reveals "self" as a transitory vehicle for helping truth emerge and be recognized. Through gentle and persistent examination, meditation helps extirpate the roots of suffering by revealing to us that our desires are born of fear and attachment and have no real existence or value.

As I entertained this idea and pursued the spiritual path laid out in this system, I took steps along what is known as the "Noble Eightfold Path," Buddha's program for a spiritual life dedicated to the eradication of suffering. The first steps are:

1. You acknowledge that suffering exists, and you determine to pursue its end. The Pali word, "dukkha," is usually translated as "suffering," but it has a more profound meaning, connoting a deep and persistent thread of unsatisfactoriness woven through all of life.

2. You work to develop and maintain a depth of ethical, moral and conceptual knowledge. To Buddhists, this means understanding how the world works, how "karma" (more or less, spiritual cause and effect) works, and how Buddha's teachings address those realities. Views condition action. More than making us Buddhist scholars, this step on the path is meant to focus us on changing the whole orientation of our existence, from pursuing cravings toward pursuing a spiritual path that addresses the suffering behind desire.

This path is undeniably spiritual and unforgivingly mundane. It is a discipline. At its heart is the focus of the mind: the one-pointed concentration that blossoms in meditation.

The "Four Truths" and "Eightfold Path" are designed to contain the mnemonic touchstones that lead you toward living in a way that lets you directly experience and clearly see life for what it is. Only when you do that can you recognize and address the sources of suffering. This, along with objectless meditation, forms the spine of a very exacting and demanding spiritual practice that can be *devoid of symbol, myth, belief and centuries of dogma.*

Of course, these things exist in many strains and schools within Buddhism, as they may in any organized religion with a long history. There are cultural barriers to fully understanding some aspects of Buddhism, just as there may be for secularized Western Jews approaching Judaism. My point, however, is that what may draw Jews to Buddhist practice – especially the Soto Zen form, which is perhaps the simplest and least adorned with ritual and belief – is its utter quiet and simplicity, its empirical approach, and its explicit directions for addressing not only spiritual concerns, but worldly ones as well, of which the cessation of suffering is foremost.

This outline may help frame why I went into Buddhism as deeply as I did. Larger social forces were at work, in America and in the Reform Judaism of my youth, that led me away from Jewish learning and practice; and in my own personal, emotional and spiritual life I was typical, in many ways, of the disaffected, secularized Western Jew who sought simplicity and authenticity.

Ironically, while I studied Zen meditation, the gentle pursuit of seeing the truth helped me see that my true nature is that of a Jew. And yet, to be a Jew is to seek, to struggle, to contend and to yearn. There is a historical continuity to Judaism in which a Jew seeks his place. The struggling and yearning of Judaism and the openness to experience and non-attachment in Buddhism were hard to reconcile.

David.

Dear David,

I think that part of the appeal of Buddhism for Jews may be the fact that it is exotic. The new, the foreign, has an automatic appeal. Some men will always be attracted to other men's wives.

Akiva.

PS Why do you give me a title? My name is Akiva. If you persist, I am going to call you Grand Master David, Seer of Chicago, Light of the West; or something to that effect. Regards.

PPS Or:
The Illinois Illui (an *illui* is a Talmudic genius)
or:
David, Druid of Deerfield...

Dear Rabbi ....
I'm sorry, let me start again:

Dear Akiva,
As I mentioned to you when you so graciously came to my house after an exhausting trip, my son thinks of you as the Elvis of the Jewish world.

You have reached a level of mastery in study and in life, and calling you Akiva, without the pointed permission you just gave me, would have been difficult indeed. However, your permission, in addition to my horror at the prospect of being called by the names you proposed for me, prompts me to call you Akiva and to forever abandon the "rabbi." Henceforth, Akiva.

David,
If your son thinks that I have anything in common with Elvis, he probably means: "In the ghetto."

Akiva,
All he will say is: "Don't be cruel."

But enough of that.

When you ask: "If there is no God, what is the source of the obligation to follow the Eightfold Path?" I think you've identified what may be at the very heart of the different orientations of Judaism and Zen.

Some schools of Buddhist practice (such as the Tibetan form) have whole pantheons of deities, enlightened beings, and magical realms that act as a kind of guiding and obliging force. The Zen Buddhism that has taken hold in the West does not emphasize this. In fact, the Zen teacher I studied with has said that Zen practice can fit well within any other religious practice, because it neither affirms nor denies the existence of God: it addresses the form and nature of existence as we know it, and as we can know it.

Zen Buddhism is not concerned with the question of whether there is a God, but with discerning and becoming open in each moment to what the nature of reality is. This was the nature of Buddha's enlightenment – it was a moment of great realization and not a moment of prophetic vision or connection to God or gods. The cultural roots of Buddhism are in Hindu India, where an elaborate panoply of gods played myriad roles in daily life and in the mythological system of society. Buddha was actually trying to break the stranglehold of the elitism and corruption of this system and the accompanying enslavement to beliefs and superstitions which he saw as perpetuating suffering.

Zen does not relate to the notion of God because in developing a clear, moment-to-moment realization of the constant newness and unfolding of reality, the very question of obligation, of a God who wants certain things from us, would occlude our ability to see and apprehend that reality, and set up a dualism that Buddhists believe is a false premise from which much suffering springs.

The source of the "obligation" to follow the Buddhist path is the world and the way it works. In other words, the obligation in Buddhism is to strive to end suffering – one's own, and that of others, because suffering is the product of spiritual ignorance. It follows, then, that it's not an obligation, but a choice. The Buddhist belief in karma holds more or less that in clinging – choosing to cling – to the notion of a discrete self and answering to its cravings, one is perpetuating one's suffering in this and subsequent lifetimes, and that the whole progression through several lifetimes is a movement toward enlightenment, away from craving, ego primacy and suffering.

This is why, when one goes through the Bodhisattva initiation ceremony, one repeats, three times, a confessional verse that is central to breaking the chain of living in and causing suffering:

All my ancient twisted karma
From beginningless greed, hate and delusion
Born through body, speech, and mind
I now fully avow.

Doing good and refraining from harm, then, would be not an obligation, but a choice to participate in the vanquishing of suffering. One of the oldest and most famous examples of this is the Teaching of All Buddhas, which appears first in written form in the 5th century CE:

Refrain from all evil,
Practice all that is good,
Purify your mind:
This is the teaching of all buddhas.

Or, as the 7th/8th century Indian monk Shantideva wrote, "One law serves to summarize the whole of the Mahayana [the school of Buddhism in which Zen is a major form]: The protection of all beings is accomplished through the examination of one's own mistakes."

It might be said that Buddhism does not focus its energy on a realm where obligation exists. Obligation, in fact, indicates the dualistic

view which Buddhism seeks to penetrate (there is me, and there is
some other Force obligating me to behave in a certain way). The
notion is that the path toward Enlightenment is trod through many
lifetimes and that the progress one makes depends on the dedication
with which one chooses to walk that path, by examining one's own
mistakes, by refraining from evil and embracing good, and by
avoiding the clinging desires of the flesh.

David,
Perhaps you are telling me that although I am not *obliged* to work to
end suffering, if I meditate sensitively on the subject I shall simply *see*
that the ending of all suffering is the proper goal, and that will become
my desire.

But if desires are to be extirpated, what will motivate or drive the
process of moving towards the ending of suffering? Or towards
enlightenment, for that matter? You say that the elimination of
delusions and attachments leads to a profound upwelling of
compassion for all sentient beings. Surely this amounts to a *desire* to
help and benefit them? The desire to end suffering is certainly a
desire. There *must* always be *that* desire, surely? More than that – the
desire to end desire must itself be a desire.

The answer must be that this is not the sort of desire that needs to be
extirpated. There are different kinds of desires, and this kind is fine –
it is pure, subtle and sophisticated. The sort of desire that must be
overcome is the selfish, grasping, immature kind, the kind that is an
expression of ego. But that is Judaism exactly – if there is one
underlying idea that runs through all of our spiritual work, it is this;
our goal is the refining of character to the point where the personality
is fully expressed, but without the faintest hint of ego. I shall try to
develop this idea further as we communicate; it is absolutely
fundamental.

Akiva,

The desire to end suffering can be fuelled by greed and egotism – desire for fame, thirst for worldly success, even a subtle vanity about how "spiritual" you're becoming – and in such a case one can inadvertently work in opposition to noble goals by not understanding the desire that fuels them (this would fall under "Right Effort").

A phrase in the Bodhisattva Initiation Ceremony says:

> *Walking the path of the bodhisattva (awakened or enlightened one) is accomplished through the spirit and actuality of renunciation...*

Renunciation is an unsurpassable way of harmonizing body and mind with the Buddha way. When you give up attachments, you are free.

Here we must distinguish between a kind of lust, and a kind of determination – a kind of longing, and a kind of disciplined shedding of earthly attachment. This latter, I think, is not a very Jewish idea. As Jews, yearning is part of the very fabric of who we are, our modern condition, our ancient practice, our souls. We yearn for the restoration of the Temple, for connection to God, for return to Israel. In Buddhism, it is this very kind of yearning that leads to suffering, and to causing others to suffer.

With your question you have identified one of the most vexing and interesting aspects of Zen thought: the "non-dual duality" of our existence. We are both separate and suffused with all reality, both distinct beings and one with the greater reality. So we recognize this, and in it, we recognize desires that are at once desires and not desires – the way two drops of water, when close together, seem to bridge that final imperceptible distance by leaping toward each other. Just so, when one recognizes the path towards releasing suffering and desire, one is suffused instantly with an awareness of the non-dual duality of all things, and this is why the study of koans is so famous an example of the development of Buddhist awareness. A koan gently forces the mind to see duality through the non-duality that enfolds it, and to overcome logical and rational limits to experience a radical and wordless level of comprehension.

My Zen teacher once asked me to keep a note affixed to my desk or bulletin board, which says simply "Not Two." Every time I look at it I'm reminded that the object of my sight, my thoughts, my senses, or the issues I'm struggling with, and I, the beholder of and participant in those issues, are not, in fact, separate. It does not say "One," because "Not Two" and "One" are not necessarily the same.

To wrap back around to the question I began addressing, there really is no "obligator" and "obligated" in Buddhist thought. The closest thing to an obligator is Buddha Nature itself, that purified state of mind through which suffering passes like water through a sieve. As such, our own natures await our realization that desire is, like us, "Not Two."

Suzuki often addressed the issue of God because he saw that Westerners come from traditions in which the question of God's existence is a vital one. He did not reject the existence of God, and in fact, said:

> *"... if you think that God created man, and that you are somehow separate from God, you are liable to think you have the ability to create something separate, something not given by Him... Soon we forget who is actually the "I" which creates the various things; we soon forget about God. This is the danger of human culture. Actually, to create with the "big I" is to give; we cannot create and own what we create for ourselves since everything was created by God. This point should not be forgotten... Everything you do should be based on such an awareness, and not on material or self-centered ideas of value. Then whatever you do is true giving."*

David,

Certainly we yearn, as you point out. But Buddhism also yearns – for the end of suffering. Is that not a yearning? What is the difference between their yearning and ours – is theirs healthy and ours neurotic? Theirs dispassionate and ours anxious? What exactly do you mean? Are we not all yearning deeply for a better world and attempting to translate that yearning into a program of action for change? Where do we differ on this?

It is essential to know that we have a mitzva to yearn, the mitzva of *tzipiya li'y'shua* – longing for the redemption. Why is this a necessary element of the developed spirit? What exactly is lacking in one who does not yearn? There is a famous allegory on a related subject in the writings of Rabbenu Yona that offers a deep insight here:

> Prisoners in a jail effect an escape – they dig a tunnel under the wall of their cell and squeeze through. All except one: one prisoner remains, ignoring the avenue of escape. The jailer enters to discover that his prisoners have flown, and begins beating the one who has remained.

This is a difficult allegory to understand. Why is the one who remains being beaten? He appears to be the one who is acting properly; after all, he is the only one obeying the law. What has he done?

The meaning is this: in remaining, he has escaped more profoundly than those who have fled. The escapees have broken jail; it no longer contains them, that is true. But the one who remains *has redefined the jail:* when he shows that he is there voluntarily, he shows that this is no jail at all. While the cell was intact, he appeared to be imprisoned; but now that it is clear that he has no desire to leave, he reveals that the jail never held him. A jail is a place that holds those who wish to be free; those *who wish to be there* are not held by it. The jailer is angry not because this inmate has done something as simple as escaping, but because he has declared the jailer and his jail to be entirely irrelevant. The others have left the jail; he has utterly destroyed it.

One who does not long to see the higher reality revealed, who has no desire to see this world of suffering perfected, has *redefined imperfection*. If he does not long for redemption, he has redefined exile. Such a person does not understand redemption. He has found himself in darkness, and instead of seeking the light he has simply redefined the darkness.

One who is spiritually awake does not redefine imprisonment as freedom, or darkness as light. He recognizes his situation's limitations and longs to move beyond them, but that does not prevent him from fully developing all his limited possibilities, and indeed, he rejoices in that.

To be sure, it takes a delicate poise of spirit to long powerfully for a better world while yet experiencing the joy of this one; a kind of reaching beyond that is no contradiction to the repose and serenity that must be cultivated here. (In *mussar* training, this underlies the discipline of *z'rizut b'menucha* – alacrity in repose.) Anyone who has had the merit of being close to Torah masters will recognize that balance; it is palpable in their presence.

My brother-in-law, who was Rabbi Simcha Wasserman's physician and disciple, was fascinated by his constant joy – it emanated from him, sparkling out in all situations. He once asked his great teacher: "How does the Rav maintain such *simcha* (joy) always?" Rabbi Wasserman fixed him with those unforgettably clear blue eyes and answered: "In any situation, I ask myself what can be done. Whatever can be done, I do. What cannot be done, I do not worry about."

(What a formula! Most of us never do all that should be done, *and* we worry!)

I will return to this theme when we discuss the problem of joy.

With regard to the piece you quote from Suzuki: if Buddhism does not relate to God, as you have indicated, what was he talking about? Did he use this language as a metaphor for the larger reality, the totality of the Universe? But that is not God; nothing could be more mistaken. God is not the Universe, and God is not a metaphor.

You cannot be ambivalent on this point. If you are going to relate to God, be silent long enough to hear what He says. And if you are not, let that be clear. How can you "not relate to God" and then bring Him into the conversation? What does this mean? Was he speaking to the Western point of view – speaking to Westerners in terms familiar to them, perhaps, even though those terms are outside Buddhism's frame of reference? But that would seem to be misleading. What is going on here?

Akiva,
I don't find it misleading at all. In fact, I find it delightful. It is respectful of Western religious tradition and yet goes right to the heart of Zen thought.

As I've said, Zen neither affirms nor denies the existence of, to borrow your phrase, an "Obligator," other than things-as-they-are. Suzuki was a master teacher who understood that the Western frame of reference was built solidly around the concept of the existence of God. He came to the U.S. at a time when conventional approaches to religion, government, leadership, family structure, were all under intense scrutiny, if not attack. Few of his early students could have failed to respond to this teaching because it went to the heart of how they understood themselves in relation to the cosmos. He wanted to penetrate assumptions without casting aspersions on religions he knew little about.

David,
I would like to point out a further depth in the idea of obligation: *"Gadol ha'metsuveh v'oseh...* – Greater is he who is commanded and does than one who is not commanded and does." This principle of the Talmud states that one who acts in obedience to a command is greater than one who acts spontaneously. This is counter-intuitive; surely spontaneity is greater? Surely an action that I perform freely is greater than one that I perform because I am obliged, constrained to do so, from without?

One of the classic answers to this question is that when one is commanded to act, one is immediately confronted by resistance – the lower self steps in and says "Don't tell me what to do!" The ego, the "I", that root of the personality that seeks to express itself and nothing beyond, refuses to be subdued. To fulfill a command one must overcome this inner resistance, and here lies a secret of inner growth. Self-control is at the heart of all personal growth, and it is developed by the discipline required to obey. By contrast, when one acts spontaneously there is no resistance to overcome; the action is relatively easy, and so it has relatively little potential for growth.

(We are not disparaging the value of spontaneity; it is an essential feature of a vibrant inner life. But we mean a spontaneity *that has been created and formed entirely by obligation.* The spiritually developed individual who acts spontaneously will *always* be acting in accord with what is right. At the highest level, the spontaneous mode accords fully with the source that obligates. The *tzaddik* has fully identified his own motivation with the Divine command; he wills it with as full a heart as his commander. The commanding officer orders, but the soldier has already obeyed. See Ethics of the Fathers: "Make His will your will...." It must be your will, spontaneously and fully, but a will that has been formed in the image of His.)

But there is more here than meets the eye. When you act spontaneously, you are expressing yourself. That may be a great thing, but it can never be greater than you are. At best, a spontaneous act is a full and true expression of the one who performs it. If I am the source of my own command, I express only myself when I am true to that command. But when the source of my command is outside myself, I express that source when I act; a connection is forged between that point of origin and myself. I have reached back to that source, extended myself to its level, locked into it. The source originates the obligation and I carry it out; we join in a partnership that expresses us both.

When I fulfill a Divine command I express the Divine. I have become no less than a partner with the Divine; the individual who acts in accord with a Divine commandment has locked into the infinite and reveals in the world what the infinite source of that action intends to reveal. The word mitzva (commandment) is based on a root meaning "together," partnership. Greater is the one who acts because he is commanded, and his greatness will reach as far as the root he expresses.

The depth here is that in overcoming the private, limited self, *because* one overcomes that self, one arrives at a greater Self. Note that this level is deeply discovered in obedience to commandments. The Torah path reaches for the cosmic and beyond; for the Self that has no limits, not even those that may reach the fullness of the Universe.

Akiva,
Some thoughts in reply:

You say: "The issue then becomes not what Buddhism (or anyone else, for that matter) says about Him, but what He says. So we must go to revelation, one way or another."

A Western Buddhist response here could be this: the world is what He says. Every day, it proclaims Him in myriad ways. And in walking the path toward enlightenment, we walk wordlessly toward a kind of revelation, when we come to understand what we are and in what ways we exist and do not exist.

"...we mean a spontaneity that has been created and formed entirely by obligation."

A Buddhist is right with you until that last word. One cannot obligate oneself or be obligated from outside. One simply is and does, as one unfolds oneself (the Lotus blossom is often used as a metaphor for the many-petaled unfolding at the surface of a more oceanic condition). If there is an Obligation, it is to All That Is, of which we are a part, no matter what we do, know or believe. We move ourselves along a path that the Buddha showed us not because of an obligation, but because of a recognition that this is the way to escape the suffering we create for ourselves. We have only to realize the way ultimate reality invites us to be and to see, and then work with all our heart to realize it.

"The Torah path reaches for the cosmic and beyond; for the Self that has no limits, not even those that reach the fullness of the Universe."

Are we perhaps reaching for the same thing, but reaching in different directions? A useful oversimplification: Judaism first reaches outward toward the Divine, and Buddhism first reaches inward. Judaism then reaches inward to make the adjustments commanded, and Buddhism takes out into the world the knowledge cultivated in sitting meditation. It goes back to the experience of revelation or enlightenment: God came to the Israelites, but Buddha "came to his senses."

The steps toward enlightenment in Buddhism are not commanded. They are awakened to. Is it possible they are the same thing expressed in different ways?

Obligation, Ancient and Modern

David,

They *should* be the same thing. Remember that Abraham, long before Sinai, derived the Torah from *within himself;* he intuited the commandments, the objective Divine obligations that build the Universe, by looking inward. But as I have pointed out, that process is reliable only to the extent that you are pure. For those of us who are not yet spiritually clarified, it is better to look outward to the Source; explicit Torah is an immeasurably more reliable reference than a consciousness of doubtful clarity.

You know, it strikes me that the very idea of obligation is not attractive to modern sensibilities. This is the age of freedom, after all – do not tell me what to do. I value my freedom, I act spontaneously, I express myself. Obligation sounds the wrong tone; it does not resonate with my post-modern consciousness. I do not object to work, mind you, or to concentrated effort or significant privation, as long as I am free to choose those. Now if Buddhism does not base its program on the idea of obligation, I wonder if that is an element in its popularity? Is that part of its appeal to our modern brothers and sisters?

Is it the fact that we have come to value our autonomy above all else?

(In modern medical ethics, for example, a field of particular interest to me, the highest value is the patient's autonomy. But this is not highest in the Jewish hierarchy of values; we have higher priorities, such as the saving of life. Without going into the details and the exceptions, the general principle is that a Jew is not free to reject a life-saving option, his autonomy does not extend that far. It is not his life to discard in the first place; it is a Divine trusteeship to be loyally guarded.)

Are we prepared to undertake even a long and arduous journey towards fulfilment and perfection only as long as no one tells us what to do? Are Jews who are following Eastern paths expressing the irony of exchanging one set of rules for another – following a disciplined system, obeying dictates of the exact steps necessary to get to the deepest level of self and beyond, and all the while really only escaping from God? After all, Judaism begins by mandating the same steps – the Ten Commandments, for a start. If you happen to be a Jew you already have a system that teaches right thinking, right speech, right action, compassion, discipline of sensuality, limited use of intoxicants, veneration of the teachings, veneration of the sages, appreciation of wisdom, devotion, detaching, conquering delusion – so why would a Jew go to Buddhism? The critical difference seems to be God. But surely that is the place to start, not to avoid!

If you leave out God, you are missing the point. You are missing the most important point there could possibly be – in fact, so important that virtually any chance of its being true should obligate the intelligent mind at least to investigate its claims. A mental, spiritual and character developing program whose purpose is not to make contact with the Source would seem to be missing essence. In Torah terms we would call that a *derech eretz* training program, that is, a training in how to travel. But that makes sense only for one who is intending to travel. If the tools are real they enable a journey to the real destination, not just a tour of the local landscape. If you train for the journey and you never travel, what is the point?

It seems to me that Buddhism sees journey as destination. The two are conflated, each moment of journey is its own destination; "there is only the moment," as I think you have put it. We would see such an extreme existential reduction as absurd: why travel in order to travel? In Jewish thinking, a journey is justified by its destination. That is its motivation and its meaning. When the journey has a destination, *the journey itself* becomes meaningful, that is a deep principle that I shall try to touch on when we discuss joy; but the fact remains that every meaningful journey must lead to a point outside of itself. In the world of spirit, destination must transcend journey.

(There is a secret depth here – we see each moment transmuting into eternity; there *is* an eternity in each moment, but that is because it moves to another time and place in which it will be revealed and experienced in its *tikkun,* or perfection. *That* is called the resurrection; but that is another story.)

Which brings me to a more general point: there is *always* a source in Torah for any true idea found elsewhere. This must be – Torah is the genetic material underlying all reality; any genuine element of reality must be coded in it. If you delve deeply enough you will find it. But modern Jews who have never been taught this are looking elsewhere, and when they find meaning or inspiration elsewhere and resonate with their discovery, what they do not know is that they have stumbled upon a track that runs parallel to Torah for a distance.

This theme is pervasive: our Jewishly uneducated Buddhist Jew has been smitten by the image of a prince who reached enlightenment by seeing that the values around him were false; he is lost in admiration for this iconoclast who began an entirely new path that has led millions to a better life, a path that could literally save the world if only the world's people would follow it. But Abraham is that figure! We go back to such an individual – Abraham was three years old when he began to penetrate the falsehood of the society around him. He destroyed his father's idols, literally and figuratively, and began a new path that changed the world entirely, the West as well as the East – in fact, our sources clearly indicate that the wisdom of the East is built on principles of spiritual teaching that Abraham sent to those parts as gifts with his sons.

(See Genesis 25:6 where the Torah states that Abraham sent his sons – by Ketura, better known as Hagar – to the East with gifts; see the commentary of Rashi, and Tractate Sanhedrin 91a, where it is explicit that those gifts were spiritual. They were elements of Abraham's own spiritual work, rudiments of esoteric wisdom from which an entire world of spiritual knowledge could be built. See also the Sfat Emet, Likkutim on Jethro, on the inner meaning of this and on the point of our re-connection with that wisdom later in history.)

And all this long before the Buddha – Abraham was born in the year 1812 BCE, just over 3,800 years ago, about 1,300 years before Buddha began his teaching. Eight hundred years before Buddha, we stood at Sinai and received the Torah. When Buddha was born, the first Temple era had just ended; prophets still walked the land. (Prophecy ended in the year 312 BCE, during the second Temple era.) So we had a great iconoclastic "enlightened one" long before Buddhism began; we were a nation of prophets with a Torah that teaches what Buddhism teaches as its basic principles of human development and goes far beyond; deep into the reaches of prophecy, a phenomenon far beyond any self-generated enlightenment. Abraham reached a certain level of enlightenment at the age of three, a greater level at the age of forty-eight, and attained prophecy at the age of seventy-five. Prophecy is to enlightenment as light is to darkness; I choose my words carefully here.

So what does a Jew discover in Buddhism that he could not find in Torah, if only he knew it? Our enlightened one achieved a greatness at an early age that was only the first flowering of a development that ultimately reached prophecy and spawned a new world in the deepest sense. Buddhism, for all its teachings, its acute insights into the nature of reality, its path of developing human sensitivity and practice, is a later reflection of a Torah that is cosmic in its depth and scope. Buddhism may carry its loyal disciple to the outer limits of the Universe in consciousness; Torah carries the Jew beyond the Universe to its Source, to that which dissolves the very notion of limits.

And all that is not the most radical part of Abraham's contribution. As I shall try to clarify in our discussion of the commandments, his real contribution was something greater yet.

And if the story begins with a prince, isolated from the world of suffering, who went out of the palace, saw that suffering for the first time and decided to do something about it, that is the story of Moses. The story of Prince Siddhartha's awakening parallels his: Moses was a prince in Pharaoh's palace, detached from the people's suffering; he went out and saw it and began his path to the enlightenment of prophecy that led to his becoming the world's teacher.

(David, knowing the seeker that you are, I must share this insight with you into the beginning of Abraham's higher journey: there is a classic question concerning his chosenness – why was he chosen? The relevant section in Torah begins: "And God said to Abram, 'Go...'" There is no preamble, no reason given for that choice. In the case of others – Noah, for example – a reason is given; Noah was exceptionally righteous, as the verse clearly states: "Noah was a righteous man ...." But why did God speak to Abraham? Why is no reason given? There are many levels of answer to this question, but I would like to tell you what the great Chassidic thinker, the Sfat Emet, says: the Torah here is not saying that Abraham was chosen at all. *God was speaking to all men, but Abraham was the only one who heard.* God was not speaking to *him*, he was speaking to anyone who would listen, and Abraham was listening. The Torah is simply taking up the story of the one who heard. And of course, God is still speaking to everyone; the question is only who is listening.)

I see the appeal of Buddhism to the Western mind. There is in the East a self-effacing, calm, centered poise that refined Westerners find fresh and attractive, especially in its counterpoint to Western self-promoting hype and bluster. (I well remember how struck I was, as a youngster interested in Japanese martial arts, when I heard the comment of Sensei Enoeda, a karate master of almost incomprehensible skill, on winning the all-Japan championship one year: as he came off the mat he was heard to say softly to himself: "Many mistakes still.")

But how shall I find the words to express to you that for all this it appears to be no more than the steps we teach to begin the path to Torah? These are the basic tools of self-control, refinement of consciousness and character that we expect from students of Torah as the groundwork for engaging a wisdom that only *begins* with this training. A system that teaches, refines, enlightens and opens consciousness is not enough for us. Our goal is something else, our task and our path beyond the realm of human awareness. We look to the infinite and we have the audacity to reach into the infinite. A system that encompasses the Universe may be great. But compared to its Source, all the Universe is very small indeed.

Idolatry

David,

I have more than once come across Buddhist Jews who are troubled by the question of idolatry. Does Buddhism embrace or at least tolerate idol worship? Is the Buddha worshipped? Do statues of the Buddha have the status of objects of idolatry? These are issues for Jews; and not only for traditional or observant Jews, it seems. Quite obviously, the deep-seated Jewish antipathy (allergy?) to idolatry is still alive and well, and even in some unexpected quarters.

The question is, does Buddhism accept, condone or perhaps include elements that are idolatrous? This is critical; when we examine Buddhism from a Jewish perspective we shall require clear answers to these questions. To the extent that we discover even the faintest element of idolatry within Buddhism we shall have to take a clearly negative view of Jewish involvement in Buddhist thought and practice. The claim that Buddhism is "portable" as you put it, that it is entirely compatible with other religions and with Judaism in particular, will stand or fall on this point before all else.

I am aware that we may find different answers to this question as we consider the various forms of Buddhism – you have made it clear that Buddhist paths differ widely from place to place and from time to time. Perhaps the Western, "minimalist" version that you have delineated presents a different nuance of this question than older and more "ornate" forms of Buddhism.

Dear Akiva,

A couple of years ago I wrote a sort of journal of my exploration of Buddhism and the difficulties of this exploration in a Jewish context. Here is a brief excerpt from that larger piece; I describe taking my wife to meet the Zen priest and the conflict that ensued over the issue of idolatry:

In response to my vague desire to learn meditation I have been sent to a Zen Buddhist meditation center. There, the priest is a woman who is a Jungian therapist. Her husband is a sculptor. I can tell she must have been through some stuff, and I can tell she's smart. These are important qualities to me.

After a little instruction and discussion, we begin sitting in meditation together. When my wife discovers that I have been sent in the direction of Buddhism, she is livid. At my meditation teacher's suggestion, my wife comes to the Zen center to see for herself that it isn't a scary place that programs its members and turns out cult-addled clones.

There, the priest, dressed conservatively in clothes that say, "Hi, I'm a Jungian therapist," greets my wife and shows her the meditation hall, the kitchen, the small library, the outdoor garden. She explains that people who come to the Zen Center are people from diverse religious backgrounds and that many of these people are still active in those religions. She even has a student who for more than two decades was a Carmelite nun.

"Why are there statues everywhere?" my wife asks.

"Well," my meditation teacher says, "the statues of the Buddha are there as reminders of the essence of what we call 'Buddha Nature.' They represent a certain kind of centered, aware, solid presence that we each have and can cultivate within ourselves."

"In my religion," my wife says acidly, "we call that idol worship. It's strictly forbidden."

"Well – " my teacher begins.

"Oh," my wife interrupts, "by the way, it's my husband's religion, too. And it's the religion we're raising our children in, just so there's no confusion."

"I understand," the meditation teacher says.

I begin staring intently at my shoes.

"So why do you want to get my husband to practise this entirely different religion?" my wife asks. "What's in it for you? Is it kind of like saving souls?"

"He came to me seeking instruction in meditation," the teacher says evenly. "I can see that it's something that's very important to him and that might benefit him. And when someone seeks instruction from me, I first try to discern whether they're serious about it. I can see that he is, and it's not in my nature, or my job description, if you want to look at it that way, to refuse people instruction in what I've been trained to teach them."

"I hear there's a lot of bowing in Buddhism," my wife says. "Do you bow?"

"Yes, there is bowing," my teacher says.

"What do you bow to?"

"It depends on what part of a service we're in – "

"Oh," my wife interrupts, "so it's not just meditating. It's a regular religion, with services and everything."

"Well," my teacher says, "it's true that Buddhism is a religion – "

"And so what do you bow to, again?"

"We may bow across the meditation hall to each other, after a sitting, or we may bow to the Buddha statue at the head of the hall – "

"If that's not idol worship, I don't know what is," my wife fairly spits.

"But that statue does not represent a deity. There is no worship per se in Buddhism. In bowing to the Buddha – "

"You can call it whatever you want," my wife says.

"We bow to the statue of the Buddha because we're recognizing and honoring Buddha nature, which – "

"I think I've seen enough," my wife says, turning to me. "Come on, let's go."

My teacher regards my wife evenly for a second. My wife is breathing hard. Her nostrils are dilated. She is seething with revulsion and anger. The teacher tries once more.

"This is something he may pursue, though," the teacher says. "It may be important for him that you – "

"No, I don't think so," my wife says, standing.

The teacher says, "So, this is a conversation you'd rather have with yourself?"

David,
Allergy, that's the word.

What exactly is the Torah approach to idolatry? How do we understand this subject both philosophically and in terms of halacha, definitive Jewish law?

To begin, I would like to demonstrate that the conventional idea of idolatry as the worship of mere fetishes is mistaken. The subject is more subtle than that.

The Torah's prohibition of idolatry prompts some particularly puzzling questions. Firstly, when the Torah prohibits us from serving "other gods" (or "other powers"), exactly which "other gods" are being referred to? The common conception of idolatrous gods is that they are no more than figments of fertile imaginations. Worship of graven images is seen as exactly that: worship of statues, pictures or other physical objects. But if these "gods" are no more than lifeless statues or simply dreamed-up ideas, why does the Torah relate to them as if they are real? Many verses refer to gods other than God as if they are very real indeed: "Who is like You among the *gods*, Hashem (the Name)?" "For all the *gods* of the nations are small gods"; "For Hashem is a great God and a great king over all *gods.*" Who are these "other gods"? If they are mere fetishes, no more than human delusions, if they do not really exist, surely the appropriate injunction should be: "Do not get involved in falsehood; do not attribute reality where there is none; do not live in the realm of pure imagination."

Secondly, we note that the Torah's *greatest prohibition* is idolatry; this is the first of all the negative commandments ("You shall have no other gods...") and at a deeper level contains them all. But surely if idolatry were no more than a ridiculous misconception the Torah would not prohibit it thus. It would be enough to say: "Do not be gullible," or even "Do not be fools"! The root prohibition of the Torah must surely be posed against something of very real existence and danger.

We are forced to conclude that in the sources of idolatry lurks something very real indeed.

Think about it: what exactly is the meaning of a person bowing in worship to a carved statue? What sort of person cuts a log of wood in half, uses half for firewood, carves the other half into some statue or totem, and then bows down to the work of his hands asserting that it made him? Or at least that it has a power beyond his own? Surely such an individual is more in need of psychiatric than religious help!

Why would people do such things?

To ask this question from a deeper perspective in Torah terms: we note that the Torah uses names for these "other gods" that are names of God. *"Elohim acheirim"* (other gods); *"eilim"* – these names are profane versions of authentic Divine names, said without holiness, to be sure, but the same names nevertheless. Although God's "Name of actuality" is never used thus, we certainly find His other names so used. Why? Names are of essence in Torah; where is the commonality between objects of idolatrous worship and God Himself? Why does the Torah not use names for idolatry that convey the idea of empty illusion exclusively?

All this implies that we must take the issue of idolatry much more seriously than simply dismissing it as primitive nonsense irrelevant to people of mature intellect.

Let me share with you an approach to this that I have gleaned from my great teachers, based on a particular understanding of Maimonides. Maimonides writes that both idolatry and astrology are nonsense, entirely empty, based on pure imagination, and he speaks sharply about those who give these things any credibility. Yet many instances of astrology are found throughout the Written and the Oral Law and are presented as real and valid. How did Maimonides understand these? What about astrology is real, and what is nonsense?

To approach this issue, we shall need to understand some of the deeper levels that form the foundation of Creation. Our deeper sources describe many interlocking levels to the Creation. In a chain stretching back, beginning at the very Source of existence, many worlds are connected in sequence. Each of these higher worlds infuses the level below it with existence and energy, and together they "bring out" yet another level below them. This process continues in myriad complexity until finally our finite world results.

Each of the levels in this devolving chain of causation has its own uniqueness, but let us focus on one in particular for our present purpose. Between all the higher worlds and our concrete physical one, there is a stage that is intermediate, the second-to-last in the overall sequence. This stage, or world, is not directly perceived by us, but *is accessible.* Its function is to transmit the higher energies down to this world. It is, if you like, the interface between all the higher worlds and ours. It is at the limit that can be perceived from our perspective. This intermediate level is the world of the zodiac, known as the world of *mazal.*

In fact, the root of the word *mazal,* commonly translated as "luck," means a "flow," as in the flow of a liquid; it represents the "flow" from a higher level down to this one. There could not be a more inaccurate translation than "luck." The concept of "luck" implies total randomness; *"mazal"* is just the opposite. It is only the fact that the directing Hand behind it is *hidden* that leads us to perceive things as random.

(And of course *"mazal tov"* does not mean "good luck!" To wish someone that would be a pagan travesty of the first order. What business does a Jew have bestowing the wish for luck, in the sense of pure random fluke? On the contrary, when we articulate the blessing of *"mazal tov,"* we mean to invoke a flow of energy, of blessing, from the Source of all blessing. We are expressing the wish that this event, whether it be a wedding or some other significant life event, should be blessed with an auspicious connection to its source; in other words, we mean to express the very *opposite* of "luck" in the sense of random chance. This error is just another example of our current spiritually shattered state. Where we should be strengthening a tenacious attachment to our ultimate Source, we find ourselves invoking the random and meaningless forces that govern the spin of a wheel – can you imagine a more pathetic comment on our situation?)

Astrology is the science of understanding that intermediate world and using the knowledge of its structure and changes to understand or predict events in the physical world. Strictly speaking, it is not reading the future at all; *that* is prophecy. It is simply reading the *present.* One who knows the stars can tell approximately what will happen here because the causative energies are disposed that way *now,* the forces are already in motion. For a simple analogy: if you show a seed to an expert, he will predict what tree will grow from that seed many years hence even though you may see no more than an undifferentiated seed. The expert is not seeing the future, he simply knows seeds! And particular seeds become particular trees naturally and predictably. That is exactly the point about astrology – it is not a transcendent wisdom, it is a knowledge of the root of the natural.

The root dimension of the zodiac elements "splits" the higher energy into various "channels," each channel being the root of certain energies within nature, and these defined and specific energies manifest as the details of the natural world and its events.

At the risk of venturing too far into the technically kabbalistic, let me try to clarify this idea. This is a world of finite, differentiated particularity. Here things are separate. The deeper reality is Oneness, the manifest reality is multiplicity; or as it is put in some sources, the reality is one, the revelation of that reality is many.

Now the higher levels that emanate from the oneness of the source must somehow become the multiplicity that is revealed in this world; there must be a zone in which the one becomes many. That intermediate world is the world of the zodiac. In that world, fragmentation occurs, one splits into many. It is a world that "looks up" to oneness and "looks down" to multiplicity; it is the transition zone.

A very simple (dangerously simple) depiction of this idea might be a basin of water that has holes in its undersurface. The water in the basin is one, no part of the water is discernible from any other, but as the water pours out in individual spouts under the basin it takes the form of single, individual channels, each fully differentiated from all the others. These are the "pipelines" (best translation I can manage of the kabbalistic terminology) that bring down the elements of specific dispensation that energize the particular phenomena of existence and change in the manifest world.

In the body, this is represented by the hair. The body represents all aspects of the spiritual worlds; each feature of the human body reflects an element of the higher reality, is in fact a projection of that higher element. The hair reflects the breaking out in fine, separate "pipelines" of what is all one within. The head contains the seat of consciousness in which all is grasped as one; all thought is a function of one consciousness, but outside the head the manifestation takes the form of many separate individual strands. In fact, hair grows at the root of those parts of the body that are organs of effect, of producing effect in the external world from an inner source: the arm is the organ of effect in action; genital structure is perhaps the deepest faculty of expressing outward production from an inner source. This is also why the male body in general has more hair than the female, and why Esau was hairy and Jacob was not, and is connected to the obligation of a married Jewish woman to cover her hair. But to explain all that would take us far from our immediate subject. Let me just point out that the Hebrew word for hair, *se'ar,* is the same root as the word for a specific, limited, measured portion, *shi'ur,* and for a gateway, *sha'ar,* an opening that allows through only a certain limited amount at a time, and *Se'ir,* Esau's place of residence.

You know of course that there are twelve zodiac elements. In Torah thought, the number twelve always denotes the split into multiplicity; thirteen always denotes the unity of multiple parts. The relationship between the one and the many that these two numbers signify is a theme that runs throughout all of Judaism. The stylized representation of our three-dimensional world is a cube. The cube has three dimensions and six faces, but it is fully characterized in extension and size by its edges, the twelve lines that bound it. These are known in kabbalistic thought as the twelve meridia of all manifest reality. But you will realize immediately that there must be a thirteenth: these twelve are all parts of *one* cube, they join to form one whole. The center of the cube, the unity of the lines, is the thirteenth. So twelve indicates separation, thirteen indicates unity. The Hebrew word for "one," *echad,* is comprised of letters whose numerical total is thirteen. The Hebrew word for "love," *ahava,* has a numerical value of thirteen – love means the coming together of parts to form one.

This is why thirteen is a "Jewish" number – Jacob and his twelve sons (unifying root and its branches) constitute the Jewish people whose function is to reflect and demonstrate the ultimate Oneness; there are thirteen Articles of Faith; we end the Passover *seder* by counting thirteen levels of Torah expression. In contrast, in the society around us there is a pervasive aversion to this number. There is a fundamental difference between our grasp of the tension between oneness and its parts and theirs.

The zodiac elements are twelve because they are exactly the transition from one to many; they represent the split, they stand at the root of the manifest world, the world of the many.

Now how does this apply to idolatry?

Idolatry, in essence, is the idea of relating not to the supernal Source of all existence, the ultimate Oneness, but *to the channels that bring down energy* into the world, the "openings of the pipelines." An idolater focuses on the zodiac (the "worship of stars and zodiac" is the common Torah terminology) or on the various forces of nature: the sun, the wind, the rain. His graven images are tangible representations of these energies (an idolater who literally worships his piece of wood or stone as divine has transgressed the prohibition of foolishness long before the prohibition of idolatry). Of course one who relates only to the ineffable Source could never create a physical representation; one whose perception goes no deeper than a source of the natural can.

Maimonides says that originally, close to the beginning of history, people acknowledged God alone. Then came a stage when they reasoned that since He uses agencies such as sun and moon to accomplish His will, surely it would be fitting to give honor to these as His emissaries, His viceroys. They began to accord honor to the intermediaries as well as to God. And eventually, they ignored Him and remained focused on the channels only. Such was the development of idolatry. What needs further study, though, is this: what was the underlying motivation in this error? Such slips are not casual.

The underlying reason for forgetting the Source and remembering the intermediate levels is the most basic of all vested interests: the focus on self.

The real difference between worship of the Source and worship of intermediaries is this: one who serves the Source is concerned about what his obligations are; what does He demand of me? How do I give myself to Him? One who serves the intermediaries is concerned about *what they can do for him.* The intermediaries are, after all, the proximate source of all human needs, all natural functions of the world. The idolater looks to the immediate source of power, love, wealth – in fact, of all his needs – and asks: How can they serve me? He does not need to look further.

One of my revered teachers used to say that idolatry is like the behavior of an individual who enters a department store and wants an object which is too expensive for his liking. He offers the clerk behind the counter a bribe so that he should hand him the object. He is prepared to pay the price of the bribe but not the full price of the object. He relates to the departmental clerk but does not concern himself with the owner of the store – the owner does not deliver the goods, the clerk does. So too an idolater: he is prepared to pay some price for his needs, but not the full price; the full price that constitutes genuine service is *all that you have, all that you are,* and that is too much for him. He seeks to pay off *the source that delivers the goods,* that is his sole concern; but the Owner of the whole enterprise is not his concern at all. *Where can I get the goods?* The One who stands behind the Creation is irrelevant when you seek only "the goods."

The heart of the difference is this: true service understands that God is everything, I am only to serve; idolatry understands that *I am everything,* and *my gods are to serve me.* The Talmud puts it this way: Righteous individuals – their God stands over them, as it says "And God was standing over him" (at Jacob's dream of the ladder), whereas evil individuals *stand over their gods,* as it says "And Pharaoh was standing over the river" (the Nile was the Egyptian deity). Diametric opposites: who is primary, and where is reality? If God is primary and He is the source of reality – that is correct worship. But if I am primary and reality is the world of my personal desires, that is idolatry.

You will note that images of idolatrous worship are very often human in form. Idolatry is really worship of the self, and the graven images are projections of that self.

(This leads to a question we must ask about Buddhism. If the underlying motivation of all activity is the termination of suffering of all sentient beings, does that not put us at the center? What is the end-point of the program to end all suffering? If it is the well-being of all sentient beings, that would make our freedom from suffering the ultimate value. In a godless system, I suppose you cannot go further than this, we *must* be the end-point; but you can see how diametrically opposed this is to Torah thinking. According to Torah teaching, we *are* the ultimate beneficiaries, but that is to be in the next world, not this one. Here we are to serve; in the next world we are to enjoy.

The ending of suffering is not the underlying motivation in Judaism; our well-being is not the focus of our efforts. It may be the result, but it is not the motivation. God's motivation, so far as He reveals it to us, is ultimately to give us pleasure; ours is to do what He asks. If you see yourself moving in an impersonal, non-sentient Universe, you may be the final level of your own agenda. But that is not the Torah conception of the Universe.)

So astrology is the science of the intermediates, and idolatry is their worship. The elements of idolatrous worship are not false; they are the channels, the intermediaries, that stand between the ultimate Source and the manifest world. They "transmit" from the Source into the world; that is their function. That is why they share names with God Himself – they are the channels of His manifestation. Looking "up" to those channels for information or prediction is astrology (astrological prediction is forbidden for reasons other than idolatry – I will say something about that later); worshipping them is idolatry.

Looking to them is far from a misguided looking to entirely fictitious figments of human imagination; that is indeed the direction from which all energy here arrives. But looking *only* to them, looking *no further* than them is the problem – a correct perception looks beyond them to their Source (Jews should have eyes for the Source *only*). The element of foolishness and emptiness in idolatry is the belief that the intermediaries *are a source in themselves*, that they have any *independent* power; *that* is primitive nonsense.

I hope this is all clear. "Other powers" are not imaginary at all; these powers, forces of nature at the level of sun, moon and stars, are the genuine transmitters of Divine energy to the world. Their names are His because they parallel the emanations of His manifestation here. What is false about them is the notion that they have any independent power, that they are sources in their own right. There is a hand that gives: idolatry focuses on the hand and ignores the Giver behind that hand; true spirituality seeks to cleave to the Giver.

How does this relate to Buddhism? There is little difference in essence between the worship of an object or phenomenon and that particular form of idolatry that is the worship of a man. I mean worship, not veneration: the veneration due to a sage is an integral part of Torah. The disciple's respect for his master – that is essential. But it is not worship; there can be no ascribing of divine status to any human. That would be anathema.

So where does Buddhism stand on this issue? Is the Buddha worshipped or merely venerated? Do Buddhists bow to the Buddha or merely bend in humility? Do they bow to any specific form or image? If you clarify these points, we can analyze them from the perspective of halacha.

Bowing

Akiva,

Yes, there is bowing in Buddhism, a lot of it, and there are altars with human figurines towards which one bows. Zen Buddhists especially are pretty clear that what one is bowing to is Buddha Nature – one's own inherent ability to achieve and live within this nature, the nature of the Buddha himself, and to one's own serious intent to pursue it. They say that the statue at the head of the meditation hall is merely a symbol of these attributes, toward which we maintain an attitude of humility, and they further emphasize that the statue is not seen as a deity.

When you look carefully, you note that there are several smaller altars placed about a Zen center, usually each emphasizing some different aspect of the Buddha or Buddha nature. You can place incense in these or simply meditate before them, or observe them, if they connect you to some state or idea toward which you are trying to open. The historical personage of the Buddha is not the only figure one would see; there are several other figures both historical and allegorical, and in this regard Buddhism clearly shows a kinship with Hinduism. The statues themselves are not viewed as intrinsically holy.

There is a story about this:

> *A rabbi is confronting a Buddhist priest about the practice of idol worship. The priest gently but firmly insists that Buddhists do not engage in idol worship.*
>
> *"Why, look about you!" cries the rabbi. "Nothing but statues of the Buddha, each with incense before it, bedecked with garlands*

of flowers, people bowing to it! How can you have the audacity not to recognize it as idol worship?"

The Buddhist priest at this point calmly walks over to the altar and picks up the statue of the Buddha, a handsome statue painted in gold leaf. He turns to one wall of the temple, and with all his might, hurls the statue of the Buddha at the wall. It shatters into dozens of pieces.

"I hope you will agree, honored friend," the priest says, "that no worshipper would dare subject an idol to such treatment. And so, in all due respect, I must ask you: would you at any time be so bold as to treat your Torah in this way?"

David,

Let us look at the halachic issue. What is the halachic status of an act of obeisance to a statue? What if such acts are not construed as worship but simply as acts of humility? What about bowing to nothing in particular, simply bowing as an act of subduing ego, an act that you indicate forms part of Buddhist practice?

Bowing is problematic from a halachic perspective. Bowing before any thing is one of the classical forms of idolatrous service and is categorically forbidden. There are some specific exceptions, such as bowing to royalty, which do not concern us directly here. Bowing to people in general is much less problematic than bowing to objects – in martial arts training, for example, bowing to an instructor or an opponent is permitted, bowing to a sword or other weapon is not.

Now you indicate that bowing, in the particular form of Buddhism we have been considering, is performed to no person or object in particular; it is simply obeisance as intrinsic subjugation or humility, an act of annulment in itself.

This too is problematic in Judaism.

What lies behind this prohibition? Please note that my thoughts on this are not necessarily relevant to the *fact* of the prohibition; that is, it is forbidden whether my line of thinking about the underlying nature and meaning of the act is correct or not, and I would not be stubborn about my interpretation anyway.

Obeisance is an act of submission, of acknowledging a reality above the immediate self. I fold, I bend my vertical posture, in the face of a greater presence.

In kabbalistic teaching one of the hallmarks of human uniqueness and dignity that manifest in the body is its vertical posture; it is one aspect of the Divine image.

(The other is a certain emanation, a subtle glow, on the human face that is rooted essentially in wisdom – this varies in proportion to the development of the individual. The face of a sage demonstrates a unique quality – that is why it is popular in Torah circles to display photographs of the faces of great Torah sages; this is not mere adulation, it is education. One feature to be noted on each of those faces is a paradoxical combination of palpable weight of responsibility, awareness of suffering, and yet a surpassing serenity. It never fails to amaze me; when we find the opportunity I shall try to show you in detail how that resolved duality is yet another projection of the Jewish meshing of individual identity and responsibility with transparency to a reality greater than self.)

So folding the vertical posture in the act of bowing represents an annulment of that stature, a submission of the image in the presence of its source.

Now what is the meaning of obeisance, submission, to no external presence? If there is no external reality, to whom am I bowing? If there is nothing outside of me, the only possibility is to myself, and that is either absurd or enormously, flagrantly, idolatrous. I am well aware of the Buddhist descriptions of bowing as an internal, intrinsic act of humility; but humility within the self, *if there is nothing outside of the self*, is not cogent because in that case I can be submitting only to myself. In fact, if I assert that I am all that there is, I have come dangerously close to defining myself as only God can properly be defined.

And if there *is* an external reality to which I submit, before which I humble myself, then if that reality is not God I have just as surely entered the zone of idolatry – obeisance to things other than God is forbidden, as we have noted. Bowing to the Universe at large does not improve the situation; as we have noted before, the Universe at large is big, but not nearly big enough.

All humility, all submission, in Judaism is ultimately to God. (Note that in Jewish thinking even respect due to a *person* is deeply traced to respect for the Divine spark inhabiting every individual. Note also that with regard to bowing to a human king, there is an element of Divine royalty carried within human royalty – the blessing we make on seeing a king is: "Who has given of His glory to flesh and blood.") He is the only reality, and obeisance in Jewish practice is an acknowledgment and assertion of that fact.

The only other possibility I can see is that Buddhism means to teach that there is no self at all; bowing is a physical statement of that idea. There is no one bowing; the bow is an act of dissolution of self. But as I have tried to show, that is just plain wrong in Jewish thought. There certainly *is* a self; what we are seeking to humble, to annul, is not self but self-assertion, not the fact of self but its disproportionate ego. There is no problem with seeing the self objectively, just as any other aspect of reality should be seen objectively. We do not seek to become blind to self, we seek only to see the self as transparent. Transparent, not absent.

We can put this another way, too: the kabbalistic sources say that when God manifests clearly, the self does in fact disappear; it disappears because the Oneness of all things has been revealed. So we could agree that the self disappears, but only because God appears. What this means in terms of bowing is that a bow that annuls the self is a bow to God. Bowing must dissolve all reality other than the only real Existence.

You realize, I am sure, that here we have come back to our old argument about God, not about bowing.

Akiva,
Once again, we may have a difference of perspective and not of practice. Zen teachers are very clear that the Buddha is not a deity and that Buddhist statuary is not venerated. It is a means to draw energy to reflect on ourselves. It is the lightning rod, not the lightning.

When we bow towards the Ark in a Jewish service, what are we doing? During the service there is a moment when people bow from the waist. Don't you think that the distinction between this sort of bowing and the sort of bowing I've described in a zendo *is a pretty fine one?*

If the distinction is not a fine one, (and that's what I'm guessing your answer will be), then I hope you can further illuminate the Jewish approach to bowing.

David,
You are right; the distinction could hardly be broader. Our bowing is *always* to God. Our self-annulment is valid exactly to the extent that it acknowledges Him. The bow that you refer to during the service accompanies the words: "We acknowledge You..." We do not bow *to* the Ark; we bow in that direction because every synagogue is constructed facing Jerusalem. This is because all Jewish prayer is directed through the site of the Temple, an idea I am not going to explore here. We do not bow to anything else; not to *anything* and not to *nothing.*

Are you aware that there is a line in the prayer known as *Aleinu* that is relevant here? This line has been omitted at various times in Jewish history because it is liable to be taken as offensive by other religions who may assume it refers to them. The line speaks of idolatrous nations "...who bow to nothingness and emptiness..." The simple meaning, of course, is that idols are "nothing and empty." But it has been suggested that there is another overtone: we mean to distinguish ourselves not only from idolatrous nations who bow to empty forms, but also from those nations who bow to "nothingness" and "emptiness" itself. A Buddhist Jew needs to take note of this.

What is the place of bowing in Jewish practice? You may be interested to know that it is central. It certainly expresses the idea of submission, of humbling the self, but there is more to it than that. The deeper sources discuss the concept of folding the body, bringing the upper half to overlay the lower half; this is exactly the fetal position. (The Talmud gives a full description of the position of the fetus in the womb, and the commentaries explain the meaning of this folded posture. For now, I shall mention just one idea on a non-kabbalistic level: the Talmud says that the fetus is folded like a *"pinkas,"* usually translated as a notebook. The Maharal of Prague points out that a more accurate translation is a ledger, the kind of notebook that a storekeeper might use to keep accounts. The idea is that the fetus in the womb is like a new, closed ledger; at the point of birth it is opened and the inscribing of accounts begins.)

Bowing is part of Jewish practice. This motion is integral to prayer; accompanying the mind and the mouth, this is the *body's* act of prayer. The custom in the Torah observant community on Rosh Hashana and Yom Kippur is to bow fully, that is, we kneel and bring our faces to the floor. In previous times, in the Temple, full prostration was practised, the complete annulling of stature in humility.

Let me add a little more depth about the idea of bowing as submission. The Talmud states that one who fails to bow appropriately during prayer is reincarnated as a serpent. What is the meaning of this apparently extreme assertion? What lies behind this image?

Bending the spine must be done; if it is not done in this life, it must be done in another. We have more than once noted that the purpose of growth is towards humility; bending the spine is the act and the posture of the humble. That *must* take place; man's freedom is only how he chooses to do it – now as an act of submission and self-negation, or later as an imposed lesson in that art.

The serpent represents the fully humbled spine. Recall the punishment of the serpent, the agent that tempts man to refuse to bend himself before his Maker. That serpent walked erect; the consequence of his action is to lose his ability to walk vertically forever. The spine that is unbending when it should submit, that walks tall when it should walk humbly, will be brought to crawl.

An episode described in the Talmud sheds light on this. A certain yeshiva during the post-Mishnaic period was repeatedly visited by a particularly fearsome spiritual being. I am not going to explain what is concrete and what is symbol in this narrative, or the nature of these beings; let us simply note that they are brought into existence by the action of human imagination, are extremely dangerous, and attack the most elevated individuals most intensely. (Today we virtually ignore this particular danger; our spiritual level is so puny that we are no temptation for this type of adversary. Today we damage ourselves; no external spiritual enemy is needed.) A plan was formulated to deal with the problem: a great and saintly sage was due to visit the yeshiva; the plan called for him to be hosted there but not invited to the home of any member of the academy so that he would be left alone at night in the study hall. The assumption was that he would be attacked by the being, and the equally confident assumption was that he would deal with it effectively. That in fact is exactly what happened: he found himself alone facing what manifested as a fearsome serpent with seven heads. The Talmud relates that each time the sage bowed, one of the heads was destroyed, until ultimately the danger was permanently obliterated.

One of the later commentaries, the Maharsha, explains that the serpent represents the misplaced pride and overbearing ego that we are here to destroy, the rigid human spine that must be taught to bend. This is the serpent that defeats Adam, that induces him to express himself instead of his Creator. Bowing is the act that expresses the humility that must be cultivated. Each bow destroys another element of its nemesis, expresses another step in the conquest of the undisciplined ego, and ultimately clears the scene of the poisonous beings that are the products of our own unbalanced self-confidence, really no more than projections of our own imagination.

Obviously, this piece of Talmud requires more explanation and analysis; I bring it only to demonstrate again that bowing is part of Jewish thought and practice, to illuminate an aspect of its power, and to show that this too is not something a Jew need go to Buddhism to learn.

Akiva,

In Buddhism, I am placing myself at the disposal of the attributes that are represented by the Buddha statue. I bow to the other meditators as a way of showing respect for them. I bow to my teacher for the same reason. I bow upon entering the zendo *because it is the space in which this kind of respect is to be offered, and where the difficult work is to be done.*

One must remember that Zen originates in China and Japan, where bowing was a sign of humility and respect more than worship. That cultural attitude informed much of Zen practice, and the cultivation of humility is a constant reminder that one just does what one does, without trying to become or feel special, powerful, exalted.

As such, in bowing, one shows respect and constantly cultivates humility, and this is in large part why bowing to statues of Buddha is defended as not being idol worship.

When one enters and leaves the meditation hall, one bows. When one prepares to sit in meditation, one bows to the pillow, turns, and bows to those on the other side of the hall. When seated at a formal silent meal, one bows in thanks to the servers.

Bowing offers an opportunity for cutting through the dualities of self and other, sentient being and Buddha. Suzuki put it this way: "When you bow, there is no Buddha and no you. One complete bow takes place."

What Judaism may see as idols, Buddhism sees as intermediaries: aids to progress that we place at strategic points so that we can be reminded of the many facets of awareness we must continually cultivate.

Incidentally, your analysis of idol worship notwithstanding, I might argue that part of what chases Jews from Judaism is that we have reduced God to the status of a mere idol: *a finger-wagging symbol of negative caution who merely* represents *what God* used to be *to our forefathers.*

David,

Sadly, you are right about that last point. Nothing left but symbols; empty relics where once there was life. Sound without meaning; bodies without souls. That is what is left when non-authentic Judaism takes over. The soul is lost.

Let us look at one more angle of the subject of intermediaries. How does a Jew relate to the world of the zodiac? What is the correct perspective from a Torah viewpoint? What is unique about our place in the hierarchy of stars and nature?

As always, we look back to our "enlightened one." When Abraham is told prophetically that he will have a son, he argues with God: "How can that be," he asks, "since the stars predict otherwise?" Now how do you understand a man arguing with God Himself on the strength of astrological prediction? Surely God's explicit word overrides any possible astrological clues? But the answer is that the stars too, are His words. He writes the book of the heavens. The stars document the flow of energy through the intermediary channels, as we have learned. Therefore Abraham asks: "But Your word to me is contradicted by Your word in the stars!" That is the source of his perplexity and that is his question. And God answers by teaching him the great secret of Jewish existence: "And He took him outside" and showed him the stars; simply, outside his tent, but mystically, *outside the sphere of the stars.* You are not bound by those channels, God teaches him. They are natural, they define the inevitable; you are transcendent, you define your own destiny. Abraham merited to be carried above the world and the zodiac because he lived in a superhuman way: he withstood trials in a fashion that generated transcendence. If you live on the higher plane, it becomes real. The Torah phrase is: *"Ein mazal l'Yisrael"*; the Jewish people are not inevitably bound by the natural world of the zodiac.

The Talmud relates incidents illustrating this principle, and how even one mitzva can change a destiny. In one such incident a young girl was destined to die on her wedding day, according to expert astrological prediction. During the wedding meal she took a hairpin from her hair, unconsciously inserted it into the wall near her – and transfixed a serpent poised to strike. On enquiry it transpired that in the midst of the celebration she had taken food to a beggar who had remained unnoticed by all the guests. Such an act is not "natural"; no part of the material world transcends its own nature in an act of selfless awareness of another's need at a time of deep and justifiable self-involvement. A mitzva is performed, an act that generates transcendence, and a destiny is altered.

A mitzva is an action that lives on the higher plane; it reaches beyond the stars. Recall that the root of the word "mitzva" means "togetherness" as well as commandment, because a mitzva brings together the one who performs it and the One who commands it. An act that has the potential to lift its principal into direct relationship with the Source of all existence transcends by far all the merely intermediate levels. We relate to the Source; we bypass the intermediaries. Failure is to be locked into the mechanical and the inevitable: the Jerusalem Talmud states that the consequence for a Jew who seeks astrological prediction is that he becomes *locked in* to that prediction; if he insists on being part of the natural it becomes inevitable for him. The entire purpose of the Jewish people is to live within the natural only to transcend it, to rise to the dimension of the Source.

Accessibility

"Although Buddhism can get very ornate and very intricate, its basic tenets are extremely simple, and it is therefore not only extremely accessible, it's also portable: *that is, it does not conflict with the practice of other religions. You can practise Buddhism and still be a Jew. After all, I'm merely cultivating mindfulness, watching my breath, realizing the interconnectedness of all things and beings, and striving to recognize and uproot the causes of suffering.*

Judaism, on the other hand, is confoundingly inaccessible, and the deeper one tries to go, the denser the thicket of laws, and texts, and beliefs, and practices gets."

David,
Is the Buddhist Jew who levels these claims of inaccessibility at Judaism one who does so from a position of knowledge? Has he attempted access? Has he pursued the study of Torah as assiduously as his Buddhist studies? Does he know what is complex and what is simple about Torah?

Or does Torah appear dense and inaccessible to him from the outside?

In fact, Torah is as complex as the world and as simple as its unitary core. To approach this we shall need to examine both the simplicity of Torah and its complexity, and then address the mystery of their paradoxical coexistence.

Firstly, Torah is extremely simple, to borrow your phrase. Its teaching is nothing other than "God is One." This is the axiom, the foundation, and the totality.

But Torah is also as complex as the Universe. The Torah is the cause of reality, the underlying template of the world. (Torah is not a *description* of the world, it *precedes* the world in the sense of a film that is projected onto a screen; Torah is the film, the Universe is the screen. I shall try to explain this more fully.) The world is as it is only because Torah is what it is. The world is an emanation, a projection of Torah – there must be an exact correspondence between the source and its projected image, between cause and effect.

Now it follows that if the world is complex (and it *is* complex), then of course the Torah must encompass that complexity; it could not be otherwise. For every detail in the manifest world there must exist in Torah a particular corresponding source.

(Why the world itself must be complex is a question raised in the kabbalistic sources, and it opens a fascinating path, but I am going to resist the temptation to discuss that now. We are considering how Torah and Buddhism relate to the world and our place in it; the prior question of why the world is the way it is falls outside our purview for the present. Buddhism, too, must relate to the world as it is.)

So the Torah contains the world's complexity; both at root level in the sense of cause, and at the level of Instruction in the sense that Torah teaches the correct understanding of, and relationship with, the world of its making. Torah is exactly as detailed as the world it generates and regulates; it must be so.

And yet Torah is ultimately simple. As I have indicated, its deepest axiom is God's Oneness. Here we mean specifically the Oneness of

His Name: His essence is unknowable to us and we do not discuss it; what is given to us is a Name. This Name indicates the Oneness underlying all complexity; not a bland simplistic oneness in the sense of homogeneity, but a oneness of complex parts. The Name itself indicates the Oneness that unifies; Oneness that contains the roots of all things at a level where the roots are yet one. In fact, the Torah teaching of God's Oneness is exactly focused here: the effort is to appreciate that all *things*, all *parts* are One. Not that there are no "things;" not that separation and differentiation are specious and false, but *despite* separation and differentiation, all is One.

This obviously needs further discussion, but I suspect that a Buddhist will find this idea not unfamiliar. (Where we differ will be on this: is the oneness that summates all things no more than that – a harmonious flowing together of all manifest reality – or is the oneness of the world *more* than the sum of its parts? It seems to me that the Buddhist view is closer to the former; the Torah view is certainly the latter. Torah is synonymous with the idea that the world, in all its unified complexity, is only the external face of a deeper Oneness.)

Now how can it be both simple and complex?

The Torah idea is that in any organic system, all things that comprise that system unfold from an ultimately simple yet multipotent root. In the conception of a child, for example, the first moment contains all; in that moment of fusing of genes, all that will unfold is coded. The process thereafter is only a revelation of what the first moment held. Each moment unfolds from the previous moment, reveals it, and in itself holds the next and the root of all the rest, until finally the entire sequence has been revealed when the last moment brings to full revelation what was deepest in the first.

Compressed in all beginnings is totality. At the stage of conception, the most minute of changes may have global consequences. That is the nature of reality; source contains all, source is compressed essence.

In Torah, there are two organic sequences. One begins with Genesis, the moment of firstness in which all is coded. Torah sources make clear that the entire Torah can be derived from the first word *"Bereishit* – In the beginning...;" its manifold permutations indicate all that is to come. (An anecdote: the Gaon of Vilna had taught this axiom to his students. On a particular occasion they were seated with him at a *pidyon ha'ben,* the redemption of a firstborn son. Someone turned to him and asked where the mitzva of redeeming the firstborn son is to be found in the first word of Genesis. The Gaon replied: *"ben rishon achar shloshim yom tifde,"* meaning "you shall redeem the firstborn son after thirty days," spelled out by the acronym of the six letters of that first word of Genesis.)

The other sequence in Torah is not temporal but spiritual; it begins with the Ten Commandments. The first word of the first Commandment is *"Anochi,"* meaning "I am." (Note that this first word begins with an *aleph,* the first letter of the alphabet; the first word of Genesis begins with a *bet,* the second letter. The spiritual sequence is primary, the temporal is secondary; the first indicates unity, the second indicates the beginning of multiplicity.) Now the Sages state that the entire Torah is contained in the Ten Commandments, the entire Ten are contained in the first Commandment, the entire first Commandment is contained in its first word "I am," and that entire word is contained in its first letter, the *aleph.* I think you can see here an expression of our principle; each stage holds all the subsequent ones within it, and the process is one of unfolding each stage from its source.

So the root is simple and unitary, but it contains incipient within its simplicity all the manifold complexity that it will express. The world is a complex revelation of an unrevealed unitary root, a complex unfolding of myriad detail, but a complexity of detail that always holds within it the simplicity of the root that generates each detail. I am not claiming that this is an easy idea, in fact it represents an unfathomable mystery; but a certain level of grasp in this area falls within the ambit of the obligation of Torah study, and that is the primary reason that we grapple with it.

Although we cannot go into this principle fully here, let me give just one example for the purpose of holding it a little closer to the light.

There is an idea that in all parts of a system of this kind the whole is represented. That is, *each* part reflects the whole. From each part, the whole can be reconstructed; since each part was coded in the primal point of singleness, each part contains the whole. An application of this principle struck me during my medical education: you will note that each cell of the body contains the genes of the entire body. That is a remarkable observation – in each individual cell the entire organism is fully coded. You might logically assume that when the embryo differentiates into its multiple parts, the specific section of the genome that codes for a particular part would be found in that part: that the cells of the retina would contain the genes that code for and produce the material of the retina, and none other. Why would retinal cells need the rest of the genome? The retina never produces fingers or toes (or you would be in a lot of trouble). But that is not what happens. When the initial cell that constitutes the beginning fetus divides into two cells, both contain a full and identical copy of the original single genome. When the two become four, all four are yet identical. When the four become eight, each is still like all the others (you can demonstrate this quite clearly by separating off one cell and allowing it to develop: it becomes a full organism, not one eighth of an organism!)

And that process continues. At a certain point, groups of cells begin to specialize into different primordial tissue types, and the body's differentiation has begun. But at every point each cell receives a full complement of all the genes; in fact, one of the unsolved mysteries of biology is exactly this: what causes the initial differentiation when all the cells are identical? Why do some cells form the head and others the tail of the organism if *all* the cells have the same set of instructions? How does each group of cells "know" which part of its full genetic code to activate while allowing all the rest to lie dormant? What overriding co-ordinating instruction governs differentiation when there is no code of instruction yet known other than the code situated identically in each cell? You can see how deep this problem is; I mention it here only because it is one of those areas that illuminates mystical principles in the physical.

So each cell carries all the information, not only its own. Why are those other genes there? Only the very limited and specific gene element that is relevant in any particular cell is actively expressed, but in *every* cell, *all* the genes are present. Put another way, from any *single* cell in the body you could clone a replica of the *entire* body. Why does every cell carry the compressed essence of the whole?

That is true to our principle: the part contains the whole. Simplicity unfolds into detail, but the details, if properly studied and perceived, show their root. Torah is a training to understand complexity and its underlying bonded essence. Generalities beget specifics, specifics reveal the general. I suggest that you look into the exegetical construct of *klal u'prat u'klal*, the pattern of a generality in Torah that is followed by a specific that is followed in turn by a reversion to the generality. This is one of a group of concepts within Torah involving the notion of classes and their members. You will find it illuminating (I am sure that in your case even one example will reveal the whole).

To summarise, the correct perception of Torah is one of stark simplicity at the core, surrounded by a complexity as deep and detailed as the world itself. The former infuses the latter: the simple core illuminates the layers of complexity. As the layers are examined they reveal ever more clearly that all their myriad details are bound by organizing principles that are deeply unified, and the whole harmonizes exquisitely in a dance rich in nuances and yet ultimately simple in theme.

There is another element in your question: you mention Buddhism's *portable* nature as a feature, or consequence, of its simplicity. There is not much to say here and less to argue about: if Buddhism consists *only* of "cultivating mindfulness, watching my breath, realizing the interconnectedness of all things and beings, and striving to recognize and uproot the causes of suffering," we should not find it necessary to argue. These things are necessary and of course portable to a Jewish platform; you would not need to import them, though, because they are already there in its ancient and timeless inventory. No sensitive and spiritual path can begin without these.

It is debatable whether watching my breath as a specific exercise is necessary, but I suspect that this is more a technique employed for a purpose than an immovable article of the Buddhist approach. Incidentally, you may find it interesting to know that the breath occupies a central position in Jewish thinking, both esoteric and revealed: the Hebrew word for breath, *neshima*, and for soul, *neshama*, are one root. In fact they share a deeper common root, *sh(a)m*, which means essence in various aspects. In addition to forming the core of the word for soul, clearly a reflection of essence, this root also means a "name," always a definition of essence in Torah; and it means "there" in the sense of a destination or end-point, the essence, the purpose, of any journey or process. This is also the root of the word for ultimate destination, *shamayim*, "heaven;" in the sense of life's destination; the word *shamayim* literally spells out the plural of destination, *"shamim,"* that is, the composite of all "theres" that are possible, the culmination of all journeys, final essence. Note that the word for the earth, *eretz*, means "running towards;" the word for heaven indicates where that running ends, the destination and result of all movement. (Do you begin to understand the depth of the pain we should feel for our generation's sons and daughters stripped of the knowledge of Hebrew, for whom "heaven and earth" denote no more than concrete images worthy of no attempt at penetration? Sons and daughters for whom the sounds of Eastern languages ring with exotic allure while their own Eastern language, whose essence is every word's penetration into the transcendent, is foreign in their ears.)

The word for breath holds much more on the esoteric level, including a paradoxical meeting of opposites, but I mention these more basic elements only to follow through with my undertaking to demonstrate that the Buddhist ideas you describe are to be found in Torah. In the *language* of Torah, mind you; spiritual ideas are not things we *describe* in Hebrew words, they *are* the words, they are the currency of our discourse. This subject verges on the miraculous and it needs much more attention; I shall try to show a few of its elements as we continue to communicate.

Dear Akiva,
The Jew who levels claims of inaccessibility may be a lot like me:
experiencing that inaccessibility despite living an active Jewish life,
pursuing more Jewish education, raising Jewish children. The real
question is, exactly what is it about Judaism that is sending Jews in
other directions?

Although Buddhism is a venerable tradition, you have said that at best
it can be seen as preparation for a life of Torah. My response to this is
ironic but truthful: in my experience, Buddhism does a better job of
preparing one to live a Jewish life than does Judaism!

Dear David,
That is exile. That is how far the Western Jew has become estranged
from the real and proper engagement of his mind and heart. A core
issue here is lack of genuine Jewish education, and far worse, non-
authentic Jewish education to the point where what is known of
Judaism could hardly be more wrong. The modern Jew who is the
victim of such "education" may come to reject the version of Judaism
that he knows (not surprisingly, given his distorted picture) in favor of
something that appears beautiful, not beginning to realize that what he
has chosen is no more than a fragment of the real Judaism he has not
begun to discover.

That is the meaning of exile. This is a key concept – the Torah is in
exile; at a deep level it is far from us, hard to reach. Exile is far more
than a geographical problem.

We are exiled in a foreign culture and a foreign language.

In a foreign culture: we are children of the West, not of Torah, and we
see the world through the eyes of our host culture. We see Torah
through those eyes, too, and that is what makes it inaccessible to us.
How do you see the essential nature of obligation in a society that sees
only personal freedom? How do you see beyond the values of a
culture and a society when your eyes are formed by that culture and
that society? How do you think free from conditioning experience

when the very form of your thoughts is determined by your experience? Before you can see, before you can think, you must clear your eyes and your mind of the substance that clings to them and claims to be their essence. Before you apply your tools to their purpose you must make it your purpose to adjust those tools; but where do you find the tools for that?

We are deep in an exile of the mind. For our generation, achieving genuine access to Torah is as miraculous as any redemption. But if it is genuinely longed for and worked for, it happens. The opportunity opens, the teacher appears.

And we are exiled in a foreign language. There is no access to Torah without the language of Torah. This is a deep problem. Torah lives in its language, and although the goal of spiritual knowledge lies beyond words of any language, the path to that knowledge traverses a Torah of words. In fact, the first step on that path is to recognize that the language and its meaning are one; the beginning of reconstructing the deeper knowledge is in grasping how in Hebrew the word and what it conveys are not separate. Here lies a great secret in the theme of how vessel and content are united; how meaning can live in a vessel that transmits it and yet is one with it. The deepest Torah theme of the oneness of reality reveals itself here.

One of the most profound aspects of our exile is the discarding of Hebrew by those who should have known better. When certain communities decided to learn and pray in translation, they virtually sealed their fate. I am not going to spell out which strands within contemporary Judaism, which groups and communities are relevant here; you can fill in the blanks. I am making a general point: when the decision was taken to change to a translation for the purpose of making Judaism accessible, within that action lay two consequences: it became accessible, but it was no longer Judaism. I am not talking about translation as *explanation,* as a medium of commentary alongside the original; that is fine, even necessary. I am talking about *exchanging* the original for a translation; when you do that you lose what you are trying to translate. There is an element of good intention in the attempt, to be sure, but its result is disaster.

The argument in those circles is: "But they no longer understand Hebrew – let us give them what they can understand." A bizarre analogy comes to mind when I meet members of communities in your country who have no Hebrew at all and whose learning and services are all conducted in English, who present that argument. Imagine a desperately ill patient who can no longer digest food. A well-intentioned bystander says: "Feed him artificial food; perhaps some flavored plastic or moistened paper." The doctor responds: "He will die of starvation that way; he needs real food." The first objects: "But he cannot digest real food; and see how he likes the paper!" The challenge is to find a way to heal the digestion problem, not pander to it with useless substitutes. That digestion problem may be very real, it may even appear incurable, but the substitutes are certain death.

The solution is not services in English, Torah in translation. Teach them Hebrew! Give them the real thing. The right dose of the real nourishment will heal the digestion problem; I can guarantee you that it will stimulate an appetite. What exactly is the problem? They cannot understand Hebrew? The services will be meaningless because they cannot understand? Teach them! What is the problem with teaching their children the language of Torah? What is their objection? They learn Spanish, don't they? French, don't they? Or is it German? Those who invest in a classical education for their children include Latin in the syllabus. What is the problem with giving them Hebrew so that they can learn Torah? Is it not classical enough? Too classical?

No; the problem is that it has ceased to be relevant for them. They live in a culture that defines what is relevant, and that has become their culture.

What were their leaders thinking when they agreed to throw out the contents with the vessel? Why did they not demonstrate that Torah and its language are so organically married that their divorce kills them both? You have to be so profoundly devoid of Torah not to know this that it makes their leadership incomprehensible. What did the flock do to deserve such shepherds?

Approaching Torah without Hebrew is like regarding a stuffed lion in a museum and complaining that its roar is not loud enough. When you take Torah out of its living medium and cast away its pulsating heart; what is left? (And that is not all, David, because in the communities I am referring to, whatever is left is stripped of the practice of the commandments too. So the modern Jew brought up with that sort of education is exposed to a mistranslated empty shell, emasculated and eviscerated beyond all recognition. I would say that the dusty skin of a museum lion draped over its false bones is very much more alive than our victim.)

What will you argue in their defence? Perhaps you will say that Hebrew is no longer our spoken language; perhaps this is some justification for its neglect as the medium of learning and prayer. But do not think that in bygone eras Hebrew was the natural medium of Torah study because our people *spoke* Hebrew; that now that our vernacular is English or some other diaspora language it has become difficult to approach learning and prayer in Hebrew because it is no longer our mother tongue. That is an error; we did *not* speak Hebrew as our first language in ages past. Not since the first Temple has Hebrew been our spoken language; throughout the centuries since then, since the ending of prophecy, we have always *chosen* another language, even when we had to invent one ourselves, like Yiddish or Ladino. Even *in Israel* during the second Temple period Hebrew was not the language of the Jewish street or home (Aramaic was). For the last two and a half thousand years we have learned and prayed in Hebrew and never spoken it as our medium of common discourse; not in Israel and not in any country of our exile.

A moment's digression to give just the briefest of clues to the reason that the people of the Torah chose to avoid the language of Torah for everyday use: when Hebrew is used only in the context of Torah, its concepts and constructs point always to the transcendent. The language retains its luminosity. When you speak the language of holiness to convey the mundane, you strip it of that aura. If you do that, you can never again convey the sensitive higher meanings in the words you have prostituted; they have fallen in your consciousness and can mean only the mundane. Forever after, when you say the word and mean its sanctity, I shall hear its lower message. To understand the depth of the problem, think of the images we see when we use English words for spiritual things – who can claim that when he hears the English word "God" he needs no effort to see beyond a picture of a sage old man with a white beard reaching down from the heavens, his outstretched finger about to touch Adam's? What picture do you see when you hear "angel?" Be honest – do you apprehend an abstract concept of emanation from source, or do you see a detail of a medieval Italian painting? What do you see for "saint?" Nothing to do with a delicate gold ring levitating above the saintly head? What does "Heaven" convey? Nothing to do with fluffy white clouds hosting happy fellows holding harps? Do you see how sordid is the prostitution of language? We never allowed that to happen to Hebrew. I am not even going to begin discussing modern spoken Hebrew and what it means for Torah learning.

(Why was Hebrew our everyday spoken language during first Temple times? The key is this: during the era of *prophecy,* during that period when the higher world was manifest in the lower, when a clear vision of the transcendent was constant, when flesh and blood heard the Divine word, when the material was comfortable host to the spirit, Hebrew was the language of the everyday because the *everyday was elevated,* the mundane revealed the holy. There was not the degree of schism that we experience today, the war between flesh and spirit that is now the norm. While the Temple stood the Jewish people centered around a focus of spirit within the physical, and their everyday speech was invested with an elevation that the voice of prophecy makes natural.)

Or perhaps you will argue that translation should be allowed to supplant the original because the flock would wander otherwise; that such a compromise is justified for the sake of Jewish continuity, Jewish survival. That is a fundamental error. Firstly, that sort of compromise does not work; the flock may indeed remain, but if they do they risk death by starvation, as I have tried to show. And if the throes of starvation do not send them seeking other pastures one must wonder about their sanity.

But the error in such thinking is even deeper. Compromising Torah beyond the limit that Torah itself allows, whether in the matter of language or law, for the sake of Jewish survival is fundamentally flawed. Beyond the question of whether the compromise is likely to be effective in holding Jews, or generating greater numbers to bolster Jewish survival, there is a more basic issue here. And although there will certainly be outraged howls from those quarters in which Jewish survival is the urgent (and sincere) driving motivation for much hard work, I have to tell you this: the Jewish people's survival is not our problem. It is not a problem at all; it has been promised by the One who is entirely capable of delivering on His promises. Survival and redemption are guaranteed. They may be His problem when His children insist on being wayward, but they are not ours. Our problem is not the survival of the Jewish people; *our problem is the survival of Jews* – individual Jews have no guarantee of survival. Our work must be to attract and help Jews for *their* sake, not because the survival of the nation as an entity is at risk. That must be the underlying rationale for Jewish outreach efforts today – to learn genuine Torah with anyone who remains sensitive enough to attempt it.

Perhaps a simple analogy will help: when the tree loses its leaves in the winter, it does not die. Even though its leaves fall, the tree survives. Jews are being lost, that is true; leaves are falling. But there will be a spring, that is sure. The tree will survive. *But the leaves fall –* that is our concern; we are not trying to save the tree, we are concerned about the falling leaves. Each Jew who loses contact, detaches from the Tree of Life, is a tragic loss. We worry for them, we are concerned for their survival; we are thinking about the leaves.

So compromising Torah beyond recognition, presenting an emaciated, bereft Judaism so that we shall have numbers and that way ensure our survival as a people, is a manifold mistake that perhaps only tears can begin to express. And if you *insist* that increasing numbers must be an issue, that membership must be swelled, there is only one way to do that: deliver the real goods. If anything really attracts the Jewish heart and mind it is only the real thing. In the real language.

Akiva,

You make a critical point – intimacy with Judaism requires a facility with the Hebrew of the Torah. No other religion that I know of – certainly not Zen – virtually encodes a specific language with the origins of its experience and its system of belief, knowledge and worship.

We are more and more a post-literate society. As we assimilate, we get more and more of our knowledge from our media, from our computers, from the brief and shallow references of our hurried lives. (There is no way you could have risen to your level of Jewish literacy without being fluent in ancient Hebrew, whereas I could probably become a Buddhist priest with little more than a few words of Sanskrit, Pali and Japanese.)

If words as reality do in fact "verge on the miraculous," I hope that's something you'll talk about more. For a Buddhist, words are like selves: at once tools and obstacles to greater understanding. The profound connection between the language and the Divine presence cannot be glossed over. What more can you tell me about it?

Language

David,

The potency of the language of Torah is a vast subject. Hebrew is called the "holy language" because it underlies all of manifest reality. (There is another reason too: Maimonides says that Hebrew is known as holy because it has no vulgarities. All the words for unseemly things and functions, those things that in other languages are used as profanities and curses, cannot be said in Hebrew; they are all expressed as refined references only. In modern Hebrew, should you wish to utter a profanity, you would have to use a word from another language; all modern Hebrew profanity is borrowed.)

The root concept is that *the world was created by means of the language;* the world was "spoken" into existence. When the Torah states "And God said..." in creating, it does not mean He gave instruction; it means He spoke a word and that word condensed, crystallized, concretized into the object it denotes. In reality Hebrew words do not describe things, they *are* the things themselves (we are referring to Hebrew in the deeper sense, what we would more properly have to call prophecy. Maimonides indicates that when you heard a prophet speak, you did not *hear* what he said, you *experienced* what he said. The prophet did not talk *about* a thing; he *said the thing itself*).

In Hebrew, unlike other languages, the word for a "word" and the word for a "thing" are the same – the word *davar* means both "word" and "thing" because in essence any thing is none other than the word the Torah uses to create that thing. (Of course, this principle has a corollary – all things in the world are speaking their words, the world is created to be a dialog; we should be listening.)

Language is the medium of Creation. Now that our language has broken down we have only shards of the original language in our Hebrew and in our language in general; but in essence language and reality are one. I have already mentioned the idea that the world is a projection of the Torah: in analogy, the Torah is a film through which an ineffable light is shone; the light shines through the Torah and projects onto a screen which is the world we experience. The Torah is the film, the fabric of our reality is the image on the screen. Each detail on the film is projected onto the screen; each word in the Torah is a thing in the world. (Each is enough to fathom the other – one who knows the Torah will know the world; one who knows the world will know the Torah.)

You can see what a powerful tool this is. No other language has a hint of this; in the languages of the world words connote things by convention, that is all. (In depth, all languages derive originally from Hebrew; that is the meaning of the breakdown or splintering of language that occurred at the Tower of Babel. That generation had decided to re-create the world in their own image; they could do that because they spoke the language of Creation. Their downfall was brought about by the breaking of their language; that destroyed their ability to create and left them much as we are now – at best able to describe things, unable to create.)

There is another dimension to the Hebrew language too, that of *gematria*. This is the numerical correlate of the verbal element; the letters have a system of numerical equivalents that parallel their literate function. This means that a Hebrew word speaks its meaning both explicitly and mathematically; in a sense like the two functions of verbal expression and scientific (or mathematical) notation of other cultures. The wonder here is that the two systems overlay each other: in English you might express an idea verbally in characters of the English alphabet or choose alternatively to express the same idea in mathematical notation using Arabic numerals; in Hebrew, however, the letters and the numerals are co-extensive. The *same letters* do both; a Hebrew word expresses the verbal aspect of an idea and the *same word* read as a numeric expression gives the mathematical or quantitative aspect of the idea. I hope I am making this clear: imagine reading a perfect English-language description of, say, a bridge, and then going back over the very same text reading the letters as numbers and finding that the text is also a perfect specification of that bridge in the mathematical notation of engineering formulae. This almost incomprehensibly beautiful system is the language of Torah. (In my personal opinion, if you were accumulating proof of Divine authorship this would contribute mightily.) As we continue to correspond I shall try to give an example or two. (Remind me to show you a seemingly problematical verse analyzed by the Vilna Gaon in which the Torah describes the ratio of diameter to circumference of a circle verbally and the *gematria* of the words gives *pi* to a number of decimal places.)

How can I convey some of this endless subject to you meaningfully here? Perhaps we can look briefly at just the first letter of the alphabet; that surely is the place to begin. Let us discuss only the *aleph,* and let it stand as a symbol that we are only beginning the discussion.

The letter *aleph* indicates deep knowledge, higher wisdom, mystical knowledge – its numerical value is one, a clue to the Supernal Oneness, and it is silent. In fact it is the only completely silent letter; the idea is that it is not yet in the world, or rather, it stands between the higher world of potential and the lower world of the actual. The *aleph* brings down from that world to this, and indicates elevation from this world to that; it is the junctional zone that stands between the world of transcendence and the world of the manifest.

Consider the structure of the *aleph* א. Its components are a higher letter *yud* and a lower, mirrored *yud,* joined by a *vav,* the letter of connection (which together comprise twenty-six, the numerical value of the Divine name). The *yud* is the letter that indicates the ten "emanations" or root energies of Creation; the *aleph* connects the upper and lower of these, the root with the reflection of that root which is the revealed world.

Again unlike other languages, Hebrew letters are also words. The root word *aleph* indicates elevation; the verb *aleph* means to elevate spiritually, as in teaching. The word *aluph* indicates the highest rank, the word *eleph* means a thousand, the highest named number in Torah language. (The full Hebrew alphabet begins with the *aleph* whose number is one and progresses through all the decimal elements; the total is 999. Thereafter comes *eleph,* a thousand, or *aleph,* one, the very same word, back to the point of origin, itself expressing a deep principle in the mystical teaching.)

There are many more secrets hidden in the *aleph.* We have noted that it is silent; real knowledge has no finite sound, it is intangible, inexpressible, transcendent. The next three letters in the alphabet, the coming down into the finite, the tangible, are ד ג ב in sequence spelling *beged,* the word for a garment, the outer clothing of the invisible core. But *beged* is also the word for "treachery." The garments may lie, they may cover an identity instead of reveal it, that is their nature. The silent center cannot lie, but its outer layers, those layers that speak, may speak treachery. (The Hebrew word for an outer garment, a coat, *me'il,* has a similar quality; the same root spells a profaning, a betrayal, of the holy.)

The analysis of a Hebrew word is built on its root letters. Any word that contains an *aleph* will comprise some element of elevation or transition between worlds, and particularly when it begins with the *aleph.* The simplest of all Hebrew words, for example, is *"av,"* comprising, of course, just the first two letters of the alphabet, which means "father." You do not need me to work out how the concept of "father" expresses the *aleph* at root. The verb root *av* means to desire, in the sense of volition, the desire to extend beyond the limited self, in essence the father's desire.

And so on. David, you just cannot manage without Hebrew, I am afraid. Approaching Torah without Hebrew is like trying to swim without water. Or perhaps like trying to breathe without air. If ever the medium was the message, it is here.

Chosenness vs. Universality

"Buddhism recognizes and focuses on the interconnectedness of all things and beings. In fact, in meditation one can concretely experience this, and it is extremely liberating. Contrast this with the concept of chosenness, which is a fundamental cause of the Jewish people's deliberate separation from the rest of society – a cause, one might even say, of resentment leading to anti-Semitism and its horrifying consequences. To be a practising Jew, you really have to believe that you are part of a covenant in which you have been selected for a special task or role in life. This fundamentally sets you apart, and obstructs you from experiencing the true nature of the Universe."

David,
There are two points here to address: firstly, the idea of universality and what is assumed in your question to be Judaism's intrinsic opposition to it; and secondly, our separation as a possible cause of anti-Semitism.

With your permission, I am not going to comment on the latter. The profound and timeless hatred that is directed at us, pervasive as history itself, needs deep study. But before we assume that expressing our uniqueness accurately and loyally is adequate motivation for those who would destroy us, let us study what that uniqueness means. Before we blame the victim, let us understand him.

You assert that if you are different, "fundamentally set apart," your specialness "obstructs you from experiencing the true nature of the Universe." The first question to ask is, what is the true nature of the Universe? Because if it turns out that we *are* different, then perceiving that difference will be perceiving the true nature of the Universe. So if our goal is accurate perception of the Universe, what sort of Universe is it?

Is the true nature of the Universe a bland sameness, or is the Universe built of fundamentally different elements that are also fundamentally related? If it is the latter, then seeing and experiencing this will be no "obstruction" between the observer and the world.

Why do you assume that the interconnectedness of all things must necessarily be in conflict with the *uniqueness* of each of those things? Assuming that one can in fact "concretely experience" this interconnectedness, does one then experience non-distinction? My point is this: asserting that all things are connected (as Torah certainly does – we touched on this in our discussion about the unfolding of details from a unitary source) is not to say that all things are or should be the *same*. When the parts of an organism are properly connected so that the organism functions as a cohesive and integrated unity, its parts yet remain separate in identity.

In fact, the separate identity of each part is absolutely necessary to the survival and well-being of the organism as a whole. You would look rather silly if your body comprised only identical liver cells! A piece of music works because it comprises *different* notes *in correct relationship*. Or in that overworked but useful analogy, an orchestra is successful because it comprises *different* instruments in harmonious synchrony. Different instruments and different notes, but one piece of music; and if it is a great piece, it is great not despite but *because* of those differences and their disciplined relationship.

I am sure you see where I am heading. The interconnectedness of all things is not synonymous with sameness. The world teaches us that. Each cell comprises a multitude of components, each organ comprises many different cell types, each organ system requires its various and distinct organs, and the body lives because all of its highly differentiated organ systems cohere in indescribable complexity but perfect connection.

Should men and women aim for "sameness?" Do not male and female express the magic of their relationship in the uniting of their unique and different, indeed in many senses opposite, bodies and natures? Would the world be better if all its parts were one color and one shape?

Why are critics of Jewish "chosenness" led to assume that differences are, in themselves, bad? Surely there lurks behind this dissatisfaction with the expression of unique Jewish identity another concern (and it may be worth trying to identify that concern – could it be the *Jewishness* of Jewish uniqueness that irks?). It is obvious that parts of a whole need not, indeed should not, be identical. In the area of the esthetic, as you will see if you examine it, beauty exists where different and often opposite elements come together, each showing up its counterpart by contrast and yet somehow blending with it. That is exactly what beauty is; it is created in the harmony of sweepingly different aspects of vision or of the different notes and tones that combine to form their symphony. "More of the same" does not constitute beauty; that is just "more." Juxtaposition of opposites, contrasts, different elements correctly disposed and composed, that is beauty.

Now when we grasp the world's ethnic and cultural differences as real, are we grasping a problem? Is not the richness of their diversity a treasure in itself? Why should we as Jews not express our uniqueness – how does that expression somehow damage the greater universality that we seek to perceive and complement?

Deeper than this, it is a Jewish teaching that each individual human has a unique identity and a unique role. Should we prefer all humans to be identical robotic clones? I do not for a moment imagine that Buddhism teaches its adherents to lose all traces of personality and seek conformity of character to the extent that each becomes indistinguishable as an individual. Judaism certainly opposes that kind of conformity.

Individual humans must express their individual characters (the Talmud speaks out the uniqueness of each individual: "Just as their faces are not alike, so too their minds are not alike"). And nations and cultures must express theirs. Individuality must be expressed in a hierarchy of uniqueness: each individual as unique, each group of individuals as unique among groups, each larger and more inclusive group reflecting its level of cohesion in its unique way, all to yield the universal body of humanity that is the sum of its myriad parts working together in a vast and precise co-ordination in which each part is utterly subservient to the whole and yet utterly identified and expressed in its particular role.

When the Torah details the structure of the Jewish people it specifies individuals, families and larger groups in a hierarchical structure – individuals have functions as individuals, families as families (the family is a real entity *beyond* merely comprising its members as individuals), and the nation as a whole among the family of nations.

In this international interaction lies the potential for much mutual benefit, a rich harmony of identities and contributions – in fact, that is exactly our Messianic vision. We have essential elements to contribute (you yourself allude to the Jewish people's seminal contribution to human society in another of your questions) and we take from the nations: Rav Tzaddok HaCohen shows that one of the purposes of our exile is to absorb points of essence from the nations we meet. This is too extensive an idea to examine fully here, but part of it is this: the Talmud states that we are exiled in order to recover souls as converts from the host nations. Rav Tzaddok explains that this does not necessarily mean human converts to Judaism; it refers to "sparks," elements of the host cultures we inhabit that must be absorbed. These "sparks" are the subject of much mystical discussion; in this context they are traced ultimately to aspects of Torah that have escaped us and found an abode in other cultures – in our interaction with those cultures they will be brought home.

I mention this because it may be directly relevant to Jews who have explored foreign systems of thought and practice and are now being awakened to their own origins; like yourself they may bring home something they have found outside. This is a delicate point because not everything brought home belongs there. I would say that there are two reservations to consider:

Firstly, is the imported element valid? Is it an aspect of Torah that is coming home? This can be treacherous territory and needs senior Torah guidance; the beginner may fail to negotiate it successfully.

And secondly, is what is being imported really new? If it was always at home the process is no more than an illusion. For a Jew to "discover" things outside that are in fact intrinsic elements of Torah and feel that he is bringing something home is nothing but a testimony to his lack of Jewish knowledge.

I think that if there is a valid element in this process it must be the sensitization that has occurred outside that sends the student searching more deeply and eventually brings *him* home. It need not have happened outside, but the reality in our generation is that due to the profound lack of genuine Jewish knowledge at home it happens that way more than occasionally.

Let me tell you a story in this context; I think it brings out our point. I had the opportunity to share some Torah learning with a group of high-school students recently, and in the course of our discussion I told them a well-known tale. (If you ask me if this is a true story I shall give you the answer of a talented contemporary rabbinic teacher: "All my stories are true. Some happened and some did not, but they are all true.")

The tale is that of a Jew named Berel in a small Eastern European village known as Horodok, who dreams repeatedly of a treasure buried under a bridge in a far-off town. The dream recurs so frequently that he eventually decides he must investigate its validity. He makes the long and arduous journey to the distant town, and sure enough, he finds a bridge exactly like the one in his dream spanning the river there. Under cover of darkness he begins digging under the bridge but is soon dismayed to find himself under arrest – he has been observed by a sentry and is taken to the head of the local police, a coarse and brash individual who interrogates him. Having no really better option, he tells the truth: "I dreamed of a treasure buried under that bridge and began to dig there to see if I might find it."

The police chief responds: "Fool! Where would I be if I followed every dream of mine? For nights now I have dreamed of a treasure buried under the oven of a Jew called Berel in a village called Horodok. Do you think I am about to run off looking for the place just because I dreamed of it? What could be more ridiculous?"

As soon as he is unceremoniously released, Berel hurries home and digs under the oven in his home, and of course, he finds the treasure exactly there.

I asked the students for their response; what is the message of this tale? I anticipated hearing, of course, that the real treasure is right at home and there is no need to search in far-off places. Search at home; dreams of the far distance are misleading, exotically attractive perhaps, full of promise, but misleading all the same. To my surprise, one of the students answered: "You see he had to go far away to find out what he had at home."

I do not need to tell you that that was not the object of my lesson that day, that was not what I had meant to teach them; but it was certainly something I learned.

What we ought to be engaged in, of course, is showing people who have not been brought up with that knowledge what is buried at home. Perhaps for a few dreamers, at least, we can short-circuit the process and obviate the need to travel only to come back to their point of departure.

Is this theory of universality constructed of unique parts in conflict with Buddhist teaching? I imagine not, and I do so confidently because objective observation of the natural world demonstrates its truth. So what is the problem with Jewish uniqueness? Do those who oppose it oppose the unique color and flavor of any other culture's expression? I think not; and I am led to conclude that it is not uniqueness or difference that they oppose, not the idea of different parts harmoniously disposed in a universal concert, but rather Jewish uniqueness specifically. That is worrying, to say the least. What could be wrong with the strong and clear expression of Judaism's unique outlook on life and history? What is wrong with Judaism's overarching agenda of building a world in which each individual and each people will be free to express its character and make its contribution to a united humanity, united by attachment to the central fact of God's existence and service? An entire humanity radiating out from the recognition of one central fact and focus, all different and yet all united by their common origin and purpose. The phrase "like spokes of a wheel" comes to mind; I believe I learned it from you.

You must know that we neither seek nor encourage converts. We do not teach that all people must be Jews; quite the contrary. Those who insist can convert, but we tell those who would that it is not necessary.

Is Judaism universal in its outlook and agenda? As Rosh Hashana (the Jewish New Year) approaches I cannot help thinking of the recurring theme of the liturgy of the day: "Rule over all the world in its entirety." The question here is why "all" and "in its entirety" – surely this is repetition? In the Hebrew the same word is used twice. As you know, we never accept redundancy in our texts as mere repetition; there must be a reason for stating "all the world" twice.

One of the classic commentaries, the Turei Zahav, explains: there are two kinds of "all" in halacha. One is constituted by a majority; even though a minority differs, we refer to the majority position as "all" because that is its legal force. Where a majority outvotes a minority in Jewish law, the ruling accords with the majority entirely, it is to all intents and purposes unanimous. So a majority is as good as "all;" when a majority rules "all" have ruled.

But when we seek the final peaceful unification of all mankind, that is not the "all" we seek. Here we do *not* ask for a halachic "all," a majority which would satisfy the legal criterion, but an *absolute* "all." We are not interested in mankind *in general* perceiving the Divine and accepting His rule; for that sublime purpose a majority is not what we mean; we want every last South Sea islander, Manhattan stock trader, New Guinean spear fisherman, Chicago housewife and Californian beachcomber to be united around the fire of His spirit. No less will do.

No; being different is not the problem. To object to difference as synonymous with divisiveness is to complain that man and wife can never be one because they are different; it is to express dismay that music must be forever flawed because it comprises dissimilar notes. We come together as husband and wife *because* we are different, therein lies the secret of our bond. We are enthralled by the music *because* of its transitions, variations and tonal distinctions, that is what makes it music. This is fundamental.

Certainly we have been "selected for a special task or role in life." So has each nation, and so has each individual. Therein lies the greatness of each nation and each individual; no-one is dispensable or replaceable. *Our* "special task or role" happens to be deeply bound with the development of spirit and the revelation within the physical of an utterly transcendent Source; on the individual level it follows that each Jew must have at least some of that cosmic task allotted to him. I do not propose to delve more deeply into the specific role of the Jewish people here; I shall direct you to the large body of Torah writing that deals with this issue and to that section of our teachings that examines the role and destiny of each of the world's national groupings. When we talk about the nature of the mitzvot, the commandments, I shall try to explain our uniqueness more fully.

If Buddhism teaches the harmonious interconnectedness and integration of all manifest reality, that is valid from a Jewish perspective; but it is not enough in terms of our personal historical task. Our contribution is designed to reach further, it is the work of demonstrating the Source and the Reason that lies behind the world's unity; not simply its fact, but its explanation.

Part and Whole

Akiva,
Is there a Jewish equivalent to Buddhism's understanding of non-dual duality, that interweaving of component and unity?

David,
I am not sure that we differ essentially from Buddhism on this. Perhaps Buddhism's emphasis is more on the whole, the interconnected oneness of parts; we recognize the paradoxical interplay of part and whole. Torah draws attention to each part as separate and yet asserts the oneness of all parts in the whole.

Let us follow this seam and work it more finely.

There is an analysis of this area presented by Rabbi Dessler, a Torah thinker and teacher of the last generation. I shall attempt to summarize it for you; I hope you will find it illuminating.

For this, we shall need to study the order we perceive in the world. The world is exquisitely ordered; the very fact that it can be studied mathematically and scientifically is an expression of this fact.

There are three essential levels of order. The third or highest is the one we must examine most closely; if we approach it by examining the two more basic levels we will find the third thrown into clear relief.

I.

The first, "order for the sake of order," is the symmetry and harmony apparent in the world. This natural order permeates the Universe; the mind manifests this system of order too – the outer world always parallels the inner. It is this order of the mind, reflected in the order of the physical world, that makes it possible to think logically and consistently.

There is a resonance to these inner and outer patterns of order: when they are in harmony, we perceive their harmonious dance; when they are in disharmony, we perceive their dissonance. In a situation where order or symmetry is apparent, your response to that symmetry depends on your own inner sense of order or lack of it. If you are traveling by train with the symmetrical rhythm of the wheels on the tracks – *clickety-click, clickety-click, clickety-click* – your response to that rhythm depends on your own inner rhythm: if you are at peace, inwardly tranquil, as you may be when traveling towards some pleasantly anticipated destination, the sound is soothing, pleasant, musical. The inner symmetry and the outer symmetry are resonating in harmony. But if you are in distress, traveling to some unpleasant or dreaded destination, and your thoughts and emotions are in turmoil, the sound is unbearable. The outer harmony is mocking the inner disharmony, and you feel the pain of that mockery.

Inner order seeks to be mirrored in the outer world; a fractured inner world often reflects itself in outer breakdown.

It is interesting to note that in all forms of artistic expression, the West has seen a consistent disintegration of symmetry over the past few centuries. In all art forms the norm has gradually changed from a symmetrical, representational style, through stages of ever freer expression, to the asymmetrical and often frankly chaotic in the post-modern world. Why does the creative expression of this generation reflect a preoccupation with such dissonances? What does this say about our inner state?

No doubt more than one interpretation is possible, but if art is a reflection of the mind of a culture or a generation, could it be that a taste for disharmony and destructuring implies a breakdown of the inner sense of order?

I wonder if the inner disharmony of the West is part of the force driving its children to the East. How is the environment set up in Buddhist schools? I imagine the meditation hall is appointed in even and symmetrical style. Is there a garden laid out in calming and pleasing fashion? How would a Buddhist teacher respond to an exhibition of post-modern art?

II.

The second level, "order for its results," exists when parts are arranged so that they function. The purpose of the arrangement is to maintain the proper relationship between parts so that each can fulfill its function correctly. An example of this kind of order is an index to a library.

Rabbi Elchanan Wasserman, a leading sage of the last generation, used to point out that if a library is indexed, the more books it contains, the better; but when the index is lacking, the more books it contains, the worse. Without an index, the sheer number of books becomes the problem: if you had only twenty books you would find what you need; if you had twenty thousand you would probably not. And thus it is with the order inherent in the mind: the more organized the mind, the more useful are many facts. But the undisciplined, disorganized mind may do better handling fewer facts. One who wishes to know much must develop structured and orderly thinking; developing a powerful mind is more important than accumulating facts. The skill of great Torah minds lies in their ability to think powerfully within structured paths and yet to break the pattern when appropriate. And even in breaking the pattern a certain structure must be maintained; the truth requires a certain constraint: the paths of truth are always more limited than the paths of falsehood – there may be only one correct solution to a mathematical problem; there are any number of false ones.

III.

The third, "order for unity of function," is the level we need to ponder. This level expresses paradox; here parts come together in an echo of the root paradox of Divine oneness in which parts are no contradiction. At this level, components are organized so that they mesh in a unified whole, and the composite entity functions precisely because of the harmonious blending of its components.

An example of this type of order might be a complex machine – the parts of the machine are interconnected in such a way that the machine functions. Each part would be useless on its own; together they achieve their purpose.

This is not to be confused with the order of the previous level: the type of order that an index imposes on a library ensures the function of the library as a whole, but *each book has its own separate identity and use* – even if the index disappears and the books become completely disorganized, each book remains a book, intact and meaningful. You may have trouble *finding* a particular book, but the nature of each book has not been affected at all. In the case of a machine, however, the individual parts are *nothing* on their own, it is only in their interconnectedness that they achieve any meaning. In the library, the index makes each self-contained part accessible, but in the machine the order and organization are the *entire reason* for the existence of the parts; no individual part has any use without all the others.

Here we begin to feel the tension between individual and whole. In our machine there may be a small screw in the carburetor that is almost insignificant in terms of its intrinsic value – it may be worth less than the smallest coin. But without it the engine does not run, and if that small screw falls out and buries itself in the desert sand when you are driving through Death Valley, you will realize that it is worth the value of the entire vehicle. Without that tiny part you have nothing at all. While the engine was running smoothly that part was unconsidered and unappreciated; now that it is missing its value has become apparent.

Systems set up so that all the parts are needed before any become relevant have a unique quality: each part manifests a paradoxical duality. Each part is at once nothing and everything: nothing because without the rest of the system it is utterly useless, and everything because when all the other parts are in place and functioning, it becomes essential and critical to them all. Each part depends on all the others entirely, in this it is utterly subservient; and yet all the others depend on it, in this it is utterly controlling.

This is how we see humanity: within the Jewish people, each individual is essential and unique, utterly necessary for the cosmic purpose which the Jewish nation must manifest, and yet lost in his merely biological smallness when not fulfilling his destiny as a Jew. Each nation manifests an equivalent pattern; at a broader scale all of mankind, and ultimately the Universe, constitutes such a system. Every thing is created unique in its position and function and will ultimately reveal how critically necessary it is in the greater scheme of reality. The important thing to see here is that we are not simply books in a library to be organized effectively. We are organically linked with such intensity that we are each pathetically small relative to the cosmic expanse and yet utterly indispensable even at those proportions when we find our place in it.

Each Jew is represented by one of the 600,000 letters in the Torah (the deeper sources point out that the name *Yisrael* read as an acronym gives: "There are 600,000 letters in the Torah"). And just as a Torah scroll is completely invalid if even one of its letters is missing, even partially, so too we are fractured as a people unless each individual is present and whole.

No one can replace me, and I fill no one else's role. That is why I am here; we are not accidentally dissimilar. Note too that this expression of individuality is not in contradiction with being a servant of God; *loss of ego is not the same as loss of personality.* A real servant is not one who comes to his master and says: "Master, I am clay in your hands. I have no ambitions and no feelings, no desires and no sense of self. Push me, pull me, do what you will with me and I shall obey." That is simply an individual who will get in the way. A real servant is one who says: "Master, I am *burning with ambition.* I long to express my every faculty, my every talent, and all of my power – but for *you,* not for me." That is a servant.

I mention this because I sometimes detect a loss of this aspect of self in some who have studied and practised in the East, a conscious attempt to lose the very idea of identity. This comes across in many of the things you have written, too. Judaism does not teach that, as I have tried to show. It teaches the aim of divesting the personality of ego, of the childish "for me;" not the aim of losing the personality itself.

This duality of self-expression and self-negation is reflected in the world of our emotional responses. We respond both to the experience of being unique, single, "the loner," and also to the experience of blending into a team or crew. These responses are antithetical: if it is natural to thrill to being a single, all-important individual there should be a negative response to losing one's identity in a group; yet we find, paradoxically, that both are thrilling.

Saving the day alone, unaided, is the stuff of many a young person's fantasy. There is a special thrill in the awareness that the entire deliverance hinges on one individual; the very aloneness of that individual in acting is the source of that unique surge of experience.

Yet we thrill when we blend into a harmonious whole so that the parts become interlocked indistinguishably: a mass display of precision gymnastics in which no individual stands out and the entire human mass seems to function as one being evokes a special feeling in both participants and onlookers. Certain team activities that depend on perfect interaction generate a special thrill. If one member were to make a small move expressing his particular individual presence the entire experience would be destroyed.

We respond in these two opposite ways because that is the nature and purpose of the human experience: each of us is unique, cosmically important, yet we achieve our uniqueness precisely when we fit into a larger order perfectly. When we blend into the Universal picture exactly in terms of our private, unique qualities and abilities we thrill to the realization that no one else could fulfill this particular function, no one else could stand exactly here and do what must be done here. I fit in perfectly so that I become indistinguishable as an individual, and yet as I do so my individuality swells to the proportions of the Universe. I am nothing and I am everything. Each person reflects the uniqueness of the image of the Creator, the totality of the Universe reflects His Oneness, and in depth, the two are not in contradiction.

The thrill of fitting in is a more mature experience than the thrill of being a loner at any cost. The immature personality may choose to step *out of line* in order to experience its own uniqueness; the fact that the overall structure is betrayed and damaged is not relevant to the undeveloped mind. Immaturity cannot see the beauty in yielding the self to actualize the self; in truth, however, that is the only way to genuine selfhood.

(Of course this vision raises the obvious question for each individual: what exactly is *my* uniqueness? What is my particular task? What essential part of the Universe is mine to build? This question is critical – a life spent pursuing an unrealistic and inappropriate identity is a life wasted, and worse, it will damage the entire structure. I have written something on the Torah approach to discerning the individual's role for teenagers, for whom the issue is particularly acute; I shall be happy to send you a copy if you are interested.)

Akiva,

With regard to your comments on order and symmetry, yes, Zen monasteries and gardens in Japan are famous for their painstaking precision and design. One can find such centers in the West now, too, although the Western proclivity for asymmetry and unpredictability sometimes makes a whimsical appearance. So even this works its way into and is embraced in Zen.

Zen teachers have stressed that a special room or environment – other than quiet – is not essential for meditation, although it's thought to be helpful, especially for beginners. Nonetheless, cultivating and keeping the cleanliness, simplicity and order of the meditation hall and its surroundings is seen as an essential aspect of Zen practice.

As to how a Buddhist teacher would respond to an exhibition of post-modern art: "Well, there you have it," might be a common response.

The loss of identity you speak of is something that more ascetic aspects of Buddhism may pursue. Zen teaches you to be careful in each and every instance to understand what is really you and what's really nothing more than fearful rationalization for bad behavior masquerading as authentic aspects of yourself.

Dogen, one of the towering figures of Zen, said "Your own heart, that is the practice hall." The essential matter, the great challenge, is to know what is you *and what is the stuff that accretes upon you, like the barnacles on the bottom of a ship, impeding your progress and eating into your very fiber.*

I find what you have said fascinating, but sometimes I have the feeling that these ideas, compelling as they are, lead into a labyrinth of intellectual refinement with no exit to the practical world. How do I apply these ideas in living? How do I use them to extend my awareness, my own maturity, my own connections to others and to the Divine within them?

David,

Certainly this theme has practical applications. Let me spell out one concrete example of the paradox of self-annulment and self-expression.

In Judaism, the primary learning experience for the paradoxical expression of individuality that is sublimated into something larger is marriage.

Marriage should be a relationship in which each gives entirely; gives himself, herself, utterly and fearlessly. The result far surpasses a simple summation of two individuals; it is the product of two souls each fuelled and fired by the other in a resonating process of ignition. To achieve this you must be ready to give entirely with no thought of holding back, no reserve of any individual identity. You must be prepared to lose yourself completely in the relationship with total vulnerability; and the remarkable result is that when you give yourself away entirely, you discover yourself most sharply.

The paradox here is that to the degree that you are willing to give yourself away, exactly to that degree you find yourself. And when you have found yourself thus you must be ready to put all that you have found back into the relationship. You must give again, and more deeply. And again you will discover a new depth to your own inner being. And again you will give it away. That is the beginning of a relationship that can be called love.

A selfish generation does not know how to give; the real love that binds two people in one fiery and shimmering bond of giving and discovery is hard to find. The very idea of marriage as a commitment is not popular today – why not enjoy the benefits of a relationship without its obligations? Jewish marriage is an unconditional commitment, a total giving of body and soul, present and future; only then can you begin to talk about love.

That is the Jewish idea of marriage: two people giving so intensely that they find themselves each entirely within the other, and yet each discovering a unique identity more sharply defined that is no contradiction to their oneness.

Marriage is the beginning of community, of course. The lesson of self-discovery and expression in relationship that begins with marriage is to be carried further into family and then community. Marriage and family are essential elements in Torah; the family is the crucible in which much spiritual work takes place. We move in ever-widening circles of development: individual to marriage, marriage to family, family to community. This is one of the reasons for the Jewish custom of performing the marriage ceremony in the presence of a *minyan* (quorum of ten): despite the fact that the essence of marriage is the moving into an exclusive relationship, a *withdrawal* from society in the sense that partners in marriage become forbidden to others, yet we begin that phase of isolation from other relationships in the presence of ten, the number that signifies community in Torah. We are thereby making a statement that even as these marital partners are moving into an exclusive relationship, at the same time they are moving towards community. Here we perceive and express again the theme of exclusivity and commonality that underlies all Torah.

Jewish marriage is redolent with references to the marriage of the individual with God, the ultimate meshing of part and whole. That work is known as *d'veykut*, the cleaving of self to Source in an experience that is entirely a denial of self and yet an expression of self. So when you ask for a practical application of these ideas, marriage is a good place to start.

Self-Knowledge

"Buddhism helps one to see that there is no such thing as the 'self,' with a small 's.' Sure, there's a body, and an agglomeration of personality traits within it. But all our 'selves' are interconnected like bicycle spokes. This perspective frees us from grasping and clinging to ideas and desires – the ultimate causes of suffering.

Judaism, on the other hand, upholds the notion of self, and from the get-go puts burdens on it: 613 commandments; and sets for one goals that lead to grasping, clinging, and the endlessness of the cycle of suffering. One could say, then, that in focusing on the true nature of 'Big Self,' that is, the interconnectedness of larger Universal identity, in which we all repose, Buddhism gives a deeper, more accurate, less agonizing self-knowledge than Judaism could, and after all, it is with self-knowledge that we begin to ready ourselves to serve the larger world and avoid inflicting suffering on others."

David,
You raise the issues of defining the self correctly, the "burdens" imposed on the self in Judaism, namely the commandments, and the suffering that results from an incorrect grasp of self. I shall say more about commandments and suffering later; for now, let us focus on the question of self.

What is Judaism if not the process of transforming small self into Big Self? On that we do not differ, but as I tried to show in our discussion about God, we go further; our idea of Big Self is far more than the *"interconnectedness of larger Universal identity."* You might say that as small self relates to Big Self in the Buddhist model, for us the entire Universal reality (Buddhist Big Self) relates to God. In this sense, we begin where Buddhism ends.

But I think there is another, more subtle, difference. As we began to see in our discussion of the tension between parts and the whole, we do not seek to annul small self; we bring both small self and Big Self into sharp focus (the *mussar* teachers say that you should keep two notes in your pocket at all times; on one should be written "I am nothing" and on the other "I am everything"), we grasp both as real and significant, and we grapple with the paradox they set up. And for us, the resolution of that paradox must be in the ultimate Big Self too.

Let us explore this in more detail.

Recently, an individual who plays a leading role in academic and public life was visiting Jerusalem and consulted my teacher for general guidance. In the course of his presentation of what he sees as his life work, this person explained that the central theme of his work is helping others; he feels that his essence is expressed there. The Rabbi's response was interesting. He indicated that the Torah sees an essential step prior to doing good, and that is: first, *be* good. The questioner had to admit that he had not given enough thought to his own inner development; he had always assumed that giving is the highest mode and all that is necessary; he had defined himself entirely in his relationship with others. During that conversation he came to the new insight that doing good to others is a fine mode and goal, of course, but the self must be developed first. What lies beneath the surface here?

Many assume that "do good unto others" is the defining tenet of religion itself. In Jewish thinking that is inaccurate. It is true that "do good unto others" is central to a Jewish view of spirituality, and it is also true that expressing good outwardly is a prime vehicle for the development of inner goodness; nevertheless, Judaism begins with a primary notion of "be good" rather than "do good."

Before a meaningful relationship with another can take place, the inner self must be developed. What is the value of my relationship with you if I am nothing within myself? Only to the extent that I am richly developed is my relationship with you meaningful; only to the extent that I have generated genuine content do I have anything to give you.

Since Judaism defines the quality of relationships in terms of giving, and primarily the giving of self, it follows that the intensity and meaning of my relationship with you exist only to the extent that there is a value of self that I have to give. If I am empty I have nothing to give, and if I have nothing to give, no real relationship can exist between us.

So the development of self is primary, both intrinsically and in forming the root of relationships with others.

In the idea of love this comes into sharp focus. In Jewish spiritual thinking love is defined, perhaps paradoxically at first sight, in terms of self. Love of self is the primary mode of being in the healthy psyche, the drive for self-preservation relates to this, and it is the entirely natural state. This is deeply related to the only direct and immediate knowledge, the knowledge of self. There is a deep connection between love and inner knowledge (remember that the Torah's term for marital love is "knowledge").

The key is this: real love is not love that I have for you as *distinct* from me, but rather, my love for you is an *expansion or extension of myself to include you.* (This is the depth in "Love your neighbor *as yourself.*")

Genuine love of another exists when that other is included in the ambit of one's own being. When I have the maturity and depth to expand my grasp of myself to include you, when you become integral to my definition of myself, when you are as close to me as I am to myself, then my love for you follows automatically. I love you because at a deep level we have become indiscernible as two; we are one. As I have pointed out already, the Hebrew word *ahava*, love, has the same numerical equivalent as the word *echad*, one – the letters of each total thirteen (and I have already indicated why thirteen is the appropriate number to express parts forming unity).

This is a far deeper and richer concept of love than simply a subject-object relationship. A subject-object type of love is really a transformation of the loved object into that which feeds love of self. Ultimately, this is nothing but an immature selfishness. The *mussar* teachers illustrate this by inviting examination of a statement like: "I love fish." What sort of love is that? Of course it is no more than love of self; what is meant is that I love what fish does *for me*. If I really loved the fish, I would not grill and eat it, I would gently put it back in the water and let it swim away.

A child begins with the idea of himself as total; the world exists to serve his personal needs. Maturity begins with the realization that I am only part of a larger reality. Emotional maturity means the acknowledgement that there is a reality beyond self and obliges the control of self that is required to defer to that reality. Mature love requires the ability to expand the grasp of self to a wider radius.

Love is not simply where two meet and share; that is mere partnership. Love is generated in the process of two becoming one. Expanding the sense of self to include another is the ultimate act of love; nothing beyond that step is needed.

The relationship between parent and child is the natural example of extended self. *Because* the child is an extension of the parent, the child is loved by the parent. This too is the deep reason for the fact that parents love their children more than children love their parents: the Torah wisdom is that since love is generated by giving, not by receiving, this love is generated by the giving of parent to child. The parent gives life and existence to the child; that deep giving of self is the root of the parent's love. The child is an extension of the parent; the child is naturally loved.

The idea that love of self is the source and that love of another is an expanded definition of self applies also to the love of God. The path to that love begins with a maturing of the idea of self. When the childish grasp of self as central and served by all external existence is relinquished, a deeper and more subtle notion of self begins to replace it and love of God can begin. Our deeper sources point out that one of the names of God is *"Ani"* – "I." When arriving at the Temple for the Succot celebrations, the great sage Hillel would say: "If I am here, everything is here." Hillel certainly did not mean "I" in the limited personal sense – Hillel was known for his surpassing humility; that was his defining characteristic. Rather, a deep truth is being subtly expressed. If I am here, all is here: the teaching is that ultimate humility, sacrifice of the limited self for the expanded self, is the beginning of revealing the Divine. When I identify my own "I" with His, when my individuality becomes indiscernible from Him, I have begun the spiritual journey, and perhaps more than begun.

The Sfat Emet constantly develops the theme of the dissolution of small, personal self in the larger, real Self. Here is an elegant example: commenting on the words *"v'lo anachnu"* in Psalm 100 (written by King David five centuries before Buddha's birth), which we say as we begin each weekday, he points out that the word *"lo"* there is written and pronounced differently; that is, this is one of those places in a Torah text where the written form of a word differs from the tradition we have regarding its pronunciation. Here the word is spelled so that it means "not;" the verse therefore translates as: "He made us and *not* we ourselves," but the spoken version has the spelling of *"lo"* as "His," giving: "He made us and we are *His*." Now there is always an organic overlay of the two meanings, and here it is this: to the extent that we are *not*, to that extent we are *His*. To the extent that we learn to see that we do not exist, to that extent exactly we exist in Reality.

What is the source of this idea of the primacy of self? What is its root in the higher world?

Kabbalistic sources teach that before the world is brought into existence there is an expression of Divine existence; in the process of Creation a Divine emanation precedes the formation of the world. In the liturgy it is expressed thus: *"Adon olam...* – Master of the world who ruled *before* any thing was formed..." Leaving aside the difficulty of grasping the meaning of rule or mastery *before* there are subjects to be ruled, we note that this is an essential stage. Divine kingship exists *in itself* before Creation begins. This aspect of kingship or rulership precedes the world despite the fact that subjects would appear to be necessary for a definition of rulership.

The meaning of this apparent paradox is that the world comes into being with the pure and isolated existence of God in pristine aloneness to teach that pure and lonely self is *necessary* before movement beyond self.

Later, we say: "When all was made according to His will, then His name was called king." After all is created, after subjects are brought into existence, His name can be *called* king. Subjects relate to their king, give meaning to the idea of kingship, that is true; but nevertheless we note that before the stage of relationship with subjects He is king, alone and within Himself.

Relationships extend the individual – in the throng of public existence there is an elevation: an assembly of ten brings in a new composite presence – a *minyan* can achieve what no isolated individuals can achieve. But there is also a limitation: the private mind can soar to limitless heights, whereas in public there is always a certain levelling to the common denominator. In halacha there is a hint to this: in the laws of Shabbat, the upper limit of the public domain is ten handsbreadths above the ground. But the private domain reaches *ad l'rakiya* – "to heaven;" it has no upper bound.

The lesson of the inner focus is fundamental for a correct building of the mature and spiritual psyche. The immature tendency is to externalize all inner experience, to shape consciousness and inner responses by what they will look like externally. But this is not the correct spiritual starting point. The correct point of origin is the opening of an inner knowledge of self above dialog, above one speaking to another, above display; the beginning of a genuine, deep and immediate grasp of self.

Only when this innate primary grasp of self is mastered, when there is no speaker and no listener but only one integrated organic selfhood, can a real inner life begin. Oneness must be established before twoness can be risked. This idea is not popular in a culture of media babble, and probably not least because it is almost inexpressible. The only way to grasp the private self is by silent and intensely private meditation – I shall go into this further when we discuss meditation and the place of silence in Judaism.

One has to know how to be alone. "Do good unto others" as the defining mode of self-realization may lead to the mistaken idea that a life deprived of relationships would be meaningless. But even in isolation the mind's intrinsic richness and its involvement with Torah and the external world should provide enough material and fascination for a full program of development. Although the very idea is antithetical to the popular culture, a developed mind senses an expansion in being alone, not a fear of loneliness. The view that makes relationship essential would make a lonely experience on a desert island a torment; the view that a rich inner life is fundamental would make that experience into just another opportunity for development.

Why is self-awareness the deepest level of consciousness? Why must it be so? The answer lies in the most fundamental axiom of Torah, the axiom that gives rise to the basic architecture of human consciousness as it does to all of reality: God's oneness. The unique feature of consciousness is that it is direct; all else is perceived via the interface of the senses. That interface forces a wedge between self and what is perceived. Perception of the external through the medium of senses necessarily introduces the question of the objectivity, indeed the reality, of all externalities; there is no assurance that what is perceived outside the self is reliable. Consciousness itself is a direct, immediate, unedited phenomenon, and that sets it quite apart. This is the beginning of knowledge and this is the development site of the mind's learning to know. In depth, this is really all that can be known. To know any thing, the mind must expand to include that thing. All other knowledge is simply information; real knowledge is always based on self-knowledge.

In Jewish sources the centrality of self is clear. The Maharal of Prague sets up the actualization of self as one-third of the spectrum of all human action; for example, in his analysis of the Mishna in Ethics of the Fathers. There, the Mishna states: "The world stands on three things: Torah, service (of God, nowadays primarily in prayer), and kindness (to others)." The Maharal shows that Torah represents the development of self, service represents the relationship with God, and kindness, the relationship with others; these are the three primary fields of human activity. Torah represents the relationship with self because without Torah the self remains undeveloped as human; without the spiritual growth that Torah generates, the self remains animal. So Torah is the method of self-development *before* we begin talking about developing a relationship with others. Of course, Torah includes the other two areas intrinsically too, but the Maharal is pointing out that Torah relates to development and elevation of self as its primary focus. Note that Torah is mentioned first in the Mishna; not kindness to others, and not even service of God. Not only can I have no real relationship with people if I am entirely undeveloped, I cannot have a real relationship with God either. That is the clear message.

Of course, real development of self must move locked in step with development of a relationship with God. Any other version of building the self would violate the obligation of ego negation. Nevertheless, a conscious element of spiritual movement must be the focus on self as a clear and distinct component of the basic triad of man's areas of growth.

Consider another Mishna in Ethics of the Fathers: "If I am not for myself, who is for me?" Do you begin to hear the resonance of the "I" here as both the personal "I" and the ultimate "I" together? And the Mishna continues: "And if I am only for myself, what am I?" because development of self must include sensitivity to others; if I am entirely wrapped up in myself to the exclusion of others, what quality of self can I achieve? And what am I worth?

Wherever you look in Judaism, you will see these three as the basics – self, relationship with God, relationship with others. At a deeper level they are intertwined (as you might expect); they are facets of the same jewel and this is the reason that you will find one or other of them presented as *the* basis in various places; there is no contradiction. You are aware that all of Judaism can be subsumed in the mitzva of "Love your fellow as yourself." The Talmud says explicitly that all of Torah is contained in this dictum, the rest is commentary. (The Talmud rephrases this Torah principle in the converse: "What is hateful to you, do not do to others;" in practice this is the way to begin.) I see that when the Dalai Lama is asked which religion he follows, he answers: "My religion is kindness." If that axiom sums up Buddhism as religion, a Jew does not need to look there to find it.

With regard to your point that we must *"avoid inflicting suffering on others"* – you say that "small self" is the cause of suffering. There is no need to argue about that. The self we are both looking to develop is indeed a larger self, and I have tried to show Judaism's vision of that larger self as the meshing of the clarified personal self with its Source, the ultimate Self. That sort of self does not perpetuate suffering.

So yes, Judaism upholds the notion of self. But that is not in conflict with *"the interconnectedness of larger Universal identity in which we all repose."* On the contrary, the idea of self, strongly and clearly defined, is essential to the process of truly attaining awareness of the larger Self.

From a Jewish perspective the problem is not self and awareness of self but rather the *wrong grasp* of self. What we identify as the problem is the vision of self *for its own sake*, grasped and clung to (as I imagine a Buddhist might put it) instead of sublimating ego into the real Self. This is perhaps the single most important idea in the Jewish vision of our work here; that is, to elevate the self and the world, not to leave them behind – we always acknowledge the reality of the lower, the limited, but we see our work as transmuting that into the higher and the unlimited.

We enter the world and elevate it, and we enter the world of the self and elevate it. Personal desires no larger than the immediate, immature self are clearly to be erased, here we have no argument. If you can develop to the point where you want what He wants, you will have come to the correct wanting. "Make His will your will" is the expression of the Mishna; we are looking to sublimate desire, not to annul it.

Belief

"Now, Buddhism in some forms does entertain certain ideas that might be called belief, but if we're talking here about Buddhism in its sparest and most common Western form – specifically, Soto Zen – then one of its great strengths would be that you don't have to believe. You *experience for yourself. This is what made Shakyamuni Buddha such a revolutionary spiritual leader. He saw belief systems as forms of enslavement, either to political systems or to mirages that inflamed suffering. In Zen, you simply experience. Belief is a kind of smokescreen that obscures reality."*

David,

The question to ask here is: what did he mean by belief? If he meant wrong beliefs, of course he was quite right to oppose them. False beliefs are enslavement itself. It hardly requires argument to establish the harm of holding false beliefs; nothing could be more in discord with the spiritual path. There is no room to disagree here.

If that is what he meant, then the next logical step is simply to clarify which beliefs are right and which are wrong. Which beliefs relate to objective fact and which do not? If we are talking about Judaism, the question will become: is the object of Jewish belief true or false? Do the claims of Judaism and Jewish history relate to fact or not? To the extent that the object of our belief is true, such belief will be entirely in order. The problem will then become establishing the veracity of Judaism's claims, and I hope to show a little later which direction an approach to that challenge should take.

But I suspect that he may have meant something deeper. He may have been opposed to belief itself. Did he perhaps mean that belief, *regardless of the truth and objectivity of its objects*, is problematic? Let us examine this more subtle position. I think we shall find that it is correct, and again we shall not need to differ.

If belief is a personal and subjective thing entirely unrelated to evidence, purely an inner decision to hold a certain position with no regard to the facts, then it can be worth very little even when it turns out to be right. What I mean is that a belief that happens to accord with fact is no better in essence than one that does not because *since the belief was not based on fact,* that it turned out to be correct is pure luck, and that of course has nothing to do with the path to enlightenment. Belief as such has no place in the development of inner clarity; the question of which beliefs accord with fact and which do not is really irrelevant here. What we are seeking is knowledge, not belief.

But, I hear you asking in surprise, is Judaism not a belief system? And if our direction thus far is correct, have we not excluded belief systems as the road to knowledge, even those that are true? If Judaism's foundation tenets are not knowable objectively, surely holding those tenets is belief and therefore a smokescreen and an enslavement?

I would like to go into this further because a major principle is at stake here. In fact, *the* major principle, nothing less than the first mitzva of the Torah – namely *emuna*, which is commonly translated as faith or belief. (Maimonides holds this to be the first commandment; others hold that it is even more fundamental than a commandment, it is the substrate on which all commandments depend.) What is *emuna*, and how are we to avoid the "belief problem" we have in common with the Buddhist teaching you quote? And if Judaism is not a belief system, what on earth is it?

The key here is that we are dealing with a mistranslation. As I have tried to show, the Westerner who has no Hebrew faces a pervasive problem in his attempt to come to grips with authentic Judaism. In Torah the medium and the message are inextricably bound; in Torah, without the medium, the message is almost inaccessible. A translated word necessarily carries the concept of the culture that its language serves. The English word gives a concept that has all the connotations, nuances and overtones of the culture of the West. Not infrequently, translation into English expresses the diametric opposite of a Torah concept.

If we define the Jewish idea of *emuna* accurately, that is, if we translate the word correctly, I think the question and the problem will disappear. The conventional translation is belief or faith; but if that means blind belief or a leap of faith with no factual objective backing, then the Buddhist reservations about that type of belief are of course correct. Unfounded belief, arbitrary faith, holding positions unrelated to solid evidence, is certainly a recipe for spiritual (and often physical) disaster. That is a sure way into a world of delusion.

Words like faith or belief will inevitably lead us into the trap of seeing falsely. In Western usage, belief and faith relate essentially to the unknowable, they are necessarily blind ("blind faith"). You do not *believe* something you see or experience, you *know* it. Relating to that which you *cannot* know is called belief; that is the appropriate use of the word.

But that is the wrong translation. *Emuna* does not mean blind faith and it has little or nothing to do with belief.

I am going to delay translating *emuna* correctly until we have laid down some background; before we attempt a correct definition we must demonstrate that belief cannot be the right idea.

I think we can do that like this: if *emuna* means no more than subjective personal opinion, we are faced with a problem: if you have no evidence for a thing, why should you believe it? If belief is entirely personal and subjective, no more than a whim or fancy, what recommends it to the intelligent mind?

The general attitude in the secular West regards faith in exactly this way; it is personal, private, and rests on no objective facts. Asking for proof that a particular belief is true is neither sensible nor necessary; matters of faith cannot be proved. You believe because it is meaningful to you; that is all. (Here is a quote from Scientific American, July 2004, page 23: "Religious faith depends on a host of social, psychological and emotional factors that have little or nothing to do with probabilities, evidence and logic.")

That type of faith, the arbitrary attachment to purely subjective belief, is worth very little; and as you say, harmful and even dangerous.

But on the other hand, if the object of faith is knowable, why talk about belief when what you believe can be known? Surely that should be called knowledge and we should have no use for the notion of faith?

To put it plainly, if the existence of a reality that transcends the natural rests on solid evidence, then faith and belief are inappropriate terms. If you can demonstrate or experience the existence of God, then we should talk only of the process of coming to know that existence. Belief would be the wrong direction here.

And again, if there is no solid evidence, why believe it at all?

In summary, how can *emuna* ever be meaningful? The existence of God is either definitely knowable, or it is not. If it is knowable with a definite clarity, then *emuna* would seem to be the wrong idea. But if God's existence is *not* knowable objectively, then *emuna* would seem arbitrary, no more than a personal emotion, really. And quite possibly a smokescreen, a confusing, deluding and enslaving thing. So what is *emuna*?

What we mean by *emuna* is not belief. We do not commit ourselves to something that is the product of imagination. We have not committed ourselves to God throughout history because we decided subjectively and personally that such commitment was a good idea. Our commitment is based on *knowledge*. We assert that the object of our "faith" can be established and known. That knowledge is enlightenment itself, and that is the real value, not belief.

In fact, clarity of knowledge is exactly what we are seeking. Torah study is a demanding and rigorous training in objectivity. Torah students are not encouraged to accept anything uncritically and thoughtlessly; they are encouraged to think powerfully and logically. Torah learning is not an appeal to the emotions; it is a very demanding appeal to the intellect. To study Torah effectively you must be able to ask the most penetrating questions and learn to accept only completely satisfactory answers; only the highest standards of thought and logic are valid. We are not afraid of questions. On the contrary, asking difficult questions that cut to the root of an issue is the basis of learning.

Now if it is true that the knowledge we seek can be attained, two questions arise:

One, of course, is how do you acquire that knowledge? How do you come to know the entirely transcendent? I shall deal with that question when we discuss Torah from Sinai; for the present, I shall simply note that Judaism presents the means to acquire that knowledge.

Our subject at present is the question of belief as opposed to experience, raised by your exposition of the Buddhist distaste for subjective belief. I would like to stay focused on that, and that leads to the second question – why talk of faith? At the very least, those who have *reached* a clear knowledge should have no use for the idea of belief; for them there is nothing left to believe, there is only knowledge. Do we say that for prophets and others who have reached these sublime levels of development there is no *emuna*?

Here is the key: the correct translation of *emuna* is not faith but *faithfulness*, loyalty. The concept is this: when you have acquired spiritual knowledge, when you know clearly that what meets the eye is not all there is, the question then is *will you be loyal to that knowledge?* Will you live up to it? The problem of *emuna* is not how to gain knowledge of the spiritual world, it is the challenge of being *faithful* to that knowledge. In the gap between impersonal truth and direct personal experiential contact with that truth to the extent that no disloyalty can enter, *emuna* becomes a possibility and an obligation.

Emuna derives from the same root as *ne'eman,* meaning faithful or loyal. Even the most superficial examination of the word in Torah will show that it cannot be translated as faith in the sense of belief: in the verse *"Va'yehi yadav* emuna *ad ba hashamesh* – And his hands were loyal until the sun went down;" Moses' hands stayed where they were, they remained *loyal* to their task. The verse cannot be translated in any other way – hands cannot have faith or believe anything.

Or the verses that describe God speaking to Abraham and then state: *"V'he'emin baShem..."* You cannot translate this verse as "And he (Abraham) believed in God;" it is quite clear that God was speaking to him directly – there cannot be praise for someone who believes in something that he personally experiences. No, the idea is not that Abraham believed; a prophet does not believe, he knows. The praise here is that he was *loyal,* he stood strong and went through the most difficult tests and ordeals; that is appropriate praise, and that is *emuna.*

A unique feature of the human condition is that we can know something with clarity and yet act in discordance with that knowledge. In *disloyalty* to that knowledge. You may acknowledge that a certain action is wrong and then do it anyway (who can claim that this is an unfamiliar problem?). Free will means exactly that you can act in disharmony with your intellect. Understanding a thing and all its consequences clearly does not guarantee that you will live in accord with your understanding, that you will be loyal to it. Not at all. It takes work to live up to the truth. That work is *emuna.*

Emuna relates very little to the idea of blind belief; it relates far more to the work of disciplining the heart and harnessing the hands in loyalty to the head.

We experience this problem constantly; in a deep sense, this is the human problem. On a simple level, anyone who has ever struggled to stay on a diet will understand. The fact that you know you have to do this in no way ensures that you will. Clarity of mind is one thing, behavior consistent with the clarity is another.

As a physician I have often been faced with the challenge of patients who harm themselves against their own better judgment; it is one of medicine's deepest frustrations. Let me tell you of a case in my own experience that demonstrated this problem to me in the most forceful way: during my internship in surgery, a patient with Buerger's disease was admitted to our ward. In this disease, the blood vessels become obliterated if the patient smokes; people with this condition are exquisitely sensitive to the nicotine in cigarette smoke and their vessels respond in this way. If they stop smoking, the disease process is arrested; if they continue smoking, they can lose digits and even limbs due to interruption of the blood supply to these parts. This particular man was a highly intelligent engineer in his forties who was admitted because of a threatened limb – his leg was blue and in danger of gangrene, which of course would mean an amputation. He knew all about his disease, and that he could halt the progress of his pathology if he stopped smoking.

He continued smoking and we had to amputate his leg. The next time I saw him was a year later; he was being wheeled down the hospital corridor in a wheelchair, with no legs, still smoking, on his way to losing an arm.

I have never forgotten that sight, and I have often since pictured him, standing with a cigarette in his hand, about to light up, and weighing the options – simply flick it away and save his leg, walk, run, play with his children; or light up, inhale and face the inevitable. How do people do such things? How do intelligent, aware people make such mistakes? Is it possible to understand this? But we all do that, of course. We would never make another man's error – that would be ridiculous, not even a temptation; but when it comes to our own areas of test somehow we blunder. We have the knowledge, but we are unfaithful to it.

Akiva,
Because we live in such an information-saturated age and culture, we are inclined to be more skeptical than ever. Even the most solid of proofs have been doctored. Even the most unassailable truths have been revealed as cynical manipulations. The greatest leaders have repeatedly been exposed as crooks, or worse.

There lies the torment: can we ever really *know? And without certain knowledge, how Jewish can we ultimately be?*

David,
You are right. There is always an element of the unknown. Although the translation of *emuna* as faith or belief is inaccurate, it contains a seed of truth (distortions and falsehoods that are persistent always do). What is the aspect of the blind, the unknown, in *emuna*?

As we have noted, the nature of an ordeal is that even when it begins with a clear obligation to act in a certain way, great strength and courage may be required to carry out that course of action. You know what is right, you know what you have to do, but it may be enormously difficult actually to do it. Will your knowledge oblige action? Will you derive within yourself the fierce loyalty needed to bind what is right to what is expressed in action? That is the problem of loyalty; but what generates this problem – why is there a gap between the knowing and the doing?

When Abraham is commanded to leave his home on the journey that begins Jewish history, he is not told the destination. "Go from your land, from your birthplace and from your father's house to the land *which I shall show you.*" This is the classical structure of a test. The point of departure is clear; there is no doubt that he must go. The test is that the journey leads into the unknown; what he will find and what he must go through on that journey are not clear at all. The destination will become clear *only when he gets there;* the entire journey must be made only on the strength of the command to travel.

This is where we meet the element of the unknown in ordeals, and this is the element of truth in the world's translation of *emuna* as blind. If there is a blindness in tests, it is this: the destination is always hidden. You can never know what the end of the road will be until you are there *because the end of the road is really the greater form of yourself that the journey is building.* Each life ordeal is an opportunity to become what you must be; you will know the meaning of that only when you have made it real.

Abraham's journey is towards himself, of course. "*Lech lecha....* Go to yourself." He must walk the path that leads to a revelation of all that he can become and beyond. He must leave who he is now and go towards the greater man he has the potential to be; we must all walk that road. To see the result while yet in motion is impossible; if you were shown the result before you had worked to reach it you would see only a shrunken and distorted version of that result because your vessel is yet too small, you are still in the process of becoming, your consciousness is still constricted. Imagine trying to explain to a small child what he will be when he is grown mature and wise. He will condense your vision down to some or other amount of candy.

If you are trapped in a glass prism, no matter how much white light is shone upon the prism you will always see the spectrum's colors individually. Shining more light onto the prism will not help, you will not be able to see it – until you break the prism. Only when the limits of your present situation are shattered will you be able to see beyond those limits. When life locks you into a particular paradigm you see everything in its light; you *must* see everything that way. Real growth begins with breaking your own present form; until you shatter your zone of comfort and familiarity you will see everything that fits it and nothing else. First you must leave where you are; only then will you be able to see the new. You cannot see over your own horizon.

Before the journey begins, all you can know is the direction. The person of real faith is prepared to follow wherever the road of truth leads, no matter how difficult that road and no matter how unclear the destination. The point of departure is clear; the destination is unseen. The spiritual journey demands a commitment to walk that road without the comfortable assurance of knowing where it leads. *That* is faith.

When you hear spiritual commitment insulted, when you hear it said that one who walks that path is a weak-minded blind follower, a mindless ritualist following guidelines unthinkingly, remember that exactly the opposite is true; the path of *emuna* requires a fearless commitment to walk the difficult and lonely road of the truth with no preconception of what the destination will be.

As a people, we meet our destiny at Sinai – the revelation is clear. But the test is *after* Sinai, when revelation fades – will we be loyal then? In that revelation the first mitzva of the Torah is spoken to the Jewish people – the mitzva of *emuna:* "I am God" – and that truth, that knowledge, sets up an obligation to be forever loyal. Nachmanides says "Our eyes and our hearts must be there (Sinai) always." Experience, knowledge, is the beginning; *emuna* is the work that follows.

In the gap between the clear point of departure and the hidden destination is the proper place of *emuna*. Traversing that gap requires faithfulness, loyalty to the path. So *emuna* does in fact relate to the unknown, in that sense "belief" may be apposite; but the base, the ground, the point of departure, the motivation and obligation to travel are rooted solidly in the known. We know and we do not know. As we travel, each unknown reached becomes the known; we move from belief, if you like, to knowledge, and each stage of the journey, each element of destination reached in clarity becomes a new point of departure for a journey into a new unknown.

Akiva,
In the realm of the knowable, God, to many Jews, remains frustratingly out of bounds.

The result is an ambivalent relationship with the very notion of divinity that occludes our intimate connection with God Himself, and with our Judaism. We keep veering away from it and coming back to it.

David,
You are right; there is a deeper issue here, another aspect of the unknown on the path to knowledge. It is essential to note that there is no possibility of absolute knowledge (the knowledge that is called prophecy requires separate discussion; it is not relevant at this juncture in history and is not our subject now). Quite apart from the element of the unknown that we have examined, there is also an element of the *unknowable*. Not only because the ultimate and absolute Source is inscrutable to embodied humans; I am not referring to that. I am referring to the nature of human knowledge itself. No knowledge, indeed no experience, is absolutely reliable. You have only to think of the convincingly real experience of a dream to realize how flimsy our convictions about reality can be. Even knowledge of the simple fact that you are awake has no demonstrable proof – in a dream you are also convinced that you are awake; that is exactly why a dream can be so ecstatic or so terrifying.

We never reach an absolute knowledge. The Torah analysis of the necessity for this uncertainty in the Creation is a central subject, but I am not going to examine it here; for now, I want only to note that it is so. *All* knowledge is imperfect, never absolute. Even our immediate experience is not *absolutely* reliable. One of the consequences or applications of this fact is that we always need to act at least somewhat beyond our proofs. There is always a gap; there must always be *emuna* in commitment and action. Demanding absolute experiential clarity is unrealistic. A mature realist knows that no matter how he may long for absolute contact with the world of the real, he is always at a distance.

It is unrealistic and unreasonable to demand absolute knowledge before committing to any particular action. The appropriate standard to demand is not absolute proof or absolutely incontrovertible evidence, but rather *sufficient* evidence. What we need, indeed all we can ever have, is *sufficient* evidence. You will notice that we do not demand more than this in any practical area of life; we act when the evidence is good enough. Even in life-and-death matters we do not demand absolute evidence. When the facts have been weighed, when the situation has been analyzed and a direction becomes clear based on the balance of evidence, we act if that balance is clear enough.

In the realm of the spiritual, it is hypocritical and dishonest to demand absolute knowledge before committing to a path of spiritual growth when we do not demand that standard in any other area of our lives. The individual who refuses to take the world of meaning and spirit seriously because the evidence is not incontrovertible is quite possibly seeking to avoid that world; in other areas he moves when the evidence is adequate – why does he apply a more rigorous standard to the world of his spiritual obligations?

No; doubt always exists and the evidence will never dispel it completely. The evidence must go beyond *reasonable* doubt, as the legal phrase has it. The standard must be *good enough* knowledge, knowledge solid enough to predicate action, not absolute knowledge.

If the evidence of our Torah and our history are judged to be adequate, they oblige. They need not be absolute; they are not absolute. But they are certainly good enough.

And in this element of obligatory uncertainty, we discern again the place of *emuna* We do not reach a knowledge that obliges action absolutely. Free will is always given; a choice must always be made. That zone of choice is the zone of *emuna*.

I hope this begins to clarify the Jewish approach to belief.

Doubt and Certainty

Akiva,

I think emuna *is the heart of the matter. When I sit in meditation, in a Zen sangha, I am haunted by God, and by questions: Is this idol worship? Am I "getting it," or am I lost? This vast opening I sometimes experience, is it Buddha Nature, or is it God? Are they the same thing? When I sit in meditation, my Judaism rises within me, and it asks: "What do I know of God? What will I ever learn here?"*

My humble hope is to continue focusing on those aspects of Buddhism that from my perspective most appeal to Westerners and lay people like me (I wish "dilettante" were still a compliment). I must say that one reason for the popularity of Buddhism is that the primacy of rational thought may be eroding. We Americans have, as we often do, abused the very best aspects of our natures and our political systems so that our best inclinations are in danger of becoming our worst. Rational thought at one extreme becomes legalistic, picayune, and dismissive of all that occurs and exists that defies logic. The appeal of Buddhism uses logic (and paradox, and silence) to propel one beyond logic to a level of understanding beyond mind. I clearly will need to work on explaining this better, but where it applies here is in the silencing of the noise we experience in our worlds and in our heads.

Our increasing collective ignorance fuels itself, breeding more ignorance, until the layers of the Torah, both written and oral, seem flattened and archaic to us. Emuna *in its construction and in your explanation are not foreign to me, nor would they be to most Zen practitioners. The knowledge that forges and forms* emuna, *however, is receding from us.*

If Buddhism hears from God, it hears not through Torah, nor mitzvot, but through streams and sky and death and age and meditation.

David,

You are right that deep knowledge is receding. In depth, all our existential tension stems from doubt. In ordeals and in life in general we struggle most profoundly to identify the correct path – and it may seem impossible. Very often the problem lies not in finding the strength to cope with adversity – you feel you would go through fire willingly if only you knew in which direction. If only we could be sure that this or that particular path were correct in an absolute sense, that it would not let us down unpredictably, we would find the raw courage to walk that path. But that is not our experience: we choose a direction, convinced that it must be the correct one, and tomorrow we are forced to wonder how we could possibly have seen things that way yesterday – the situation appears exactly opposite now. And of course, the next day we feel even more confused – eventually we lose confidence in our sense of direction altogether. Life is a halting, faltering business – three steps ahead today, two backwards tomorrow, and often no more than helpless circles with the dismay of crossing our own tracks repeatedly.

Let us dissect this matter. Our mystical tradition calls this world "*alma d'sfeika*" – a world of doubt. The world is a confusing mixture of good and bad, true and false. It is also called "*alma d'shikra*" – a world of falsehood. The deepest essence of falsehood is that it contains an admixture of truth: if not for that component it could never exist, and therein lies the confusion. In fact, the most dangerous forms of falsehood are those closest to the truth – they are the most deceptive.

What is the source of doubt underlying this "*alma d'sfeika*"? The Torah's account of how the human condition came to be what it is details this breakdown. Adam was faced with the primal choice – to obey the Divine command and refrain from eating the fruit of the "tree of the knowledge of good and evil" or to disobey. The world he experienced was perfect; the tree held the power to loose evil into the world.

Why is the tree referred to as "the tree of the knowledge of *good and evil?*" Surely it should be named "the tree of the knowledge of *evil;*" it is the source of evil in the Creation, why *good* and evil? But that is the point exactly – if the tree were of evil only, that evil would be so easily identifiable, so odious, that no one would engage it; it could never present a temptation. It is the knowledge of good and evil *combined,* confused, that is the problem. "Knowledge" always means intimate association, intrinsic bonding; the tree combines good and evil so thoroughly that after its fruit is ingested the human becomes a tangled knot of both elements. No situation is entirely clear thereafter. Never can we completely separate our lower selves, our vested interests, from our pure core dimension. And *that* is the problem.

At root, this is the reason we reject the claim you describe as the Buddhist idea of intuiting the correct path by simply experiencing reality: we are no longer purely objective. Ideally, we should indeed hear "through streams and sky and death and age and meditation;" originally that was exactly the way: Abraham intuited the entire Torah from an examination of the world, he derived all the mitzvot from within himself (the Midrash says he learned Torah "from himself;" another Midrash says "his kidneys became his teachers"). He did not need the Torah as an external guide; but we are no longer able to do that. We cannot know which inner voice is objective and which is the subtle echo of our own vested interests.

Do not underestimate this problem. In fact, *the deepest vested interest is the one that tells you that you are the reliable objective arbiter of your own values,* your own perception of reality. Mark this well. No matter how deep the meditation, you are always perceiving your own version of reality. This is inherent in the fabric of our reality now: we need to refer to an external standard, now we must relate to the revealed Torah for clarity. I do not expect this to be accepted without a fight, David; the vested interests are too strong for that. But it is true.

"Streams and sky and death and age and meditation" – these things speak; you are right. In the original pristine world they were all that was necessary. The Ten Commandments were not yet spoken, only the "Ten Sayings" of Creation had been spoken, and they were enough (the Sfat Emet says that they are higher than the Commandments; the fabric of reality speaks and commands at the highest level). The streams and the sky speak, and for ears that were pure they spoke with unmistakable clarity, but for our coarse ears they speak far too broadly.

After sin enters the world, all is confusion. A subtle hint is enough for a sophisticated and unclouded mind, but for a dull mind clear instructions are necessary; now we need the clearest of explicit instructions. The Commandments are spoken to those who can no longer hear the wind in the trees and interpret its music reliably.

That confusion is the root of all sadness. The root of the Hebrew word for "weeping" means to be lost in confusion (*bechi* means crying, and it forms the root of the word for a "maze"). The word for a "tear," the eye's issue in weeping, is from a root meaning a mixture (of the pure and the profane) that cannot be separated.

When Adam confronted that tree he was pure and the world was pure. Evil existed only as an objective, dispassionate possibility external to himself (in Maimonides' classic formulation: he did not experience good and bad, only true and false). But when he ate that fruit evil became internalized within himself and within the goodness of the world, and now the human mind can never resolve its doubts entirely, never read the world plainly as the open book it once was. The mystics refer to the tree of the knowledge of good and evil as "*ilana d'sfeika*" – the tree of doubt. I cannot emphasize enough how much effort this idea is worth; if there is *one* thing that can be seen clearly, it is the pervasive nature of this doubt. To miss this is fatal.

See what becomes of us after that confusion possesses us: after man eats from the tree, he hides in the garden. Hides from God, Who is everywhere. How could Adam imagine that he could hide? He knew God as no human has ever since, knew deeply and personally that He sees and knows all. But man no longer sees reality clearly; on the one hand he knows that God sees – that is why he is hiding. But on the other hand, he somehow thinks, incredibly, that he can hide. He has become a deeply pathetic figure, hiding from that which he knows is inescapable and yet fooling himself anyway. Who cannot identify at least to some degree with this behavior?

But far more disturbing is God's response. He appears in the garden and calls to Adam: "Where are you?" The Creator of the Universe, Who sees all, knows all, asks: "Where are you?" *As if He does not see.* When man attempts to hide, to blur reality into a crazy, fractured version of itself, God responds in kind, *allows* man to see the world that way; measure for measure exactly. You wish to escape Me, to feel independent, hidden from My gaze – *"Where are you?"* Man is allowed to perceive that he is alone.

The Jewish people's arch-rival through history is the nation of Amalek. The historical aspects of Torah also describe a deeper path in spiritual history – the numerical value of "Amalek" and of *"safek"* (doubt) is identical. We are supposed to bear clear witness to a higher reality; our arch-enemy is named doubt. Think into this. The descendant of Amalek who tried to destroy the entire Jewish people was Haman. Where is his name in Torah? The Talmud locates his name in the garden, at the time of Adam's sin; when God asks Adam that second question: "Did you eat from the tree? – *Hamin ha'etz"* the word *"hamin"* ("Did you?") is the name "Haman." That gap between reality and perception, the gap of doubt, opens with the sin. Note that the question: "Did you?" is asked *by God;* there has come into the world a deep problem of perception. The meaning here is that in the root of revelation of the world itself lies an opportunity for confusion (the Hebrew word for the "world," *olam,* literally means "to hide"). The world itself hides as it reveals; it is man who brings this into expression, and God responds in man's terms. He does not show Himself more clearly than you wish to see.

Amalek's historical task is to hide the spirit. Our task is to reveal it; to testify to its existence and its centrality although it may be hidden. "You are My witnesses." The function of a witness is to declare, to clarify, to establish what cannot be seen; no-one needs a witness when an event is openly visible. When we say *"Shma Yisrael,"* this is what we mean. Note that the first word of Shma in the Torah has an enlarged letter *ayin* and the last word has an enlarged *daled*. Together they spell *eid*, witness. (And perhaps your Hebrew is now advanced enough to know that if you read the only possible alternative combination of these two letters, they spell *da,* the imperative form of the verb "to know;" the depth of the testimony you are speaking here must begin in your own consciousness: *know,* and make known.) Amalek opens the gap of spiritual doubt in the world; the Jewish people seek to close it.

After his expulsion from the garden Adam cannot go back. Guarding the road to the garden are Beings wielding swords; their blades flash and turn continually. The commentaries explain this image: the turning sword is the lethal weapon of doubt. Today reality appears thus and tomorrow different. Always. And man cannot find the road back to the garden; it eludes him continually. Not only is he confused about where he is, but the road back to clarity is in doubt too. Dangerous weapons, and their blades flash again and again; a glint, a hint of clarity, and then a fading. Life is like standing on a windswept plain on a stormy night; as you stand there lashed by the rain, beaten by the wind, hopelessly lost, there is a sudden flash of lightning. In the instant of its flash you see the road ahead more clearly than by day. But as it is seen, it disappears, and if you are to make any progress it must be on the strength of memory alone. You may have to trudge through the dark for hours on the strength of a memory of a moment of light. Some see more closely repeated flashes of lightning, some see less, but no one walks in the light.

(Admixture is an inextricable feature of our world. The mystics teach that just as Adam ingested a mixture, so we are condemned to do the same in our bodies – our food is a mixture of wholesomeness and waste. Together they are good; but within the body the necessary elements are extracted and absorbed and the waste remains, offensive in the extreme. *Within* the organism of our being.

At a level of spiritual purity – when some element of the garden is attained – this ceases: in the desert the Jewish people ate manna, and there was no excretion. Pure existence can be fed by pure food, and there is no waste, no lower side of reality, no need for separation. Of course, that generation's counterpart was the cult of Pe'or – the worship of excretion and excrement. The evil forces work to focus on the lower, the impure, and to present *them* as primary. In Torah, idolatry is referred to as *"avodat gilulim"* – literally the worship of dung.)

As always, the words say it all: the Hebrew word for doubt is *safek,* and for certainty, *vadai.* Now these commonly used words are not to be found in Scripture. Nowhere does the Torah mention them; both are of Rabbinic origin. If the essence of an idea is contained in the Torah word for that idea, and we find that *there is no word* for a particular idea we encounter, it surely means that *at the deepest level, that concept does not exist.* (Recall our discussion of Torah language – each thing in the world is a projection of the word the Torah uses for that thing. The word is written on the "film" of Torah and projected onto the "screen" of reality. If no word exists in the Torah corresponding to a thing we perceive in the world, that constitutes a strong suggestion that the thing we are perceiving is illusory. *Someone has painted it up on the screen of reality*, but it is not being projected from the source.) And of course – the world as formed by its root in Torah *contains no doubt:* things either exist or they do not. There is nothing in the world that exists "doubtfully," tentatively; doubt is a problem of *our perception,* not an objective reality. (And if there is no doubt, there is no certainty either – certainty exists only where doubt is a possibility; if there can be no doubt there can be no certainty, a thing simply "is.")

The primal, pristine world is clear and open. We opacify and confuse it. The word for "doubt" is of human origin; it is a description of the damage we do to our own perception.

So our situation is confused. That is its essence. Our task is to develop a tenacious hold on the truth even when we are tempted to see it change; our goal is to break through into clarity – that is transcendence. And that is the joy of enlightenment: "There is no joy like the resolution of doubts."

Torah from Sinai

"This is connected to my previous question concerning belief, of course. If one does not believe in the revelation at Mt. Sinai, how can one call oneself Jewish? One may hear many distinguished Jewish scholars, yourself included, note that there is no revelation in history like that of the Jews at Sinai. Hundreds of thousands, if not millions, blown backwards by the voice of God Himself, and the numerous experiences of God by the desert wanderers thereafter.

But a Buddhist might say that this is little more than an excellent myth, and if you can't fully believe this myth, are you really Jewish? And if you do believe it, are you not suffering from delusion, one of the Three Poisons? In contrast, a Buddhist might say, the Buddha was, we're sure, an historical figure, whose movements were tracked, sermons documented, whose life and death are historically known. He was utterly human, and transformed himself through inquiry. No hocus-pocus."

David,

If you "can't fully believe this" of course you are still Jewish; you are simply mistaken, that's all! And if you do believe it, of course you are "not suffering from delusion" if it is true! Belief issues boil down primarily to questions of objective fact; that is always the first level to consider, as we have noted.

In the interest of accuracy, they were not "blown backwards" when they heard the first of the Ten Commandments directly from His mouth, they were magnetically *drawn forwards*. Their souls were attracted to the Source of existence, the Source of their being, with an irresistible explosive power; their *bodies* were blown backwards. And when they had been revived and God spoke the second of the Commandments, they exploded again and needed to be resuscitated again.

We heard those two commandments directly from the Divine through no intermediary, and that experience began the millennia-long intensity of our love with Him ("O that He would kiss me with the kisses of His mouth" – see the Song of Songs).

Akiva,
Concerning the Sinai experience: we are a skeptical, stiff-necked people. All I can say, with all due respect, and wishing it were otherwise, is something many American Jews would say, using the ugly vernacular: I just can't buy it.

David,
It is not for sale. It is yours already. And as for the price, that has already been paid. Your grandparents paid for it when they were dispossessed in Berlin and exiled from Barcelona; your great-grandparents paid when they were cut down in York and Cracow; their parents paid when they were hounded in Bavarian forests and Polish streets, watched their scrolls burned in Paris and their homes in Madrid.

Your grandmother paid more than enough when she sold the family stove in a Russian winter to have enough to give her children a Torah education. And she overpaid with her pain when she watched her American grandchildren walk away from that mountain in whose shadow she had lived with the graceful strength of a conviction that came naturally. Walk away without looking back, mind you, unwittingly exchanging the indescribable richness of Torah for the self-help literature of a neurotic society that has forgotten what is real, or the literature and practice of exotic philosophies that cannot offer more than what they are supplanting.

Akiva,
Sinai was either a unique occurrence, or a unique story uniquely told,
but can we ever know which it truly is, really? Won't we always be
tormented by that question, and the questions that inevitably follow?

What we see here is a failure of communication down the generations,
the communication of the everpresence of awareness of Divinity
commanded in the Shma.

David,
Understanding what happened at Sinai is fundamental to a grasp of
what Judaism is. The Sinai experience is at the heart of Jewish
knowledge; it is one of the two pillars on which our knowledge of
God rests.

You will recall that we defined *emuna* as faithfulness or loyalty to a
knowledge. Bearing in mind that *absolute* knowledge is not attainable
in any area of human enquiry, what are the means of acquiring
knowledge of God's existence? The two primary avenues of access to
that knowledge are the Sinai revelation and its unbroken transmission
throughout subsequent history, and logical enquiry based on objective
examination of reality.

(Inner knowledge, although it is ultimately more important, needs a
more sensitive exploration. We began to examine that subject in our
discussion on the expanded self. In fact, the closest we can ever come
to pure or complete knowledge is in that inner consciousness,
unmediated through the senses or even the logical faculty. In Jewish
spiritual development all work begins here; inner knowledge must
flourish. We call this *da'at;* and as you already know, there are no
words to describe it. The development of this inner clarity, pure and
simple with neither ego nor language to contaminate it, is the real
beginning of *emuna*.)

1. Experience

Firstly, we met Him. The Jewish people stood at Sinai and experienced a direct revelation; in fact, no prophet's testimony would be good enough for us if we had not begun with the most direct and immediate kind of experience. Only because we lived through that cosmic meeting are we prepared to accept the words of prophets who spoke later in history. As you say, we are by nature a skeptical people; only the highest standard of evidence is good enough for us, and nothing less than experience would have been sufficient.

Sinai requires deep study; but at the very least we should note that it was radically different from any other revelation claimed throughout history.

For example, all Jews of that generation were present and experienced the revelation, over three million people together. It is remarkable that in the history of mankind no one else has ever produced even *one witness* to any supposed revelation of the Divine (I do not mean miracles; I mean a direct revelation of God). Every claimed revelation was reported by a *single* individual who said that the Creator had spoken to him, and that individual's testimony was accepted by his followers. No one has ever *claimed* even one witness to his experience whereas we have the testimony of millions of people agreeing on what happened. Think about this.

You can reverse the logic too: imagine for a moment that the whole claim is false. That would mean that there must have been a point in our history where a *whole* generation colluded, *with no recorded dissension*, to foist the identical, colossal falsehood on all their children: that the previous generation had *unanimously* told them that Sinai had occurred, with all its details exactly agreed upon so that it would subsequently be handed down with complete accuracy forever. Personally, I think it is easier to accept a revelation!

Exactly how reliable is this transmission? To what extent can we rely on the accuracy of the handing down of the details? This is examined in our classic sources; see the Kuzari, for example, and Rabbi

Gottlieb's contemporary exposition of that work. But a few points are worth considering here by way of indicating a direction.

One of them is the timespan. How far are we, in fact, from the events? How many generations stand between us and the Sinai experience? How many links were there in that chain of transmission?

Many think that we are thousands of generations removed from that moment of revelation, that vast ages stand between us and our forefathers who witnessed it. But a quick calculation gives interesting results: we are now approximately 3,200 years after the event. If we consider a generation to be forty years, a reasonable time for parents to transmit the information to their children (and to their grandchildren, itself a specific Torah obligation), we find that we are only eighty generations away from that time ($80 \times 40 = 3,200$). There are far fewer generations between Sinai and us than we may imagine, a relatively small gap in time.

And we know who they were. We know who the individual sages in *each* of those generations were; we know their greatness by historical account and we have their original works. Our record goes back in identical written form throughout the Jewish world to the event itself; it is not a story pieced together from hazy fragments of lore. We can pinpoint the handing over of the tradition from one great Torah authority to the next, a thread running through time that can be microscopically examined (see Maimonides, for example, who lists them all in sequence in his Introduction to the Mishna). This is no vague tale stretching back into the mists of time beyond human memory. It is a concrete, crystallized, detailed account that meets the highest standards of accuracy; preserved and transmitted intact over the span of generations by the entire Jewish people in identical form despite our pervasive and wide geographical dispersion, and despite our willful, skeptical and argumentative nature.

And except for the most recent times, when Jewish knowledge has plummeted exponentially until the majority of Jews today have almost no idea of what Torah is at all, we have no record of any disagreement. We have no record of anyone claiming that Sinai never occurred or was in any way falsified. In fact, not only our records agree – even those in the West and Near East who have attacked us throughout the generations accept it; their own religions are openly based on it. While they may disagree (often violently) with each other, they all agree that what we claim actually happened as we claim it did.

In summary, the first (and more important) avenue of access to knowledge of God's existence is our personal experience – the Exodus, the Sinai revelation and the transmission of those events to us by each generation since.

2. Science

The second method of gaining higher knowledge is logical enquiry.

Let me mention only one well-known line of thinking on this matter, because it will introduce a new angle of insight into why *emuna* carries a connotation of the unknown.

An open examination of the Universe suggests that a higher intelligence has designed and constructed it. There are classic sources that present this approach and they should be studied; I am not going to examine the importance or even the cogency of this line of thinking now. I would like to point out only that proofs of this sort are always proofs *by exclusion*. That is, they do not seek to prove that the world must have a Creator by derivation from first principles, but because the *alternative* is difficult to accept – to suggest that the Universe is a random accident is problematic in the face of the evidence. You are, of course, aware that the theory of evolution sets out to deal with exactly this issue in the particular field of biology – the astonishing complexity of life needs, demands, an explanation. The symmetry, order and complexity of the world do not suggest a chaotic, accidental process. The more that is discovered about the Universe, the more its astonishing fine-tuning and organization are apparent; it is very difficult to understand that all of the world's exquisitely detailed structure is accidental.

I know you are familiar with this line of approach, and examining it is not our immediate issue; I raise it for the sake of this point: a proof by exclusion is just as valid as a proof by derivation, but it lacks a significant element – when you *derive* knowledge of something, you understand it thoroughly because you have worked up to it, starting with first principles and not missing a detail. But when you prove something only *by showing that the alternatives are untenable*, you may have proved it, *but you do not understand it at all.* You may know that it must be true because there is no other viable option, but you have no direct knowledge of what it is.

That a thing exists can be clearly known while intimate contact with its essence may yet remain at a distance.

Here we see again the two elements that inhere in the idea of *emuna*: first, it must be based solidly on knowledge, not mere "belief." And second, it contains an element of the unknowable too; or perhaps more accurately, the ungraspable. It is one thing to know that God exists, and to found this knowledge solidly on historical and empirical inference; but to grasp *what that existence is*, to make personal contact with it, is another. To begin that process we need Torah.

Scientific enquiry can take you to the border of the physical world. At that border it becomes apparent that something lies beyond, but what that something *is* requires other tools to discover. Using science you can demonstrate to a compelling degree that there is a zone beyond science; but to enter that zone you need Torah. That is why our main avenue of access to the knowledge we seek is Torah study. We use science to take us to the border and to show that there is a beyond; we learn Torah to enter that beyond.

Sinai and Beyond

Akiva,
Sinai is the formative experience of Jewish identity. But the fact that
no one else has claimed such a mass revelation doesn't make this one
"true": it simply makes it unique.

Where I get confused, and where many other Jews of my stripe would
be pulled up short, is in your statement that "we met Him...Only
because we lived through that cosmic meeting are we prepared to
accept the words of prophets who spoke later in history." What you
say next is made doubly true: "We are by nature a skeptical people;
only the very highest standard of evidence is good enough for us."

I have listened to the tape in which you give an enthralling
explanation of what that meeting must have been like. But I do not
consider myself to have been there. When you say "we met Him,"
whom do you include in that "we"? From this question proceed a host
of others that are annoying in their naivete, but which will be asked
nonetheless: where has He been since; why is there no archaeological
evidence of our sojourn in Egypt, of the meeting at Sinai, the trek in
the desert; why are there no independent first-person accounts of that
sojourn anywhere other than the Torah (and other such evidentiary
objections) and why are we as Jews so consistently wracked by dissent
and disagreement about exactly who we are, what we are called upon
to do and by whom, when His words (if His words they were) and
directions to us were so indelibly clear, and the consequences for not
following them so dire?

Were we literally "there," in some past life, or were we there by virtue of continuity, through the very DNA we carry, whose molecules had that event impressed upon them? We have already abandoned or modified so many of the mitzvot He detailed, is it possible that we have lost our connection with Him already and don't know it? How do we know if we're doing the right thing if we don't even know if He is?

I do not wish to debate this, but only to point out that most Jews that I know – most of whom are relatively literate Conservative Jews – do not, cannot believe that they met God, that God was met, or even that Torah was given at Sinai. And if they are conflicted or in doubt about this, how can they really consider themselves Jewish, foster Jewish continuity or continue the sacred work of Jews in the world?

For me to understand what you mean when you say "we met Him," I need to know this: were you and I, in some fashion, there? Because if we were not there, then either we have met him since and many of us don't even know it, or we are taking "on faith" the fact that 80-odd generations ago, He was met.

David,

Since we do not experience the original historical event as personal we must investigate its veracity in other ways, and that is why the study of the history of Torah transmission is so important. I have already referred you to works, both classic and modern, that examine this transmission history – it is basic Torah material.

Archaeological evidence: I shall attach three references detailing the archaeological evidence of our sojourn in Egypt as a start for your research on this subject. (What archaeological evidence would you like for the meeting at Sinai?)

Were we all at Sinai? In reality, we *were* all there at a deep level, and knowledge of that experience is possible. In fact, we have a tradition that one of the specific problems of our age is a dense block in consciousness that makes that knowledge hard to access. This block is an important facet of modern Jewish disaffection; detachment from the core awareness of Jewish identity is at the heart of the problem.

Why do so many Jews of this generation hardly relate to their Jewish identity at all? The Talmud states: "Every seventy years a star rises that misguides the sailors." Seventy years is the conventional measure of a generation; each generation in Jewish history is tested by a particular mistaken ideology. Great ideological movements contrary to authentic Jewish values sweep through the world and the Jewish people; each generation is tested and tempted by one of these, and many succumb in the face of a new and apparently redeeming approach to life. Seventy years later the idol crashes and a new one arises; again a generation is tempted and again there are casualties.

The opinion of great Torah minds of the last generation was that the test of that generation was the communist and socialist idea; many Jews were swept away by its promise of a perfect society. Seventy years after its grand entrance, it crashed and exited the stage of human ideology, one more failure in the long series of human ideas intended to build a universal messianic reality.

Now what is the ordeal of our generation? What star misguides those who would navigate a course through our part of history? What misperception tests and tempts the minds of Jews today?

It is quite likely the blurring of the distinction between Jew and non-Jew.

In the modern Jewish mind a transition has taken place to a universal grasp of man without distinctions. The unique nature of the Jewish people and its path through history are becoming blurred in the minds of modern Jews. The special beauty and greatness of our people, a sense of the miracle of our existence despite the concerted efforts of vast sections of humanity to destroy us throughout history; the sharp awareness of these things is being lost. There is no longer anything specifically Jewish at the center of the personal sense of identity of many Jews today.

The deepest element of the sense of self that has always lived in the heart of a Jew, that natural pride in being a child of Jewish history, is being lost. It is fundamental to understand that *this is unnatural;* the star that rises and misguides the navigators is *unnaturally* placed, it does not belong in that part of the firmament. That intelligent Jews should regard their Jewishness as irrelevant, unworthy of even a passing thought, is nothing short of miraculous.

For an idea that has been at the forefront of human consciousness for millennia, at the focal point of world history throughout the ages of human activity, to pass so far out of the consciousness of its sons and daughters that they are prepared to give it up without engaging it even superficially is remarkable. Souls hewn from the rock that formed Abraham, children of a family whose story spans history, whose ancestors changed the world most profoundly and consistently, scions of an epic of unparalleled survival – and these survivors find all this irrelevant. Not worth considering; simply irrelevant.

The Jewish mind is asleep, drugged by this unusual and unprecedented ordeal. The vibrant and aggressive Jewish mind, that sharp and inquiring mind that has examined and penetrated, discovered, conceived and invented in all areas of knowledge, has lost knowledge of itself.

Akiva,
Further to our speculations on what draws Jews to Buddhism, I would posit this: it is precisely *the relief from the burden of the* connection to a formative event *in favor of* this moment, *that draws Jews strongly toward Buddhism.*

In Buddhism, the moment is all there is. All moments unfold within and are telescoped into this one.

(There is, of course, the story of the Buddha's awakening under the bodhi tree and the events that preceded and followed it, but even though the Buddha's life is well documented there is so much myth

woven in that it's hard to tell or care whether it's real. What matters
is what has been revealed through the Buddha. That's why, when a
student asked a monk, "What should we do were we to meet the
Buddha on the road?" the master replied, "You should kill him." The
Buddha was no deity, and the monk was pointing out that students had
to radically separate themselves from veneration of a figure in favor
of close study of his ideas.)

David,

You say that Buddhism sees the moment as all that is real – "the moment is all there is." But Buddhism talks about a final enlightenment after all the necessary incarnations; is that not a point outside the moment of present existence?

Or is the idea in Buddhist thinking that there is a destination that transcends the journey, but all awareness must be focused on the present moment? In Judaism, we see the ideal as total focus on the moment as the locus of action, yet with an inner eye on destination because it is the destination that gives definition and meaning to the present moment.

You say that Buddhism focuses on experiencing the present. In Jewish thinking the proper expression of that sense of the eternal present is the next world; that is the dimension of end-point from which there is nowhere else to go. The next world is a dimension where time is not linear; there all points in time are one. There, only the moment exists in the deepest sense. The kabbalists explain that "time" in the next world *expands* – no moment is left behind, each moment adds, there is no forgetting. In truth that is here and now, but awareness of that depth is in the next world.

The mitzva that brings out this element of consciousness is Shabbat.

Shabbat is called *"me'eyn olam ha'ba"* – a taste, a small degree of the experience of the next world. Shabbat is the tangible counterpart of that existence in this world. How is this higher taste experienced? By desisting from work. Not work in the sense of exertion, that is a serious misunderstanding of Shabbat. What is halted on Shabbat is not exertion but *creative activity*. The week is built by engaging in constructive actions, Shabbat is built by *desisting* from those actions. The meditation of Shabbat is the meditation of being, not becoming.

A common misconception is that Shabbat is a day of "rest" in the conventional sense; a break from the work of the week. The proper term for that is "weekend," not Shabbat. There is nothing Jewish about that idea; Shabbat is a spiritual issue, like all of Torah and its mitzvot. The "weekend" has nothing to do with Shabbat.

At the end-point there is nothing but being, no time but the present. Each week we enter that timeless zone, and each week we bring down something of its ethereal nature into the flow of time. We are able to do that because the timeless thread that is woven into the flow of historic time begins at Sinai; that is where we entered the eternal present.

Legalism and Spiritual Vacuity

"The preservation of arcane traditions, and the inability of Judaism to adapt itself to the different times and cultures in which Jews have found themselves can account for a lot of Jewish seeking, and finding, in Buddhism. How can a spiritual tradition, with a close connection to a vibrant, present One God maintain that connection in the mind-numbing tracts of legislation and commentary through which Jews approach their relationship with God?

Many see Judaism as so engulfed in procedure and law that it, and its adherents, are utterly lacking in spiritual identity. A Buddhist almost invariably puts openness and awareness and compassion front and center, and is a spiritually enlivened being. Many Jews seem utterly unconcerned with spiritual life and development, but still proud to call themselves Jews, and it is the sons and daughters of these people who join other religions, or fall away from all spiritual practice, who intermarry, who lose any connection to Jewish identity."

David,
"...the inability of Judaism to adapt itself to the different times..."
You are simply mistaken about this. My shelves are full of books detailing applications of Jewish law to modern situations; that is exactly the nature of the Oral Law. In the field of medicine, for example, each new technology raises ethical questions and it is the province of the Torah minds of the generation to apply Talmudic precedent to each case. I am deeply involved in this; I often find myself at the intersection of modern medicine and halacha. Never yet have I failed to find the Torah resolution of a medical dilemma; on the broad shoulders of our leading authorities rests this responsibility. Their task is to identify the

correct Torah source for a particular challenge; if you page through the classic responsa spanning the centuries you will find that this has always been the case. Each age throws up its challenges and its questions, Torah answers them. It is axiomatic that the Mishna contains the principles that govern every conceivable human situation; the creative effort of our masters and teachers is to correctly identify the relevant ones and rule appropriately. This is a thrilling exercise; to see an ancient law apply consistently through all the permutations that human ingenuity brings to our lives, timeless and uncompromising yet dynamic and multiplex, is to experience the remarkable marriage of technology and morality that is one of the classical provinces of halacha.

Look up some of these responsa, you will find them illuminating. Whether it is a question of risky surgery where the alternative is certain death in the longer term, termination of a pregnancy when the mother's life is doubtfully in danger, triage priorities in kidney transplantation, permissibility of cosmetic surgery, or a problem occasioned by supersonic air travel involving the international date line, the halachic decisors have dealt with them and ruled definitively.

I could fill a book with examples drawn from my personal files alone. Here is an example for your consideration: not long ago I was asked for an opinion in the case of a patient who required emergency replacement of a heart valve. His cardiologist and cardiac surgeon favored a particular type of valve, but a senior colleague whom they consulted favored a different type, a valve with a very different profile of benefits and risks. This is a question with potentially the gravest of consequences, as I am sure you realize. Now the first two physicians are nationally recognized experts; the consultant is an international authority. The question they put to me was this: what holds sway in Jewish law – a majority of expert opinion or a minority of superior opinion? Think about that; it is not a simple matter. On that occasion I was able immediately to consult Rabbi Eliashiv, leading halachic authority in Jerusalem, and within a half-hour I was privileged to provide the solution. (The patient is fine, by the way. I shall be glad to share with you an analysis of that case, and how Rabbi Eliashiv resolved it halachically.)

Note that unlike secular law, Torah law does not change. In the secular world, changing times bring changes to the law; what was culpable homicide yesterday, actionable in a court of law, is called euthanasia today and countenanced by the law as moral and correct. Torah does not change; it expresses itself anew in each new situation. In a democracy the law itself shifts as human votes move it; in Torah the human effort is applied to bring out the inherent flexibility of Torah while remaining true to its principles. Rabbi Samson Raphael Hirsch summed it up in this classic statement: "In a democracy, the people make the law. In Torah, the law makes the people."

"...the inability of Judaism to adapt itself to the different... cultures"
What do you mean by Judaism's inability to adapt to and live within cultures? Who has done that better than us? Who has spent millennia (who has been around for millennia?) in other peoples' cultures and survived? Who has preserved a culture while living within others as we have done? This represents a protracted feat of adaptation, the achievement of a strong-minded people who integrated into the lives and cultures of their host societies but never weakened their ancient attachment. I am referring to the religious element, not the assimilationists (they *never* survive, by definition – if they really assimilate, they are lost from us); I mean those who lived intensely Torah-true lives and yet were royal physicians in twelfth-century Egypt or ministers of finance in fifteenth-century Spain, those who were unflinchingly Torah-true and yet understood and contributed richly to the host culture.

(You present "adapting to cultures" as obviously desirable; let me point out that this is not always so. If adapting to a culture means becoming like the host culture in its immorality where it is immoral, its modernity-for-the-sake-of-modernity where that implies no genuine content, then we do not want to adapt to it. We want adaptability to the good, but staunch non-adaptation to the bad. That is a particular challenge that has traditionally been met through the ages of Torah society's residence in the world's cultures.)

"...mind-numbing tracts of legislation and commentary"

Mind-numbing? *Mind-numbing?* David, you have never learned in a yeshiva. Only someone who has never grappled with the Oral Law could imagine that it is a mind-numbing exercise.

Here is an extract from some lines I wrote as a beginner in yeshiva in Jerusalem:

> Although the Oral Law was written down at various times in history to avert the danger of its being altered by the action of time and the tortures of exile, the form of its writing ensures that it remains oral – the Talmud requires a transmission of understanding from master to disciple; an encoding of great beauty. One can translate a page of Talmud accurately and not have any idea of what it means, and yet when understanding dawns, one finds that everything is there, locked into the words in a riveted structure of sublime balance and poise.
>
> The structure is multi-dimensional, the great commentaries often differ on its definition; one suddenly sees that when viewed from another angle it looks entirely different and yet obeys all the rules of form and structure in its new shape. One must learn to hold both (or more) in the mind's eye at once and when clarity in all the commentaries has been attained the experience is the intellectual equivalent of turning a multi-faceted diamond in the light.
>
> One can become enraptured with the clarifying of structure alone, but the dissecting of the Talmud's anatomy is done to bring out the deeper level, the underlying conceptual framework. The effort here is to trace the discussion to its common denominators, to find the unifying concept or theme that explains its manifold structure.
>
> One learns to descend in stages through the layers of a Talmudic discussion to a level where one begins to understand what the commentaries are saying and experiences the electricity holding everything together, the sparkle of each of the elements, their interdependency and range of consequences.
>
> Beyond this lies the level of *chiddush* – the experience of becoming so identified with Torah that from the well of one's own

being an original insight is drawn; the primordial inborn Torah in the essence of the self rising to consciousness.

This process is not performed in abstraction – even the beginner will notice that the stuff of Talmud is the very fabric of the world; the Talmud deals with everything from personal duties to moral and ethical concepts, the nature and structure of the human psyche, interpersonal relationships, the metaphysical; in short, the Universe. Depth of insight in Talmud is insight into the Universe. Clarifying the multi-dimensional constructs of Talmud is a training to see reality in its various cross-sections. Talmudic analysis of the Mishna is a training to see beneath the skin of the world into its soul. The letters of the word Mishna are also those of the word *neshama,* soul.

So much for beginners. When you meet the great exponents of those tracts you will note that there is nothing numb about their minds – when you met one of this generation's leading Torah scholars recently in Jerusalem, did you feel you were engaging a numb mind?

Mind-numbing? David, you could not have chosen a less apt description. When you have the privilege of engaging those tracts at close quarters, as I hope you soon will, you will see how mind-expanding and mind-energizing they are. Those tracts keep us alive; they keep our *minds* alive.

But beyond the energizing of mind that Torah effects, it elevates the entire personality. Torah makes its exponents wise, not only sharp. And that wisdom is secondary to the character refinement that it generates – the purpose of learning lies beyond knowledge and wisdom. When Rabbi Moshe Feinstein, the last generation's leading halachic authority, was driven home from the yeshiva on one particular occasion, he asked the driver to stop a block away from the yeshiva; as the car stopped Rabbi Feinstein opened the door and extracted his hand that had been trapped by the closing door. The shocked students travelling with him asked him why he had not shouted as the door closed. Rabbi Feinstein said: "I did not want to embarrass the young man who closed the door on my hand."

We are talking about reflexes, David. You or I could probably also stand that sort of pain if necessary; but the question is whether you or I would still the reflex response of an anguished cry when a sudden and unexpected trauma strikes. That is possible only when you have developed to the point where someone else's embarrassment is as close to you as your own pain reflex.

And the speed and power of mind that harnesses those sensitivities is hard to grasp. Let me mention a further anecdote about Rabbi Feinstein that was occasioned by the gap between Torah and secular learning:

An aspiring young yeshiva student was brought to Rabbi Feinstein by his parents. They wanted their son to attend college, but the youngster had set his heart on studying in yeshiva; Rabbi Feinstein was to adjudicate. The father, knowing Rabbi Feinstein's reputation, had thoroughly prepared his argument:

"Rabbi, the Talmud says that each person is formed by three partners; his father, his mother and God. The Talmud also says that we rule according to a majority. Now my son's three formative partners are right here: I am his father, this is his mother, and you, Rabbi Feinstein, represent God. I want him to go to college, and so does his mother. You, rabbi, no doubt want him to go to yeshiva. But we are two against one, and therefore, entirely according to Talmudic principles, he should go to college."

Without a moment's hesitation, Rabbi Feinstein replied:

"You are quite right about all your premises. But let us look at the full picture, exactly according to what you have said. You, too, are comprised of three partners, namely your two parents and God; so is your wife, and so am I.

Now perhaps the two parts of you that represent your parents want your son to attend college, but the third part of you that is God does not. As for your wife, her two parents may want your son to attend college too, but the third part that is God does not. And as for me, all three parts of me want your son to attend yeshiva. I make that five against four."

After a very brief silence, the father said: "If *that* is what they learn in yeshiva, that is where he is going!"

Can I think of a relevant anecdote based on the theme of Eastern wisdom? Perhaps this one:

When the Jews in Japan were threatened with extinction during the last war by a request of the Germans that their Japanese allies set up extermination camps to deal with those Jews under their jurisdiction, the Japanese were puzzled. Why do the Germans want to kill Jews? Why annihilate civilians who pose no threat to you? Why kill your own citizens? Why could they want us to kill these harmless refugees – what is it about them that makes their total extinction necessary?

The Japanese convened a panel to consider the German request; they were not going to butcher civilian refugees without reason. The Amshenover Rebbe, a Chassidic leader who was among the Jews there at the time, was called to meet the Japanese investigating panel to answer their questions so that Japan could decide the issue.

When the Rebbe faced the panel, the Japanese Admiral who headed it put the question to him: "Why do they want to kill you? What is it about you that makes them hate you thus?"

In a flash of genius, as life and death hung in the balance, the Rebbe answered: "It is because we are an Eastern people."

Nothing more was heard of Japanese intentions to destroy the Jews.

Akiva,
I meant no disrespect to any sages. (Yes; when in Jerusalem recently, I met your teacher as he rushed into a lecture hall to speak to eagerly waiting students. His presence was truly electrifying – a towering and peaceful but still forceful shield of light seemed to envelop him. It extended into my bones as he shook my hand, shrugged in apology and hurried in to give his talk.)

When I used the phrase "mind-numbing" I wasn't referring to scholars and sages. Of course *they get it: they're scholars and sages! But what about the rest of us? The highest level of Jewish scholarship no longer reaches even a sliver of the Jewish people. We are in danger of becoming an illumination aristocracy, where an anointed few delve into layers of knowledge for which the majority of us are ill-equipped, and becoming more so. More minds each day are not just numbed but positively alienated by their de facto exclusion from the levels of Jewish knowledge to which only the* illuminati *retain access.*

David,

Who is excluding you? Torah wisdom is there for the taking. It costs effort, there is no doubt about that, but it is available to anyone who is ready to invest that effort. Certainly our sages are our aristocracy, but theirs is not an inherited status. Torah is not inherited, it is acquired by single-minded devotion. It has been said that Torah is an aristocracy of authority, but a democracy of opportunity.

In virtually every city with a Jewish population today there is an organized Torah outreach effort; people who make themselves available to learn with anyone who asks. Our sages teach constantly; Torah learning without teaching is considered defective. A feature of modern Torah life throughout the world is the focus on outreach; Rabbi Moshe Feinstein famously ruled that every knowledgeable Jew should devote at least a tenth of his learning time to learning with someone who knows less, just as we give away at least a tenth of our income.

No one is being excluded from Torah any more than from Buddhism; just as you made an effort, I am sure, to discover Buddhism, an effort must be made to discover Judaism. It is true that there is a language problem and a lack of textual skills, but these are not insurmountable. And if it is the broader picture that concerns you, the drift away from Jewish knowledge as the generations progress, a key to that is genuine Jewish education for children. If they are given the tools, they will not experience the alienation that affects so many of your contemporaries.

You cannot stand outside an open door and complain about being excluded. Come in! And bring your children.

Cultural Perceptions

"Buddhists in the West are compassionate and caring, socially active and humble people. It may be an overgeneralization verging on anti-Semitism, but some Buddhists who are Jews might say that they are turned away from Judaism in no small measure by the way they see Jews living: in self-selected enclaves of, largely, wealth and privilege. How can a vibrant spiritual tradition lead to this kind of self-imposed spiritual apartheid?"

David,

Along these lines, you said previously: *"A Buddhist... is a spiritually enlivened being"* but *"Many Jews seem utterly unconcerned with spiritual life and development."*

Do you mean to compare a practising, knowledgeable Buddhist, one who is highly motivated in his Buddhist practice, having chosen it himself, with a Jew by default, one who happens to have been born Jewish but lacks virtually all semblance of genuine Jewish education?

It is not sensible to compare Western Buddhists to Western Jews – the Western Buddhists you are thinking of are those who have chosen Buddhism and are dedicated exponents. The Jews you are thinking of are people who happen to have been born Jewish but are not exponents of Torah Judaism by any stretch of the imagination; on the contrary, they have grown up almost entirely ignorant of Torah. You cannot meaningfully compare these groups.

The exponents of a system are not the system. You cannot necessarily judge the game by its players – your experience may not be representative when you regard the field of play; you may have stumbled on some very clumsy players. It is not fair to compare masters of Buddhism, or even highly motivated junior exponents, to unmotivated, uneducated, disillusioned modern Jews. If you must judge the game by its players, make sure you are watching the experts.

The comparison you are presenting is skewed; it represents the perception of one who has seen expert practitioners of Buddhism but has hardly glimpsed a *talmid chacham,* a real Torah sage. One who has been privileged to spend time in the presence of Torah greatness would not make that mistake. When you were in the presence of a master of this generation you described the experience as electrifying. When you have deeper contact and an opportunity to begin plumbing the depths of character and learning of such individuals, this issue will melt away.

Our exile is deep; we live at a time when few masters are left. The European Torah world was swept away sixty years ago and now you must seek its shards and remnants (and the occasional new shoot pushing its way through the mud) in the relatively narrow niche of today's Torah world. You know that most modern Jews have almost no connection with anything genuinely Jewish, let alone deep learning. And even in those narrow zones that profess to be genuine Torah one needs circumspection and good judgement to detect the real from the superficial. I am sorry, David, but that is the reality. We are fragmented in a deep exile.

So if you are going to compare Buddhists and Jews in order to judge Buddhism and Judaism (if you must; I am not sure the exercise is of any value), you must set up a valid comparison. Compare expert with expert, beginner with beginner. What is the level of observance and attainment of Buddhists who *happen* to be Buddhist, for example those born into Buddhism in Buddhist countries and societies – perhaps you could examine children of American Buddhists: are they exemplary? Or are their parents exemplary because they have chosen Buddhism in idealistic rejection of American alternatives and worked to achieve a high level? What exactly do their children look like? What about Buddhists in the East – ordinary people, not monks and exemplary adepts? Are they striking examples of spirituality or are they simply normal?

The Jewish picture you see before you is a picture of exile, and an exile that has been particularly effective in detaching Jews from their source. Remember too, that you cannot compare our modern exile with the Tibetan Buddhist exile in India; exile in modern America may be far more destructive of real Judaism than the oppression and exile of Tibetan Buddhists is of Buddhism – the smile may be more lethal than the sword. I am afraid that the air of Chicago may be far more likely to stifle Torah than the air of Dharamsala is to stifle Buddhism. On the contrary, our periods of greatest Torah learning and creativity have often been our politically darkest (the Talmud says that this is one of the reasons we are compared to olives – the oil is produced under pressure).

If you must judge the game by its players, search for the masters. They are rare and retiring, but they can be found. Or perhaps more telling, study the disciples, those "ordinary" Jews who are truly Torah observant. And if you want to observe exemplary juniors, perhaps you might look to those Jews who have *chosen* Judaism and are *its* dedicated exponents – the so-called *ba'alei teshuva,* those who were raised non-observant and have come back to the ways of their ancestors. Among them you will find much to admire.

To find mastery in Torah today you have to search for it as you would for treasure; it may be buried deep. You will have to exert yourself; you may have to travel. You will have to seek out that narrow niche where the real Torah is found. If you find it too openly on the street or calling to you from a seductive doorway, look away; if it is selling itself cheaply it is not Torah. Torah must be sought; but when you find it, you will know it.

Ordinary Jews in general over the course of history have indeed been exemplary; Jewish masters have always been, and are, exemplary. Throughout history Jews lived Torah, we were indiscernibly intertwined with our Torah; in the past two or three centuries we have experienced a precipitous decline in spiritual level. This is part of a phenomenon discussed in the Talmud and known as the "descent of the generations." But modern Jews are not necessarily Judaism.

In this generation, look to those dedicated to Torah learning. These days, they are often to be found in enclaves of poverty, not wealth. In fact, in the modern yeshiva world poverty happens to be more or less the standard; I personally know many families in that world who live on less than you probably waste. A Buddhist monk who lives on the alms that provide him his one daily meal would feel right at home there. Why this is so is not our subject; I mean only to draw your attention to the appropriate places to look for your spiritually enlivened Jews.

Rabbi Shach, Talmudic and halachic luminary, until his recent passing the Torah leader of this generation, used to sleep without a blanket. He did not own a blanket. A *blanket,* David. He used his coat; his wife used their only blanket. I know, because an individual connected with this incident told me that the only way the students in his yeshiva could get him finally to accept a blanket was when a Swiss student returned home and left his blanket behind ownerless; only when the other students assured Rav Shach that no one else needed it did the Rosh Yeshiva acquire a blanket. This is not far-fetched; I had the privilege of visiting Rav Shach at his apartment in Bnei Brak, and I can tell you that it was bare.

You may know that the Chafetz Chaim, Torah leader of the pre-war generation, had virtually no possessions. A well-known anecdote tells of the surprise of a wealthy Western European Jew who visited the Chafetz Chaim at his home in Radin; the man expressed his amazement at the spartan emptiness of the home. The Chafetz Chaim asked him: "Where is all your wealth? You do not seem to have much, either." The visitor replied: "Rabbi, I am only passing through. Where I am going, I have plenty." The Chafetz Chaim replied: "I am also only passing through..."

But these great Torah minds were rich in another way. Their heads were in another place entirely, and in that place they were drunk with the richness and joy of Torah. If you spend time in the presence of those who are immersed in learning you will begin to feel this. They live in the Talmud, they are absorbed by it to a degree that is hard to describe; a surpassing addiction might not be too strong a term. That is the locus of their consciousness, that is where they live. The depths and intricacies of Talmudic problems are the enclaves they inhabit.

When the Mir yeshiva was aboard ship approaching Shanghai during the war, one of the students came up on deck and asked: "Where are we?" Rabbi Chaim Shmulevitz, the Rosh Yeshiva, answered: *"Kiddushin daf mem"*– the page of Talmud they were currently studying. That is where he was; that is where they were. And David, that is where we should be. Shanghai or Chicago should really not make much difference to us; our real place is the place within Torah that holds our attention.

To be sure, we need to live in the world, and when we engage the world we need to do that fully and responsibly. But that is not where we live; we live in that other place, on that higher plane. There are plenty of people and nations to engage the world; they can do it more or less as well as we can. But none of them can engage Torah; that is our province and that is what we are here for. If you are looking for the spiritually enlivened Jew, that is where you will find him.

David, I could not say these things to most people. Most modern Jews would consider the suggestion that our unique purpose is to live on another plane, to engage an esoteric intellectual wisdom with all our hearts and minds, as bizarre and hopelessly outdated; you know that *more than half* of American Jews now profess no connection with *any* form of Jewish identity. We have reached a situation in which the suggestion that Torah should be the proper engagement of the Jewish mind is unintelligible to most of its children; most of them would have great difficulty even if they tried – as I have repeatedly pointed out to you they have been deprived of its very language, let alone its refined concepts and constructs. Bewildered tears are perhaps the only appropriate response to this peculiar tragedy.

I could not say these things to most people, but surely I can say them to you. Surely if there is one thing a serious involvement in Buddhism must have taught you it is the primacy of spirit, the courage to renounce egotistical materialism for hard work on the self, the ability to see through the superficiality and perversion of much of the culture that surrounds us. Surely Jews who have seriously committed themselves to a system like Buddhism at some point in their lives can relate to this, can see that there must be another way, that the world was designed for something better. If there are Jews outside the Torah world who understand the importance of spirit, who know that profound dedication to spiritual study and practice is required to walk the path to enlightenment, surely they must be found among those like you who have engaged a serious system of personal work, who have learned to renounce material convention.

Attachment to materialism is antithetical to Torah. It is not wealth as such that is the problem; it is the attachment to wealth that obstructs. Poverty in the literal, economic sense is not essential to Torah; *detachment* from the material is. The Mishna states: "This is the way of Torah: eat bread with salt, drink water by measure, and sleep on the earth..." The commentaries explain that this Mishna is not teaching that a diet of bread and water is mandatory for progress in Torah, richer food is allowed; rather, the teaching here is that bread and water *should be enough* – one may eat a meager diet or a richer diet, the point is that *it should make no difference*. When the excess becomes important, when it could not be instantly exchanged for utter simplicity, and exchanged with total equanimity, then one is far from "the way of Torah."

So if you are serious about finding the enlivening spirituality you talk about, you will have to visit those enclaves where poverty and riches keep company. Deeply visit, taste and experience real learning, and not as a tourist but as a recruit. It is not easy, I can tell you. There is hard work to be done just to engage Talmud at the first level, to acquire the initial skills, the depth and mental agility that begin the process of moving from the status of spectator to that of exponent. But hard work never frightened a serious Buddhist, I am sure.

As for "spiritual apartheid," we have already discussed the idea of separation and shown that it need not be bad in itself – in fact, separating from undesirable elements in a society is a Torah obligation. A community can be separate enough to maintain its identity and its values and yet contribute significantly to the broader society. We are in essence "a nation that dwells alone" and our Torah is valid only when it is unadulterated (that is why it was given in a desert). It lives in pristine solitude, it is purest where no admixture of values obscures its crystal clarity, and it needs no support from anything outside of itself. It is not one among many options. It is set against every other thing in the world; it is quite apart.

Emptiness

"This is a Buddhist concept that I'll have to recommend a text for. But essentially, it is that all things, all beings, are creating themselves from moment to moment, and have no inherent quality or personality. Rather, it is the overlay of our perceptions, born of our own misconceptions and our chemical and psychological interplay, that lead us to mistakenly endow things and people with qualities that, in the whole, they do not have.

This radical view, arrived at by great Buddhist philosophers of roughly the 10th century, unravels more traditional views of personality, personal experience, and of course, God."

David,
The Jewish view is this: things unto themselves are not a problem. Things seen as more than they are in reality is the problem; in fact the only problem. That is, our perception of reality must give no more to any thing than it actually has; and what any thing has is always its Divine nature and no more (and no less).

The kabbalistic sources are clear about this. The true nature of reality is: *"Ein od mil'vado"* – there is nothing other than Him. How we handle the appearance of solid reality philosophically is not our question right now (this is a central kabbalistic issue of indescribable beauty and subtlety).

The challenge is to train our perception to see that all things are dependent on their Source. As soon as reality takes on a dimension of independence, perception has become distorted.

The real problem, therefore, lies in perception. What do you see of the world? If you see things as they are, as emanations of the source, without ascribing any independent reality to them, you are seeing correctly. But when you ascribe to a thing more than its Divine nature you are distorting perception, and it is the false grasp of self that is causing the damage.

Rabbi Dessler used a memorable image to illustrate this. Perception of reality is always through a lens; the kabbalistic sources discuss the nature of this lens as either "light," absolutely transparent, or "not light," opaque in varying degrees. The lens is nothing other than the vessel of the self; all is seen through that lens. The only question is how clear that lens is. The purpose of spiritual training is to polish the lens to transparent clarity; to the extent that it is clear, reality is seen objectively. The polishing consists of working on the self to divest it of all the immature vested interests that are the expressions of ego in one form or another.

Rabbi Dessler would point out that a cloudy lens causes two problems: one is that you cannot see clearly through it; you see less of what there is to see. But there is another problem: a cloudy lens reflects the one who is looking through it. When you survey the scene through a cloudy lens you see a reflection of yourself; exactly to the extent that the lens is cloudy you see yourself, but since the cloudiness is nothing other than your own false perception, you imagine that you are seeing objective reality. More and more of the world starts to look like you, and you do not know it.

This image is a classic example of *mussar* teaching. Again, we come back to the original problem: the false vision of self.

This is why the Torah *begins* with this problem: Adam's challenge was to suppress his power of assertion of self; that is the human challenge. Note that Adam's ordeal did not require him to do anything; on the contrary, it required him to do *nothing*. His commandment was *not to eat* from the tree. His task was to allow the Divine to manifest by stilling his urge to act, to assert himself, *even in the arena of Divine service:* his ultimate function is to use his free will, his independence, to demonstrate that he is nothing, God is everything. Use his free will to give it up; assert it as sacrifice.

That was his test. "Am I to be a passive passenger? Was I given cosmic power *not* to use it? Must I sit by while the world is run by You and not show my love by acting?" And of course, that was exactly what he was meant to do; by desisting from acting independently you demonstrate Whose hand acts. *Ein od mil'vado,* there is nothing other than Him.

This is the central and the single most important element of service, or personal work, in Judaism. This is what Jewish masters built and achieved; this is precisely where their greatness lies. You will recall that the greatest master who ever lived, Moses, was the humblest ("And Moses was humbler than any man..."); that is exactly his greatness. To the extent that he is empty of himself he can be filled with Reality.

The Talmud puts it this way – "Rabbi Abbahu says: 'He who makes himself as if he is not, through him the world exists...'"

This radical view... unravels more traditional views of... God.
You are saying that a correct grasp of the idea of emptiness goes against the "traditional" view of God.

It is critical to know what we mean by God; there may be an erroneous assumption behind your comment here. All things are empty *exactly* because God fills them; they are so empty, in fact, that He is all there is. He is the vessel and the contents; again: *Ein od mil'vado.* In fact, in the kabbalistic terminology, emptiness is about as close as you can get to a correct expression of the nature of the Universe. The expression in those texts is: "He surrounds all worlds and He fills all worlds."

God is *not* one of those things that are *"born of our... chemical and psychological interplay...;"* although as long as we live in an earthly vessel we will always struggle with the subjectivity of our perception at least to some degree. It is better to conceive of God in terms of existence and the Source of existence. He is not something that lives within a broader framework; He *is* the broader framework (I have mentioned before that this is the reason that one of the Divine names is "the Place"). If you are going to relegate all perception to an illusory and unreliable function of our "chemical and psychological interplay," then even the perception of emptiness will be just as subjective and therefore unreal and unreliable, and no thought or knowledge will have any meaning or value. To study this further, I suggest pondering deeply the first chapter of Maimonides' "Laws of the Fundamentals of Torah" as an introduction.

It strikes me that the difference between Judaism and Buddhism here may be that Buddhists see reality as empty, we see it as full. They see all reality as a profound emptiness; we see it as an emptiness that is profoundly filled. What do you say?

Speaking of emptiness – on a personal note:

I notice that neophyte Buddhists often take on Buddhist names. Why? If Buddhism is portable, as you have indicated, that is, it can be imported into Judaism, if one can "practice Buddhism and still be a Jew" as you put it, why the change of name? If the core is Jewish while the practice includes Buddhist practice, what is wrong with a Jewish name? What I am really asking is: what is the core? In Torah, name is essence. A name speaks out essence, displays a compression of identity for others (one's name is *not* for oneself; if you need your name in order to think of yourself you are in deep trouble psychologically, because grasp of self should be, must be, primary in consciousness, known as it actually is, unmediated by any word or name. The first error in consciousness is to confuse thinking with words – you have indicated that Buddhists are aware of that no less than we.)

So a Jew is identified by his Hebrew name; if he has a Torah understanding he will know that his name says it all.

Do you know what "David" means? It means "emptiness." Let me enlarge a little; I hope this will make my point.

As you know, David is a royal name; not only because it designates King David but more deeply because it designates King David's ultimately royal persona, to be revealed in his incarnation as the Messiah. The Torah characterizes David as the transcendent focus known as "Kingship" in the kabbalistic system; the mystical sources define that emanation as "having nothing of its own," utter emptiness. But we mean emptiness in the Torah sense here: utter *greatness* dissolved in its Source, a full *expression* of self but *yielded* to Source, self defined entirely by the Source of that self.

Think about this: what is the purpose of a Jewish king, or more potently, the Messianic king? If the Messiah will walk the earth when God-consciousness comes fully into the world, why is he necessary – why will any intermediary be necessary in that phase of human history in which the Divine presence manifests openly? You might think he would be necessary *now*, during the dark phase of history; but why *then*, in the light? You know the Jewish antipathy to the idea of intermediaries. What does the Messiah represent?

The answer is this: the Messianic age will not be a phase in which only the Divine manifests correctly; it will be an age in which the *human* manifests correctly too, in all the glory and greatness that the human can demonstrate. And what exactly is that greatness? The Messiah will be the greatest human, the most developed and exalted individual imaginable, a king far surpassing all the kings of history in greatness, grandeur and power. He will rule with an international, incontrovertible and sublime rule, holding more power than any human ever has or will – and *he* will show that he is nothing. *That* is emptiness.

His might and power will be concentrated in a searing demonstration of one thing: that he is empty of all independent existence. In the greatest human vessel will be reflected the Divine; he will show what it means to be transparent. That is what the Divine Presence on earth means: not the Divine alone obliterating all else, annulling all conscious beings in its enormity; not simply the Divine revealed *to* the human, but rather revealed *through* the human.

The name David is spelled *daled, vav, daled*. That construction indicates the essence of the name; based on ideas revealed by the Maharal, some of its meaning is this: the *daled* indicates emptiness; its root *dal* means poverty, utter lack. (Its numerical value is four, indicating the four extensions of a flat, two-dimensional reality; in fact the shape of a *daled* is simply two lines at right angles, the stylized depiction of two dimensions with no expansion into volume.) The next letter in "David" is the *vav*; this letter indicates connection to source, addition, increase. The *vav* is the Hebrew letter of conjunction, the "and," its function is always to connect. The word *vav* in Hebrew means a hook, a connecting device. (The numerical value of this letter is six, indicating the six extensions of the full three-dimensional reality in which the flat plane has expanded into the volume of the real.) If you are following me, the process unfolding in the name David is this: poverty or utter emptiness, followed by connection with source, and the final letter is again the *daled*. David starts empty, is shown, given, everything, connected to his Source, and yet remains the same simple unaffected empty vessel he was before.

(Note that David's arch-enemy is Gog. Gog represents the kingship of Western ideology, derived from the Greeks, that will come to battle the Messiah in that final showdown between the self-reliant, empirical, human wisdom of the West and the unlimited, transcendent wisdom of Torah. Self-assertion, ego inflation, against David's ego-negation. Now the name Gog is spelled in symmetrical counterpoint to David: Gog is spelled *gimel, vav, gimel* – the root of the *gimel* means self-sufficiency, having no need to look to a source; the same root means "to be weaned," that is, to become independent of the mother's giving. Gog begins as a self-important, self-reliant individual. Then the *vav* – he is connected to the source, shown reality clearly, elevated to the fullness of all reality, and yet his last letter is the same *gimel* as the first: he remains the same self-assertive, self-inflated individual that he was before.)

That is some of the message in the name David. Why do they need Buddhist names, David? Can you enlighten me?

Emptiness is the beginning and the end, it is the central concern of Jewish development; it is the definition and the meaning of our work.

Abraham says: "I am dust and ashes." The Vilna Gaon reveals a penetrating insight into an idea we echo every week as we greet the Shabbat: *"Hitna'ari, me'afar kumi...–* Arouse yourself, arise from the dust..." Commenting on this call to the collective persona of the Jewish people at the final Shabbat eve, the end of history, the Gaon says that it does not mean arise from the dust *where* you are, but rather, arise from the dust *that* you are. There are many layers here, but one of them is a reference to the emptiness that began Jewish history in the personality of Abraham and will presage the end of history in the messianic resurrection and reconstruction.

PS Do you think you could have avoided a spiritual search with a name like Gottlieb?

Akiva,
Buddhist names are given for a number of reasons, but the central one is that the name is like a koan, or puzzle. The teacher chooses a name that has a deep meaning on which the named must meditate. On one level, it appears to make sense, and on other levels it is puzzling. It is meant to take one into the deepest heart of one's own nature with respect to the dharma, or the truth inherent in Buddhist teaching.

In a rich irony, I was given the Buddhist name "True Ancestor."

Ego and Obedience

David,
To understand more deeply the emptiness that man must strive for, let us look more closely at Adam's ordeal, for Adam was everyman. What went wrong at that electric moment? What is everyman's lesson in it?

Obedience meant bonding with the Creator by performing His will. But it required a yielding of human will. This is where the battle began and this is where it is pitched still.

Obedience to the command was all that was required. If Adam held strong and obeyed, the world would reach its perfection in a few short hours and be forever perfect. But what would be his contribution to that perfection? Only the passive non-action of resisting one solitary transgression? Surely he could be tested much more severely and prove his love of his Creator much more powerfully?

Adam reasoned that if he were to eat that fruit and bring himself and the world down from their rarefied and almost perfect spirituality into heavy physicality with all its temptations and possibilities of failure, *and then hold strong,* within that lower state remain true, that would be a far greater act of service.

He sensed that there was far more scope and potential for expression of his independent will than his situation allowed. And he was right. And he was wrong. He was right because in truth he had enormous potential; he was close to Divine in his greatness and virtually unlimited in power. But he was wrong because in going against the Divine command he would be moving out of reality.

In every expression of human free choice that is in contradiction to the Divine command there is a powerful illusion of independence, an assertion of self that is heady in its potency. But in every action in contradiction to the Divine there is a death; if He is the definition of existence, then any action against Him, no matter how powerfully real it seems, is an action out of existence.

What is the source of this ordeal? What is the root of the human psyche's longing to assert its freedom? The answer is that this independence is a deep root of the human soul. That is the origin of the dilemma; this ordeal is no mere superficial temptation. To understand this, let us look briefly at the Torah teaching of the purpose of Creation.

The Ramchal (Luzzatto), a classic source for this, states that the purpose of Creation is to give man ultimate good. Man is that creature whose reason for existence is to receive from the Creator, and to give man that ultimate good, He created the next world. The next world is a dimension in which man receives the greatest good possible – and that good is God Himself; in the next world man is to experience a closeness with God that approaches, becomes, unity with Him.

But to experience the pleasure of receiving that ultimate and inexpressible good unearned, free, would not be pleasure at all. This is known as the *"nahama d'k'sufa* – the bread of shame;" when you receive a free handout, you feel shame and helpless inadequacy. One who receives charity hardly feels alive; his dependence on others is a deep source of pain. To be given the ecstasy of closeness with the Creator undeserved, unearned, would be an eternal experience of shame, and therefore He created this world. The purpose of this world is to provide the opportunity to earn the next. This world is the place in which man is free to work of his own accord, free to generate his own perfection, to generate his existence in the next world. This world is dark and full of challenge; it is designed to provide the stage on which man operates to actualize his potential. His tools are the challenges of this world and his free choice to grapple with those challenges and overcome them.

That is the purpose of Creation. This world to work and earn; the next world to enjoy the results of the work. Our work in this world is necessary so that we do not feel the shame of living on free gifts.

But an obvious question must be asked here: why did He not simply create us *in such a manner that we enjoy free gifts?* Why put us through the ordeal of this world with all its misery and potential for failure? Why create the risk? Why not simply create a world in which we are close to Him without having earned it, without ever having experienced free will at all, and *in which we enjoy that closeness intensely?*

The answer to this question is a key to many things. If we were created such that we found ourselves given existence and pleasure passively, never having earned them, *we would not be close to Him at all.* The deepest secret of man's existence is that we are created in the image of the Divine; just as He is a Creator, man is a creator; just as He is free, man is free. God is free to create and destroy worlds, man is free to create and destroy worlds. And we are free to create ourselves: we have the capacity to develop the raw material of our personalities and our lives towards perfection.

If we were passive creatures without free will, we would be as opposite to the Divine as it is possible to be. If we were to exist eternally without having generated that eternity we would be passive puppets entirely unlike our Creator. We would be His opposites: He would be the Creator, we the creations. He would be the controller, we the controlled. He would be the giver, we the takers. And that would place us infinitely far from Him. The secret of the unity of Creation is that God and the creature He has created in His image are in fact reflections. We are deeply similar to Him; therein lies our potential for closeness to Him. At root, the degradation of the "bread of shame" is the feeling of distance from Him.

There is another nuance to this idea. A real receiver *must* be placed at a distance from the giver; if there is no distinction between giver and receiver, what giving can take place? If the receiver has no independence from the giver, both the giving and the receiving will be nothing other than an exercise of the giver. Man is set free, set at a distance from God, so that Giver and receiver are not one; that is the necessary condition for man to become a genuine receiver. Man must use his freedom of choice to annul the gap, to move back to his point of origin. He must use his freedom to sacrifice it.

Human independence has its origin in the Divine image. Building worlds is our business; we reflect the Divine most closely when we build our world. That is why Adam experienced the most difficult of ordeals: to obey meant to sacrifice, to relinquish his independence, to negate his freedom, to suppress his nature. The deepest level of his being cried out to assert that freedom; after all, that is acting in parallel with the Divine, that is expressing his Divine image. His ordeal was agonizing not because his lower self, his crude physicality, was lusting to be satisfied; he had none of that crude physicality. What was longing for expression was precisely his higher self, his Divinely modeled freedom to choose independently, his deepest essence.

That was his problem. He was certain that he had been created to express his freedom, not suppress it. What would his freedom mean if he merely watched the world perfect itself without his own heroic effort? Let me show Him that I am ready to take on all of life, and death too, to express myself in my love for Him.

The positive side: I shall live for Him; the negative side: *I* shall live for Him. That is the subtle and yet massive difference. Without that emphasis, I am His; with the emphasis, I will do *anything* to remain myself; I shall not yield my will.

Here is the paradox. While man asserts his independence he is nothing, merely a small bundle of protoplasm asserting the scope of his smallness. But when he annuls his independence, negates his ego, he melts into the reality of a greater Existence.

Yielding the freedom to choose *is the greatest act of free choice possible.* In depth that act is the highest assertion of will.

That is the human situation. We are the expression of a deep paradox; cosmically great and infinitesimally small. In sacrificing the will we assert the will at the deepest level. When we break away from Him we sense that assertion of will as a heady independence, we experience an illusion of independent reality rooted in the cosmic proportions that are the proper proportions of man, but in so doing we pass out of reality. In sacrificing the self to Him we lose independence and disappear into His reality; but paradoxically that is where we become real.

And the gap is no wider than a hair. The Talmud puts it this way: in the next world the righteous and the wicked will weep. The righteous will weep when they regard the ordeal they overcame to achieve their greatness, the negative side of their own personalities, and it will appear to them as a mountain. They will weep in wonder: "How were we able to overcome a mountain such as that?" And the wicked will weep too when they regard the lower self that they failed to overcome; *but it will appear to them as a hair's-breadth.*

We have already noted that in the work of sacrificing the ego it is easy to be misdirected – destroying the vested interests does not mean destroying the will. We are not seeking to become unmotivated robots – quite the contrary; one should be burning with motivation. The dedication of the faculty of free will to the Creator does not mean destroying all motivation and becoming an empty, emotionless vacuum of a personality. The spiritual path here is to *sharpen* the will, to hone that drive to a razor's edge, to fan the flames of raw motivation and desire into a blaze – and *fully active and flamingly alive,* to give them to Him.

A true and valuable servant is not an empty shell, a mechanical and bland being who lacks all will and interest. His will is powerful and unshakable, but it is poised constantly to carry out the wishes of the master. He has made his master's will his will; he acts as passionately for his master as he possibly could for himself because there is no difference between his master's desires and his own.

Traditions

"Shaking the lulav *and* etrog, *dwelling in booths; the dedicated reading of Torah portions about brutal savagery in war, sacrifice, plagues and torment visited upon enemies: some aspects of Jewish life and observance, and the stories by which we guide ourselves, seem to modern sensibilities arrogant, bizarre, war-like. Although it is beyond argument that the Jewish people endowed the Western world with much, if not all, of its moral code, it is nonetheless strange that we adhere to the customs and tell the stories of an ancient agrarian conglomerate of nomadic tribes when the world has changed so much.*

Much of Judaism appears impenetrable and archaic, so that it becomes the last place many Jews would look for a vital connection to the Divine. A book that recently received a lot of attention here in the States makes the claim that Judaism is dying because rituals have frozen the spiritual truth of the religion in inaccessible amber, and what's left has been expropriated by Jewish agencies using the Israeli/Palestinian crisis as an excuse to raise money to perpetuate themselves. This view is not entirely unrepresentative of much of my generation's take on contemporary Judaism."

David,
You raise two points: first, time renders certain "traditions" meaningless, and second, barbaric and terrible things are inappropriate to perpetuate; and you make an assumption: we were once an "agrarian conglomerate of nomadic tribes" and our traditions descend from there.

What you call "traditions" are mitzvot, commandments – you cite *succah, lulav* and *etrog;* these are Biblical commandments. There are two classes of mitzvot: those between man and God, and those between man and man. Those between man and man I presume give you no problem; you do not single out any of them – kindness, charity, lending to one who needs a loan, and so on. (These are all commandments of the Torah, exactly as are *succah* and *lulav.)* So I assume the problem is the man-God mitzvot. But why should these be any less relevant now than they were when they were given? You choose the example of *succah;* let us look at that mitzva briefly and see if it has lost any relevance with the passage of time.

I am going to suggest to you that quite contrary to your assumption, this mitzva is more relevant in modern times than it ever was. What lies behind this commandment? What is its meaning and what is the meditation that should accompany its performance?

Dwelling in booths is at root an exercise in ego negation; it works to build faith in the spiritual Source and not in the material domain of man's control. The *succah* requires a roof that is very insubstantial, as I am sure you know – it must be flimsy enough to allow the rain through; it is good if you can see the stars through it too. In fact, one of the root meanings of the Hebrew word *succah* is to *see through.* When you leave your permanent home (the proverbial "roof over your head") and move into a booth that has hardly a roof at all, you are developing the ability to see through the material and perceive the higher. The tempting illusion is that our security derives from the material; the *succah* teaches that if there is security, it comes from elsewhere. The kabbalistic texts call the *succah* the "shelter of faith." The festival of Succot occurs at the harvest season; the message is that exactly as you bring your harvest into your home, just at the time when you may feel most independent, most self secure, most independently wealthy, the Torah is saying: "Careful; do not detach from the real Source of all that you have." On Succot we read Kohelet (Ecclesiastes) – "All is vanity;" do not invest too much in this world. This is the constant theme of all the commentaries.

So dwelling in booths serves to sensitize you to the higher world, to draw your gaze up metaphorically, through the *succah's* thin cover and not to your mansion's concrete roof for security. This is a tangible experience of leaving the material and going out into a different kind of existence.

Is this is any less relevant today than it ever was? It could just be that it is *more* relevant now. With the development of technology, with the conquest of ever more of the material environment comes the temptation to assume that we are in control, that we are approaching mastery of our world. As we subdue more areas of the physical we amplify this danger. The ultimate danger here is not only the false assumption of competence and control, the dangerous illusion that we can take care of anything at all in our world, but at root we are amplifying ego and that is the real source of all disaster.

When you live in a solid house with technology that apparently guarantees your safety, you are *more* likely to forget from where your real protection comes. Modern culture fosters a sense of self-sufficiency and human power, a "We are in control" mindset. We need at least as much effort to control that as in ancient ages.

You chose the example of the *succah,* but we could show the relevance of all the mitzvot. The reasons and benefits that we grasp are not the ultimate reasons for the mitzvot; they are only the elements that we can relate to. The ultimate reasons lie beyond us; since the mitzvot are given from the ultimate and absolute Source of reality, of course they are relevant today. But even at the limited level that we can grasp we can show their timeless relevance.

Which other festivals are irrelevant in the modern age? Passover, that teaches the message of freedom? Shavuot, the giving of the Torah? Purim – learning to see the hidden Hand behind the natural? Chanuka – the war against the Greek anti-spiritual ideology that seeks to destroy our spiritual identity? Tisha b'Av – mourning and repentance occasioned by all the holocausts and destructions, distant and recent?

Which mitzvot? Do not tell me that kosher food is health-related, and now that our food is safe and healthy it is irrelevant. Kosher food has nothing to do with health (all Torah has fringe benefits that accompany its observance, but they are *only* the fringes). Unkosher food is spiritually desensitizing, not unhealthy. The Torah is primarily a spiritual path, not a social and medical guide.

A popular distortion of Torah suggests that the Shabbat laws are for the sake of "rest," and things that no longer require the exertion they once did are now permitted. But Shabbat has nothing to do with rest in the physical sense; what is prohibited on Shabbat is creative activity, not work, as we have already noted. The degree of exertion is irrelevant, and it always has been. Shabbat is a day of desisting from creation, a day of consolidating the week's achievement, an anticipation of the next world where all creation ceases, an experience of the destination that gives the journey its meaning.

That is as relevant as ever. As for the fringe benefits, the simple joy of family togetherness on Shabbat, with no media interruption, none of the flying from one activity to the next that defines the week, is invaluable. The high-quality time that marriage and family need, completely undisturbed, that Shabbat brings; people who have not built this into their experience can have no idea what they are missing.

Of those mitzvot of the 613 that we are able to fulfill today, what has time annulled? Kindness, charity, visiting the sick, saving life, providing medical treatment, giving interest-free loans, returning lost objects, building-safety regulations (an explicit command of the Torah)...?

And which prohibitions are not relevant now? Cruelty to animals, laws of scrupulous business honesty (the Torah prohibits even *owning* inaccurate weights and measures) – what no longer applies to us? Adultery? Murder? Theft? Jealousy? Perjury?

The menstrual separation laws? The Talmud indicates that one of the reasons for which we separate from our wives for some days each month is to maintain a spark of excitement in the sensual area of marriages that otherwise all too often descend into boredom, tired echoes of the appetite they once aroused. Is marriage now no longer a challenge?

The laws prohibiting intimate seclusion of man and woman who are not married to each other (*yichud*) are designed to prevent the unintended development of extramarital relationships; which society has transcended that problem?

Are you thinking of the specific laws that apply to Cohanim, the laws that define their particular spiritual status? But why should modernity change that? If you have trouble understanding why Cohanim should be the focus of unique laws in the first place, that is certainly worth discussion, but it has nothing to do with mitzvot that time has changed.

Perhaps you mean women's mitzvot. But again, the unique mitzvot that apply to women apply now as they always have – time has not changed the essential nature of woman. And again, if you struggle with the difference between men's and women's unique roles in Torah, that too is a subject for further analysis, but time has not changed its fundamentals.

Of course, there are those who claim that certain mitzvot were *never* relevant – but that has nothing to do with changes that time has wrought; that is a problem of plain and simple denial of Torah altogether. For one who denies mitzvot as such, time is not his problem.

Scientific and technological advances do not diminish the importance of spiritual wisdom. Do you think I could function in medicine today without Torah direction because modern medicine renders it unnecessary? How could I function without it? Abortion was practised two thousand years ago and it is practised now; our problem is not the technical, our problem is the moral and spiritual, and modern technology has not changed that. Every aspect of medicine requires spiritual knowledge; the Torah guides the process at every step. Which details are unnecessary? For example, the Code of Jewish law states explicitly that no doctor is allowed to treat a patient if a more qualified doctor is available. There is an overriding Torah obligation to give the patient the best possible treatment. This is not the place to examine that law's details and exceptions, but I can assure you that it applies today as it always has, and is just as necessary. As a Jewish doctor I need to know what is allowed and what is forbidden as much now as my ancestors who were doctors did in their day.

So modernity as a reason for the demise of mitzvot? I think not, David.

As for frozen spirituality and rituals: it is not ritual that is killing Jewish spirituality; there is no such thing as ritual in Judaism, and no such thing as symbolism, if those terms refer to *empty* practices and images. Every action, even the simplest custom in Torah practice is only a body that contains a living soul. We have no rite, no ritual and no symbol that is not the physical expression of an unfathomable depth as surely as the living body is the least aspect of a cosmic soul, only the physical expression of that soul. We have no sentimentality either; in Judaism all sentiment serves infinite spirit. There is nothing more basic in Torah than this; all of the world is an expression of the duality of form and matter, soul and body, Torah and mitzva, thought and action, meaning and expression. Of course you know that that duality is both dual and single – soul and body, Torah and mitzva, spiritual essence and the "ritual" or symbol that expresses that essence are all examples of a duality that resolves into unity in depth, the unity of Creator and Creation.

Secondly, you talk about *"barbaric and terrible things,"* for example *"brutal savagery in war"* when *" the world has changed so much."*

Has it really? Where it really matters, in human and moral terms, has it really changed? How long ago was it that the pride of the civilized world, the center of academia, the home of art and culture, the educated, sophisticated, democratic heart of Europe, murdered millions of its own peaceful and loyal citizens simply because they were Jewish? And *only* because they were Jewish; something that no species of insect has had to endure – no one has ever set about eradicating any species of insect from the world in its entirety simply because of what it is. (A harmful or dangerous species, perhaps. But annihilate a species just because its *existence* offends you?)

Those references to brutal savagery in war that you revile as bizarre and outdated now that "the world has changed so much" – was it only in the distant past that nation brutally attacked nation? It seems to me that as time goes by and the tools of brutality develop, the problem becomes greater, not less. Those tools are honed in hands every bit as brutal now as ever there were hands that used such things, but now they range further and wider, and evil that was once national has become global in its reach. Is there now less need to cry out against these things?

If you are referring to the wars that our own ancestors were obliged to engage in, let us consider those. Leaving aside for the moment the conquest of Canaan, the wars that the Jewish people fought in Biblical times were wars of self-defense – time and again we were attacked by enemies bent on our destruction and we were obliged to defend ourselves. And even then, we acted only on Divine sanction and instruction; on occasion, war was proscribed even when we were threatened – you will recall that when the Persians were poised to massacre the entire Jewish people at the time of Purim, the Jewish response was prayer, fasting and repentance, not military action.

(Why? And why at Chanukah was the response military? These two responses both seem inappropriate: at Purim, the threat facing us was *physical;* the Persians were planning to exterminate all Jews quite literally, and our response was spiritual – prayer and repentance. At Chanuka, the threat was *spiritual;* the Greeks threatened the Jewish religion, not Jewish lives. The Greek aim was to Hellenize the Jews, not to kill them. And yet our response then was physical – the Hasmoneans went to war. Faced with a physical threat we responded spiritually, and faced with a spiritual threat we responded physically. Strange, no?

The Beis Halevi provides a classic insight here. The operative principle is: "Everything is in the hands of Heaven except for the fear of Heaven." This means that we are powerless to affect anything in the world except our "fear of Heaven," our own spiritual progress. That is the province of our free will; there we are entirely free. Our own spirituality is our responsibility; that is why we are here. Now when we are threatened physically, what good will military action do if all is in the hands of Heaven? Only He can avert the danger, and so we appeal to Him – hence prayer and repentance when the Persians threaten to attack. But when the Greeks threaten our *religion,* that is, our spirituality, that is *our* personal responsibility and we go out and fight for it.

Our response is always measured by Torah; when that response is war no more and no less than when it is not.)

The nation of Amalek is a special case: our commandment to wipe out the memory of Amalek relates to the fact that Amalek's entire reason for existence is to destroy us completely – Amalek attacked us in the desert with suicidal commitment; in their scale of values, life itself is subordinate to the ideal of our demise. Other nations who have chosen to be our enemies live and wish to see us die; Amalek lives *only* to see us die. Of course, we are no longer able to identify Amalek specifically, although his ideology is obviously alive and well.

The conquest of Canaan was Divinely commanded. The Torah explicitly states that the nations inhabiting Canaan had reached a nadir of immorality and thereby forfeited their right to dwell there; we were given their land (and our retaining it was made likewise conditional on our maintaining scrupulous morality). Even then, they were given the option of leaving peacefully – the nation known as the Girgashi in fact took that option and was given a particularly beautiful land ("Afriki") as its new dwelling place.

You mention *"plagues and torment visited upon enemies:"*

If you are thinking of the plagues in Egypt, do you have any objection to the wicked receiving their due punishment after full and repeated warnings? The Egyptians cast babies into the Nile – the Nile turned to blood; each of the plagues was a measure-for-measure retributive experience in the revelation of Divine providence and justice, and ample warning was given. What is the problem here? Would you tolerate the suggestion that the evil should be allowed to perpetrate their genocides and other heinous crimes and remain forever unpunished?

With regard to the assumption that we were once an *"agrarian conglomerate of nomadic tribes:"*

The Torah is meticulous in its genealogical documentation of the generations of the family of Abraham. We entered Egypt as one family of seventy individuals and emerged over two centuries later as a populous nation of their descendants. For the next forty years we journeyed through the desert en route to Canaan. We entered the Land and lived there for 410 years until the Babylonian exile. That exile lasted for seventy years; thereafter we dwelt in the Land for 420 years until the Roman exile began. Where are those nomadic tribes? (Does the twelve tribes' journey over forty years make them "nomadic tribes"?)

Animal sacrifice is a difficult matter to understand; you are right about that. Although I doubt that I could say much that would be helpful at this stage of our discussion (when we began this correspondence I did not undertake to explain *everything*), some preliminary points may help place it in context.

Nowadays of course, we are unable to perform that category of mitzva; we do not bring sacrifices since we do not have the Temple and its service. Modern Torah thinkers have pointed out that it is not accidental that we who find this area difficult to understand are not asked to fulfill it in practice. We live at a juncture in history far removed from the prophetic era; our minds are products of an era not enlightened by the brilliance of prophecy and it is virtually impossible for us to understand what the world revealed then. We are like people trying to understand a sense by hearing it described while unable to experience it directly.

The distinction between the consciousness of the prophetic and post-prophetic eras is a major Torah subject and it is essential to grasp something of its meaning and implications before approaching elements of Torah that are rooted in the prophetic era. I am suggesting to you that animal sacrifices (and many of the other issues you raise) appeared very different to the eyes of a generation privileged with prophetic insight than they do to us now, deep in the post-prophetic darkness. We need to be cautious about passing judgement across that divide.

Of course, this reservation helps only to understand why subjects like sacrifices are difficult for us; it does not enlighten us on those subjects themselves. There are classical sources that deal with the issue – there is a well-known section in Maimonides that is relevant, and much later Chassidic sources deal with the esoteric aspects. Incidentally, eating meat altogether is not a simple matter; man was created to be vegetarian and only after the Flood was meat allowed.

I am going to ask your indulgence and not go further into this subject for now. Many elements of background are needed and I cannot do justice to it at this point in our discussion. We would need to study many things – animals in general, for one: what is the place of animals in the Creation? Do you know that animals were on a far higher level before the sin of Adam? The Talmud states that Adam sought a marriage partner *for himself* from among the animals before Eve was created.

Will you accuse me of evading the question? I have already said that this is a difficult area, and we both know that there are subjects that require much work and the painstaking construction of many elements before they can be understood. Would it be appropriate to demand an explanation of complex brain surgery before studying the more basic science necessary to understand that explanation? You would not accuse the brain surgeon of unjustly evading your request when he states that more background is needed.

(Note that the explanation need not be difficult: understanding brain surgery does not require superior intelligence; the problem is only the lack of properly ordered preliminary information and experience, not lack of intelligence. When we have learned more Torah, we can productively return to this subject.)

But apart from the problem of seeking understanding with inadequate information, there is something else here too. One may approach a Torah question not only too superficially, but also from the wrong angle. Let me try to identify this fault.

Whenever you come across something difficult to understand or accept, you cannot allow the difficulty to color the truth. The first order of business in any process of investigation must be to define what is true, not what is easy to accept. This is a major issue in clarifying the spiritual path, and the wrong attitude here is a lethal obstruction. The first step is to identify what is *right*, not what I *like*.

Starting with: "What suits me?" is obviously no way to search for the truth. But more subtle, and more problematic, is the search that begins with: "What is right?" when the real meaning is *what do I want to decide* is right. Hidden here is the agenda that will allow me to decide that unilaterally. The correct method is to dispassionately and objectively seek what is right. The next step may well be: "How does this affect me? Can I live this?" but that cannot be the first step; if it is, the search has already ended, what it will find is already guaranteed.

People can be very idealistic in holding a position to be objectively real without realizing that it is a position they chose because it *appealed to them,* not because it convinced them objectively. This is a deep problem. You will often come across a person who, convinced that a particular idea is essential to the spiritual path, finds that idea in Judaism as he becomes more Jewishly involved. He *insists* on finding it because hc has started with the conviction that it must be there. If he has enough trouble finding it where he wants it in Judaism he will manufacture it, and if that is too difficult he will re-create Judaism.

You will see this all around you. Those who have a certain idea of modernity will produce a Judaism that they see as modern; those who have certain personal problems or issues will produce Judaisms that condone those issues. This will have ridiculous expressions – if our searcher does not think God is a good idea he will produce a godless Judaism (talk about a contradiction in terms); if he does not like the Torah's requirements for conversion he will produce a new set; if he does not like the mitzvot, he will create his own (and still call them *commandments,* mark you). If he (or she) does not like a *mechitza* (partition between men's and women's sections) in the synagogue, it will disappear. I am not debating these issues; I am simply pointing out that the form of the search is invalid.

If you can find a Torah source that redefines the requirement for a *mechitza* objectively, not as the distortion of one who wants it that way, let us debate it. Why not? Find me a source for anything in Torah that stands on its own feet, not on the vested interests of the one who finds it because it is a projection of his own view, and I shall accept it. I shall have to. But do not predefine what you want and then tell me that you have found the truth when you find it. That is like a scientist saying he is going to perform an experiment to prove a particular outcome. That is not science. An experiment is done *to see what outcome it gives,* not to prove a predecided one. (When scientists make mistakes it is often exactly here.) You do not perform an experiment to prove *that* your theory is correct; you perform the experiment to see *whether* your theory is correct. The purpose of the experiment is not to show that your theory is *right;* it is to show if it is *right or wrong.* Why is this obvious in science and obscure in religion?

The logical position is to ask simply and objectively: is this element in Judaism? If it is, see it and live it. If it is not, live that too. The approach must be, can only be: what is right and true? That is the first question to ask, and it must be asked with *no agenda other than to find what is right and true.* The *second* question then becomes: how do I live up to this? What is right and true obliges, even if it does not suit me. Even if I do not like what I find, and even if it appears to be opposite to my personal starting definition of right and good, it must oblige. If I discover that God wants a certain action or behavior in the world, even if I am used to thinking of that behavior as wrong, then the logical conclusion must be that *I* am wrong. This may be difficult, but you can see that it must be this way. If I agree only with what I already hold to be true, I am the final arbiter of truth. No one else, not even God, can move me.

The classic expression of this idea in Judaism lies in the statement of the Jewish people when they were offered the Torah: "We shall do and we shall hear." We accept *before we hear what we are accepting*. Now who commits to an irrevocable contract without knowing what is in the contract? In fact, the Midrash states that other nations were offered the Torah first; each asked what was in it, and each rejected it. Note that each nation asked what was in it and each received a different answer: those who were violent by nature were told that such behavior is forbidden; those who were given to sensual immorality were told the prohibitions relating to that immorality. The Jews asked no questions (can you imagine Jews asking no questions?) and accepted. Why was each nation given a different answer? And why was each given the *worst possible* answer – exactly the element that would be sure to obstruct their acceptance?

The meaning is this: the fundamental error lies in asking, in challenging God in the first place. If God is the giver, what He gives is right. *By definition*. If you understand that He is the giver, how can you ask to judge what He gives? If you ask, you mean that you are to be the final judge of what is right and good, not Him. But if you do that, of course your particular problem will raise its head and obstruct you. The nations were not given different answers; they were simply shown the Torah and for each the issue that spoke, that objected, was the one that their personal set of values had already excluded. That is what happens when you are the judge. As we have already remarked, there is only one way to deal with God: on His terms, not yours. So the Jewish people stifled their searching and inquisitive nature to acknowledge that the truth is defined by what He says. "We shall do and we shall hear."

We do not adjust the truth to suit ourselves, we adjust ourselves to suit the truth. Even if the adjustment is hard.

Now a new problem arises: why would something that He defines as good appear to me as bad? Why is there a disparity in the first place between what He defines as good and the way I perceive good? The simple answer is that I am wrong and He is right and I must make an immense effort to shift my position, as we have said. But the matter is deeper than that. We *should* be able to rely on our intuition about what is right and good. We should be attuned to the real good; we feel that deeply. We have a deep innate sense of the right and the good and the fair.

We were *created* that way. We are created in the image of the Truth; we map to reality in the deepest way. We see that the *pre-Torah generations* were held responsible for general morality – if the Torah had not yet been revealed, this can only mean that people were *innately* aware of their moral obligations; people are *created* with a basic moral sensitivity.

The Torah itself may command behavior in a specific situation that it clearly defines as wrong in general; yet we would carry our moral hesitation across and experience a conflict in that specific case. Why are there cases like that? Why are there things that Torah defines as good and necessary and yet we may feel those things to be problematic? We do not have any trouble recognizing the goodness and morality of the prohibitions of killing, stealing, adultery, injuring, cruelty to animals and many more; we know we are aligned with the Torah on those. But a few may give us pause – and animal sacrifice may well be one of them. In this case the Torah itself raises the underlying issue: the Torah makes it clear that killing animals needlessly is wrong – the words of censure it uses are "spilling blood," the same phrase it uses for murder.

But the bitter fact is that we are no longer perfectly attuned. Some aspects of our psyche are deeply off key. Originally, there was no problem – Abraham was able to intuit the whole Torah, even the *chukim,* those laws that are not ordinarily amenable to human logic. There was no disparity between reality and his perfectly tuned sensitivity; his intuition was reliable. His superconscious ears heard all the overtones of reality perfectly on key. It could be done then, close to the beginning of time. But now, far from the source, far from the prophetic level, deep into a long and perverted history, we are no longer able universally and reliably to intuit the pattern of reality. Now the only option is to learn to accept even the parts that are not obviously in tune with our psyche, because if a thing is right, as I have labored to show, it obliges whether we like it or not. When you are dealing with the truth there can be no compromise based on personal desire. That and the truth have nothing in common.

Now there are many to whom this line of thinking is not going to appeal, I am afraid. It will not be easy to shift away from the "Me first" and "My thinking must be right" and "Don't tell me what to do" freedom generation. Lots of vested interests and cognitive dissonance are going to raise their strident voices here. But these things must be said anyway, even when they do not appeal.

So let us keep the question of animal sacrifice open for now. For the present, when you think about this subject, keep the context in mind: this is an instruction of the same God who prohibits the causing of needless suffering and killing, and indeed *commands* compassion. (Do you know that it is *Biblically* prohibited to eat before feeding your animals? "I shall provide grass in your field for your animals, and you shall eat and be satisfied" – the Talmudic exegesis of this verse points out that feed for animals is mentioned before human eating, hence the obligation to feed one's animals first.)

When you slip into thinking of animal sacrifice or Biblical wars in barbaric terms, you need to remember that these are parts of the same Torah that abominates killing and abhors the causing of needless suffering to man or beast. More than this: the same Creator who commands animal sacrifice has created us with natural feelings of empathy for animals in the first place.

But more important than all of this, what is really at issue here, underlying our entire discussion, is whether Torah is a man-made, time-bound and essentially imperfect document, or a God-given absolute standard of perfection *every word of which must be true*. Is the author God or man? That is the pivotal question. (If God is the author, all the issues we have discussed become problems of personal acceptance, not problems of right and wrong. You cannot debate the morality of sacrifice if you know that God wants it; doing so means that you do not understand the idea of God.)

And of course, it is axiomatic in Torah that God is its author (the Torah itself says so. The alternative would make the "author" not only human but a liar.)

Now if we hold that every word of Torah is Divine, does that make us fundamentalists? Well, if "fundamentalist" means unwavering attachment to fundamentals, of course we are. But if "fundamentalist" means an insistence on the most superficial, one-dimensional literalist mindlessness that tends to generate crude fanaticism, certainly not.

The key here is to understand that there is a human author too: that is exactly the province of the Oral Law. The Oral Law is an endlessly deep and subtle reading of the Written Law, itself given at Sinai and yet transmitted and refracted through the hearts and minds of the Sages. But when you examine that human contribution, make no mistake: the sole focus of the Oral Law is to fathom the Divine agenda, not to impose its own. The result is a law totally true to the Divine intention and yet shimmering with human brilliance and creativity. It is an indescribably rich weaving together of Divine root and human grasp. Nothing could be further from the modern and entirely pejorative notion of "fundamentalist."

Now this claim introduces a new problem: how can the Oral Law be both Divine and human? Can a corpus of wisdom and law genuinely admit a human element and yet retain its claim to be the Divine law? I am afraid the depth behind the answer to that question is accessible only in the deep study of the Oral Law itself. I could make a clumsy attempt, laying out for you some of the technical and textual proofs, but compared to a first-hand experience the result would fall so far short that it would be a travesty. To see the process in operation for yourself, to examine it at close quarters, will make any theoretical discussion from a distance irrelevant. So there is no real alternative; David, you will have to engage it for yourself.

PS: Some time ago I had an instructive meeting; I think it teaches our principle in reverse. A Jewish woman who has committed her life to Hinduism and yoga came to ask me some questions about Judaism. She happens to be firmly feminist in her views, and I presumed that separation of the sexes in Judaism was going to be an issue. I braced myself for the attack.

It never came. Her school of yoga always separates the sexes; they regard the mixing of men and women to be distracting and never allow it. She had absolutely no problem with Judaism on this issue. If the yogis do it, it is wise and good.

Now consider what is happening here: this woman has accepted a system and its tenets. All its details are fine because the system is fine; that is, having accepted the whole system as correct and binding, she would not consider changing any of its details. She does not consider it necessary at all; the whole is good, the parts must be good. What about the fact that one part conflicts with the way she sees the world outside of that system? After all, she is a modern feminist. But she has decided in terms of her yoga practice that the details are all good and must be good; this conviction is so secure that she carries it over into her life outside of yoga with no problem, not even when there may be a potential conflict. Her modern secular feminist friends may challenge this issue; she is unmoved, and even in Judaism she sees it as fine and good.

I think the correct analysis is this (although I would not be stubborn if you suggest an alternative): she has a hierarchy of value systems. Her yoga comes first, her feminism second (and her Judaism third). Now the higher system in the hierarchy defines the values before the lower; if a feature of yoga conflicts with a feature of feminism, yoga will win (and there is no need to change that when you get down to Judaism). If you see someone who cannot accept a feature of Judaism, you can assume that they have accepted a "higher" system that defines their values, and that is why that feature is a problem; the system higher in their hierarchy must win. It may be a poorly defined set of values that is hardly grasped as a cohesive system – it may be a general post-modern, permissive, secular mindset, but it is there at the top of the hierarchy, and it must win over anything they place lower down.

At each level, I think the logic is: if you buy in, you buy in. You buy the system, you buy its parts. After all, the system *is* its parts. If you change the parts that define the system, you cannot call it that system any longer. You respect the parts as you respect the whole; if you change or delete a part, you may damage the whole, it may no longer be what it was before.

So why do people think they can tamper with Judaism's elements and still call what remains Judaism?

Akiva,
What you may consider tampering with Torah, I might consider interpreting. My perception is that Jews have reinterpreted continuously. Who determines when the system has changed to the point where it must be called something else entirely? Who is the final arbiter of what is Jewish?

On a more personal level, I must say this: if the Orthodox community is really interested in outreach, it is going to have to stop holding its collective nose at the stench of secularism. Those of us who are not highly educated and meticulously observant, but who strive to keep learning and growing, will not respond in large numbers in the face of the unspoken assertion that we are beneath contempt. Will condemnation and contempt be more effective than instruction born of deep understanding?

David,
What changes and what does not is a deep subject that is itself part of the Oral Law; there is always a core of foundation principles that never change. These principles emerge in Talmudic study; as you immerse yourself further in Torah with an objective mind they will

become familiar to you. As we have already noted, the Oral Law is a composite of Divine root and human development; exactly where the Torah gives the Sages the authority to change and where it does not is part of the fascination of Torah study. This area is among the most important, and also among the most distorted today. As I said before: there is simply no substitute for your own investigation.

As for disparaging secular Jews – within the Torah community that is interested in outreach, who holds secular Jews in contempt? There is a world of difference between holding certain secular *values* in contempt and being contemptuous of secular *individuals*. Of course there are values that we hold to be deeply mistaken and yes, worthy of contempt. One who tolerates all values equally has no values. But one can love a person and disagree vehemently with his values and his behavior; that is exactly how one ought to relate to a brother whose outlook one understands to be wrong, and that is the correct educational attitude to adopt.

Commandments – Actions of the Spirit

David,
There is another aspect to the commandments that I would like to consider, a fundamental aspect that I believe will show up sharply where we differ from Buddhism (and to the best of my knowledge, all other spiritual systems). In order to do that I must ask you this: what is the place of the ascetic in Buddhism? What is the Buddhist view of the celibate, monastic path?

Akiva,
The approach to monasticism varies from school to school. Zen in Japan and China did (and does) have monasteries, because it was generally believed that only by retreating fully from the world and its siren songs could one extirpate the desires that keep one from fully realizing the causes and sources of suffering. This includes desires of the flesh.

Modern Zen has emphasized the practice of the "householder:" one who lives in the world, embraces worldly duties and responsibilities and recognizes them not as obstacles but as steps along the spiritual path. Eihei Dogen, a 13th century monk and Japan's most important Zen master, moved in his later writings from emphasizing the householder practice to the monastic practice, and from insisting that anyone could attain enlightenment to focusing on the work to be done in the monastic setting.

Modern practitioners of Zen typically go on retreats of a week or longer. The days are highly structured and ritualized, and consist of periods of sitting and walking meditation, meals taken in silence, and interviews with Zen priests and teachers. This is thought to renew concentration, focus and dedication to the practice. It is extremely difficult to sit for long periods of time, both physically and mentally, and sometimes it's sheer torture. But bursting through these difficult periods, one can attain new levels of understanding of and harmony with one's own nature and its interconnection with all things and beings.

David,
There is a fundamental idea here; perhaps more than anything we have discussed yet. If there is a categorical difference between Judaism and Buddhism in terms of practice, it is here.

It is commonly understood that Abraham's major contribution was the doctrine of monotheism. He taught an idolatrous world that there is only one God, and that idea is synonymous with Judaism. But I have to tell you that that picture is not accurate. The idea of one God was very firmly established before Abraham. (Idolatry, as we have seen, is the practice of relating to *intermediaries* as if they have independent power, not the failure to recognize God altogether.) Knowledge of God was standard.

Think about this: Abraham lived at the same time as Noah; he was fifty-eight years old when Noah died. Noah certainly knew God; he spoke to Him directly. Not only that: Noah was only the third generation from Adam; his life overlapped with those of a number of people who had known Adam personally (Methusela, for example; take a look at the account of the generations in Genesis paying careful attention to the dates and ages). So Abraham lived contemporaneously with Noah, who was a contemporary of people who had met Adam – can you imagine that at that stage of history people had forgotten about God?

Another question: at the time that Abraham came on the scene, there was already a yeshiva teaching Torah – the yeshiva of Shem and Ever (Shem was Noah's son). They were teaching the true Torah; you will recall that when Rebecca experienced difficulty in her pregnancy, she went to ask the prophet Shem for an explanation. On his way to the house of Laban, Jacob interrupted his journey to study there for fourteen years.

(Although the Torah was given at Sinai only much later, these earlier generations had access to it through studying the Creation; we have referred already to the idea of intuiting Torah from the Creation.)

Now if there was a yeshiva where great people were teaching the Torah of one God *before Abraham,* people great enough to give prophetic advice to Rebecca and to teach Torah to Jacob, what did Abraham add? How can one think that Abraham initiated the awareness of God when it is obvious that that awareness had not been forgotten and was being propagated at the highest level? You can see that there is a mistake in the conventional teaching that Abraham is the father of monotheism. (As I have tried many times in our correspondence to show, almost all of the conventional ideas about Torah in the non-Torah world are as wrong as they could possibly be.)

There are other questions too: why in fact did Rebecca go to Shem for advice about her mysterious pregnancy problem? (She perceived that the child in her womb had dual tendencies – both to sanctity and to idolatry. Shem told her that she was carrying twins, Jacob and Esau, and that accounted for the split.) Why did she not ask Abraham, her father-in-law? He was certainly the greatest prophet alive in the generation – why ask Shem?

And why did Jacob find it necessary to study Torah in the yeshiva of Shem and Ever? His father Isaac and his grandfather Abraham had taught him Torah for years; what would Shem and Ever add? Jacob spent fourteen intense years there, studying without ever properly sleeping (the verse states that he lay down to sleep only after he left).

We can add another question too: Abraham lived through the Generation of the Dispersion – the generation during which mankind built a "tower" in an attempt to wrest control of the Universe away from the Creator. That was a generation, united under its king Nimrod, that manifested tremendous evil; their plans were thwarted only when God Himself "came down" and fragmented their language, frustrating their efforts. We referred to this episode when we discussed the nature of language; the point I wish to draw from it now is this: those people tried to kill Abraham; the Midrash states that Nimrod threw him into a furnace. He survived miraculously, and they were forced to tolerate him only because they were unable to eliminate him. They hated him to that extreme because he opposed their ideology; they wanted independence from God and he was teaching God's sovereignty and authority (all this is explicit in the Talmud and Midrash). He was a threat to their plans, a rebel against their movement.

Now the question that arises is this: why did they not attempt to kill Shem and Ever? They made every effort to kill Abraham; they could not tolerate him because of his teaching. But Shem and Ever were teaching too; they too were propagating knowledge of God and His Torah at the highest level, as we have shown. And yet there is no record of the generation's displeasure at Shem and Ever's efforts at all. Why were they tolerated as no threat to the new world order while Abraham was not? If monotheism is what the generation condemned him for, Shem and Ever were at least as guilty, surely?

To summarize our difficulties: what did Abraham bring to the world as the amazing novelty that started the Jewish people and changed history forever, if Shem and Ever were already teaching spirituality at the highest level? What exactly was new about him? What was the revolutionary nature of his enlightenment if others had already shown the way? Why was he a groundbreaking initiator and not simply a talented pupil?

The answer is this: Abraham did not begin the path of the spirit; *he began the path of bringing spirit into flesh.* His contribution was not in the sphere of knowledge. Others had already explored the higher reaches of the spirit and were well versed in the highest wisdom when

Abraham began his journey. What he pioneered in the world was the process of bringing that wisdom down into the physical, showing how to express the highest level of consciousness in fingers and toes of flesh. *That* is the radical idea of Judaism.

The absolute uniqueness of Judaism is *not* its God-consciousness; it is the teaching that the *body* can be drawn up into sanctity. It is not the teaching of the holiness of spirit, it is the teaching of the holiness of the physical. Examine the world's spiritual systems; you will see that they grasp the conflict between spirit and flesh, the primal battle between soul and body in which body seeks to dominate soul and bring it down to serve its animal agenda. And they define a solution to this most basic of all conflicts: abjure the flesh, discipline the body by starving it of its sensuous feed, become an ascetic, celibate, enter the monastic mode. The highest exponents of the world's spiritual systems are monks and nuns, celibates and ascetics who have renounced the body in order to transcend it.

But Judaism *requires* engaging the body; requires marriage, requires the experience of bodily pleasure, regards permanent celibacy as a sin. Our path is not to separate body and soul but to engage the body and elevate it to the level of soul. For us, the body is not the point of departure for the spiritual voyage; it is the vehicle.

The body must not be left behind while mind and spirit transcend. It must be made to serve mind and spirit. *And that is the meaning of the mitzvot,* the commandments. The mitzvot are *physical actions* (there are *very* few mitzvot that are performed in consciousness alone) that express spirit. Every part of the body is commanded to act; each limb and organ performs an action that expresses Torah. Mitzvot are to Torah what body is to soul.

Abraham did not bring the idea of pure spirit to the world; he brought to the world the radical idea that the body, that fallen, subversive, treacherous and lecherous body can and must be elevated to purity. Its functions and actions are not to be suppressed, they are to be expressed as holy. The world perceives the shame and the problem of male-female intimacy, its potential to erode spiritual refinement; we perceive its holiness. The world perceives the danger of alcohol, its tendency to replace mind with earthy physicality; we use it for elevation. The world understands that the body must be renounced, that is the only way to free the soul; we give the body full expression in actions that are harnessed to serve spirit. That is how we discipline the body; we do not command it to be silent, we command it to serve. That is the basis of the mitzvot.

Let us return to the questions we posed and understand how this radical idea answers them. What was new about Abraham? Not monotheism. It is true that he reversed the trend to idolatry and polytheism; his generation had lost focus on the one God and chosen to relate to a world of intermediaries, he battled that mistake and is famous for it. But he did not originate the idea that God is one. His novel teaching was the idea that the body can be lifted out of its fallen state of opposition to spirit in becoming the loyal and fully controlled vehicle for spirit. He brought to the world not the idea of Torah so much as the idea of mitzva.

(The numerical value of the name Abraham is 248; that is the number of positive mitzvot and that is the number of human bodily parts. I am sure you see now why these equivalences must be.)

What were Shem and Ever teaching? They were teaching God-consciousness at the highest level. But the Torah they taught was not the Torah of mitzvot. It was a meditational program of sublime quality, and it required detachment from the physical; if you like, their yeshiva was a mountaintop retreat where their disciples detached from the physical world (they denied themselves sleep as part of the intensity of their training, as we know from Jacob).

Their Torah was the Torah of separation, the rarefied and exalted Torah of pure spirit. If you wish to see its equivalent today, visit a Himalayan retreat, or a Tibetan or Nepalese monastery; they are the distant descendants of the school of Shem and Ever. They were experts in the understanding of the separation of mind and body and the conflict between them. That was exactly their expertise; they knew how to overcome the perennial conflict between body and soul by holding them apart.

Why did Rebecca ask Shem about her pregnancy conflict? Because he was the absolute expert in that field. When the conflict between man's opposing tendencies manifests, when there is a pull toward sanctity on the one hand and toward the material on the other, he was the master. He was able to tell her that she was carrying twins; a Jacob who would respond to the call of the spirit, and an Esau who would respond to the call of the flesh. That was not Abraham's expertise; his work was the unification of those opposites, not the insight that teases them apart.

Why did Jacob find it necessary to study in the yeshiva of Shem and Ever? Why not find what he needed in his father's and grandfather's teaching? Because he was on his way to the house of Laban the liar and swindler, the grand master of taking apart body and soul. That is the deep meaning of lying and swindling; the inner does not find parallel expression in the outer, there is a florid discrepancy between them. Further, we have a kabbalistic tradition that Laban and Bilam were incarnations of the same soul; Bilam was sublime in his prophetic elevation and yet he sank to bestiality in his bodily actions – the Sages point out the clues that show his bestial relationship with his donkey. Here you have the extreme version of separation of body and soul; not a body disciplined in asceticism to free its soul, but a body relinquished to the realm of pure matter while its soul is elsewhere. (The Hebrew words for "donkey" and for "matter" are one identical root.)

When Jacob was about to enter that realm of split between body and soul, the house of a Laban who represented that dichotomy with full force, he prepared by studying with Shem and Ever, the experts in the art of controlled separation of those elements. Abraham's Torah was not the right one for that; he was teaching the harmony and unification of inner and outer, of soul and body. To survive in Laban's house the necessary skills were not those; there you needed to understand how desperately dangerous the illegitimate split can be.

When Jacob meets Esau on his way home, after many years of living with Laban and remaining pure, untainted by Laban's brand of evil, he announces to Esau: "I lived with Laban..." The commentaries point out that "I lived" (*garti*) has the numerical equivalent of 613, the number of mitzvot. Jacob was implying that he had lived with Laban and despite that spiritually hostile environment he had kept all the commandments. But there is a subtlety to note here: Jacob did not simply imply that he had remained pure, untainted. The focus of his statement is the commandments, specifically. *That* was the challenge; that was where the battle had been: do you live with Laban and forget to bring the spiritual down into the physical, floating in the higher realms of mind while *acting* treacherously, or do you maintain your consistent bringing down of mind and spirit into action in the expression of the commandments? *That* is the work of a child of Isaac and a grandchild of Abraham. Jacob's success in a world of evil was not only the continual learning of Torah; it was the continual practice of mitzvot.

Why did Nimrod and his generation try to kill Abraham but not Shem and Ever? Because they had no objection to a mountaintop retreat teaching pure spiritual exploration. What harm could that do? Let those monks reach into the world of spirit in detached contemplation. Let them teach that as much as they wish. *But do not tell us what to do.* Abraham was a threat because he was not teaching spiritual theory, he was teaching spiritual practice. If you followed him, you would have to live, in every nuance of your every action, in consistent expression of the theory, and that was the problem. How to behave, not only how to think.

I hope a clear picture is emerging. You can see how fundamentally misunderstood all of this is today. We are Jews in our observance of the commandments; all of them, with each movement of each part of our bodies. We are not Jews because of Jewish wisdom and generally moral behavior; that is fine and well, of course, but it is not Judaism. We are children of Abraham because we work to sanctify our bodies; what marks us off from the community of the world's wise and moral adepts is primarily the way we eat our food and drink our wine.

This is an endless subject. Let me point out only one or two details to indicate a direction for further thought: the Talmud states that one who learns Torah but does not intend to fulfill it does not have Torah either. Why? After all, this individual has learned, he has acquired Torah knowledge. *But that is not Torah;* Torah exists *only* where it will extend into mitzva where possible. That is what Torah means. Torah has an absolute precondition; it must seek the expression of its commandments or it is not Torah at all.

Elsewhere, the Talmud teaches that one who learns but does not fulfill would have been better off dying at birth. Why? Why such a harsh judgement, and why exactly at the point of birth? The meaning is this: the fetus learns the whole Torah in the womb (and forgets it at the moment of birth). Birth is for the purpose of living in the world in order to re-learn and to *express* Torah, to perform its commandments. A person who lives in the world without that dimension was far better off as a fetus – the fetal situation is the highest state of pure knowledge possible. If life is not to be the *practice* of Torah but only the exploration of the *wisdom* of Torah, a fetus is better at that.

Torah is inextricably bound up with its mitzvot. The highest wisdom must come into the lowest part of the body. (Consider the name Jacob: *Yaakov* is written as a *yud*, the letter that always indicates pure spirit, followed by the word *ekev*, meaning the heel. Our task is to bring that dimensionless point of origin into the least sentient and lowest part of the physical frame.)

That is what mitzvot are about – the connecting of spiritual and material. Take the mitzva of circumcision: this mitzva most powerfully represents the sublimation of flesh to spirit, the elevation of sensual to spiritual. The word for circumcision, *brit,* has a numerical equivalent of 612 – in this one of the 613 mitzvot, the essence of all the others is contained. That essence is the idea of covenant, and at a deep level, the root of the covenant that is being forged here is the covenant between body and soul.

The Kuzari points out the absurdity of this area of human activity: the lowest zone, the part that naturally generates shame when exposed, also generates the most unimaginably elevated function of the body – the igniting of a new life in its own image. This dichotomy between lowliness in the anatomical, functional realm and supreme elevation is almost incomprehensible. That is the paradoxical nature of the human soul investing the body, and nothing points this out more clearly than the Jewish body's stamp of holiness that is its circumcision. The terms of our covenant with God are exactly those: using the physical world, not rejecting it; but using it in His service. Just as we develop self while destroying selfishness, we embrace the physical for its elevation but reject it for itself.

That is the meaning of the separation from the world you will find discussed in all the *mussar* works: not a separation from the earth, but a separation from earthiness. These works all teach the obligation to separate from the physical and sensual – apparently an ascetic teaching, and yet we are *commanded* to marry and held to account if we abstain from the physical. Even a nazirite, who must abstain from wine completely for a time, must bring an offering of *atonement* for that abstention when it is over. The resolution of this apparent contradiction is clear: a Jew must never engage the world for its own sake; from that we abstain entirely. Physicality for its own sake is not part of Torah; that will certainly bring one down into coarse earthiness. But physicality for the sake of elevating the physical, using the material as a vehicle for the spirit, is exactly the proper use of the material; from that we may not abstain.

You see this sharply in our relationship with wine. We have noted that in many of the world's spiritual systems alcohol is forbidden entirely, certainly for the priestly and monastic individuals who would reach holiness. But in Judaism wine is a central feature in all movement from physical to spiritual. We use wine at occasions of connecting the two: at a wedding, where two physical bodies will elevate their relationship to the spiritual; at a circumcision, where we begin the process of sanctifying the body; at *kiddush,* the blessing sanctifying the first moments of Shabbat where the mundane domain of the week meets the transcendence of Shabbat; four cups of wine at the Passover *seder,* where we celebrate exile's transition to redemption, slavery to freedom.

Wine powerfully represents the danger of the physical; if taken in excess it converts consciousness to unconsciousness, dehumanizes to the extent that the drinker becomes entirely part of the physical, nothing more than a mindless body. And yet, used correctly, it has the capacity to open consciousness, to facilitate a state of elevation. The deeper sources note that although wine is a physical substance it obeys the rules of the spiritual: all physical things degrade and disintegrate with time; this is the rule for all things in the material and biological world no matter how carefully those things are handled and nursed. Conversely, things of the spirit improve with time; wisdom deepens with age – even as the body of the sage sags, his wisdom gains. But unlike other physical things, wine *improves* with age. Uniquely in the world of the material, wine reflects the quality of the deeper, the secret hidden within the material (the Hebrew word for wine has the same numerical value as the word for secret).

You know that at *havdala,* the ceremony that marks the exit of the Shabbat, we also take a cup of wine. At that moment of sensing the departing spirit of Shabbat, that moment of descent, we use wine. Now we have been saying that wine is used at moments of *elevation.* What is the meaning here?

The idea is this: certainly the week begins with the sadness of sensing Shabbat fade. The relinquishing of sanctity is palpable. We smell spices to revive the spirit. But the week's beginning means a new opportunity to build, to elevate our present status towards another Shabbat that will be higher than the last, that will reflect another week of work and growth *added* to the previous ones. This is a "descent for the purpose of ascent," a higher and greater elevation than before. That is exactly the Jewish idea – we descend into the mundane and the material, but we do so only for the purpose of elevation.

Torah lives only in its application; even its most rarefied wisdom is real only when it has some attachment to the world of action. Even the mystical aspects of Torah must somehow fulfill the criterion of being relevant to practical action. But the mystical wisdom, by definition, is separated from the practical – how can it have a practical application? The answer to this esoteric problem would take us far from our immediate discussion; I mention it to show how pervasive is the idea that the Torah lives in its connection to the world of action.

Why is "objectless meditation" not our primary focus? Why, if it is so important to enter the zone of pure unfettered consciousness, as it certainly is, do we not do this as a major component of our practice and devotion? I think you can begin to see the answer: the essence of Judaism is the translation of that rarefied zone into action, the bringing down of that clarity and purity into the world of physical space, time and motion, and *that* is where our focus remains most firmly fixed. Of course we have to reach beyond the world, of course the silent center must be accessed and deeply assimilated, but to spend the major part of our time and effort there would be disproportionate.

In "The Path of the Just," the classic Torah work on the path to sanctity, the highest of the ten stages of ascent is described like this: "The *physical actions* of the individual who has sanctified himself with his Creator's sanctity become literally sacred. He is as if walking in the next world while yet in this one... a person such as this is considered as a sanctuary..."

The Cult of Jewish Victimhood

"Some feel that Judaism as a whole perversely revels in its victimhood on the one hand, and that the current version of Zionism is imposing this very kind of victimhood on others. In contrast, Buddhism espouses detachment from forms of identity, from all places or things, that would lead to this kind of suffering. Many Buddhists (and particularly ex-Jews) might point to relentless reminders of the Holocaust on one hand, and the current strife in Israel on the other, and simply say: 'You see? This is what comes of a religion that clings to ancient ideas, to myths and to lands. Show me a country torn apart by Buddhist strife.' (One might respond that Buddhist priests in WW II Japan advocated mindfulness while killing the enemy, but that's another story.)"

David,

I think this criticism is based on a misperception. In my experience, there is very little focus on victimhood in the observant community. Certainly, terrible things have happened to us and we remember them, but it is generally the non-religious who tend to cling to victimhood as a source of Jewish identity. Torah Jews are by and large too involved in Torah learning and practice to dwell on victimhood.

Nevertheless, let me attempt to unravel the issues you raise.

Firstly, *"Judaism... revels in its victimhood... reminders of the Holocaust..."* Is remembering victims "revelling" in victimhood? Is remembering the victims and bringing to conscious awareness the fact that we have not yet merited redemption (as we do most intensely on Tisha B'Av) to be termed "revelling in victimhood"?

You say that Buddhism teaches "seeing things as they are." When you look at history, both distant and recent, and perceive the hatred that is levelled at us in every generation and acted out in violence in most, are you not seeing things as they are? For one who lives under the declared and protracted threat of his own extermination, what makes the difference between seeing things as they are and revelling in his victimhood? Exactly how dispassionate do you have to be to qualify for the former and deflect the charge of the latter?

Incidentally, emotions are important, David. They are to be controlled, channelled and used in service like all aspects of our lives. Just as we use and elevate all aspects of the real and the practical, we use and elevate the realm of emotion. To be sure, emotion is sanctified only to the extent that it is controlled, like everything else in our power, but it can and must be sanctified (as you are aware, that is part of the province of *mussar*).

Now when we relate to the points of brutality and torment in our history, how do we do so? You will note that we do not "revel"; on Tisha B'Av we mourn the elements of destruction and exile, we do it intensely, sitting on the floor in fasting, weeping and focusing clearly on our failure to rise to the level of merit that redemption requires. On Passover we recount the moments of exile too, but it is a festival and we do so over cups of wine in a spirit of the joy of the festival. Here we are relating to the redemptive element; we see the other side of the picture. Same picture, two sides. Same history, two opposite emotional responses, each as appropriate.

Let me recount a vignette of an incident I witnessed in the presence of a great man.

I had the privilege of being close to Rabbi Simcha Wasserman, one of the great Torah personalities of the last generation. His father was a disciple of the Chafetz Chaim, the great Rabbi Elchonon Wasserman who led the yeshiva in Baranovich, and who was murdered during the war. Our families are related and we had the honor of Rabbi and Mrs Wasserman's presence at our Passover table one year in Israel when Rabbi Wasserman was in his eighties; the experience stands out in my mind larger than life. I cannot convey what it means to be in the presence of Torah greatness, and particularly that of the previous generation of European greats.

Now Rabbi Wasserman virtually never spoke about his own personal experiences, but during the meal we somehow managed to persuade him to tell us some of the history of his earlier years. I think he felt that this was the right occasion for us to know some of what had been that generation's experience, and he began recounting certain events. In the course of his calm, quiet telling he mentioned some harrowing episodes in passing – the time he was left for dead on a Russian street after a pogrom and was saved by a young non-Jewish girl; the time he was in an infectious diseases ward in a hospital during the war between the Reds and the Whites when anti-Semitic locals entered and killed all the patients in their beds; only the infectious ward survived because the thugs were too afraid to enter. And all the time his customary gentle smile underlining those striking grey-blue eyes, and the tone of serenity – after all, it was a festival.

At one point during his telling of events that related more to Mrs Wasserman's family (her father, a leading Torah sage, and the rest of her family were annihilated), a soft sigh escaped her. I shall never forget the interaction between them that followed. Rabbi Wasserman turned to his Rebbetzen and said in his quiet, warm, even Yiddish: "Feigele, are you complaining?" Instantly she answered, in the same tone as his: "No, no; of course not," and the conversation, the teaching, resumed.

Second, *"Judaism.... revels in its victimhood on the one hand, and.... the current version of Zionism is imposing this very kind of victimhood on others."* This very kind? But our historical victimhood has no similarity at all to the modern form that Jews are alleged to be perpetrating: we have been brutalized throughout history simply because we are Jews. What is happening in Israel today, certainly from the Jewish side, surely has more to do with survival than with bigotry? You have spent time there – have you perceived that Jews there are interested in victimizing anyone simply because of their ethnic or cultural identity, simply because of who they are? Did you meet anyone there who is interested in constructing means of annihilating civilians because they are intrinsically undesirable? Is not the central issue there survival? What in fact is the logical alternative? To give the land to those who lust for our obliteration and leave? Leave for where? Back to Germany, perhaps? Poland? France? Where exactly?

Third, *"the current version of Zionism:"* Do not confuse modern Zionism with Judaism. They have very little in common apart from an interest in the same land. One is political, the other is spiritual. The secular "current version of Zionism" has little to do with Torah. Many of our Jewish contemporaries in the secular camp would be as surprised to learn most of what I am trying to share with you in this interaction as any Buddhist; genuine Torah is unfamiliar to them too.

In recent research in Israel it was found that in a high-school class of secular Israeli teenagers, only two had ever been inside a synagogue and only one had ever seen a *sefer* Torah. In Israel, David.

In fact, in these terms probably the only difference between secular Israelis and assimilated American Jews is that in Israel everyone knows *which* Judaism is meant; you may observe it or you may oppose it, you may know it or have no knowledge of it, but the version of Judaism that is the subject of the battle is agreed – it is the Torah-from-Sinai version, of that there is no doubt. In America, there are so many Judaisms that a child growing up among them cannot possibly know what is real and what is not. In Israel it may wear different colored uniforms and head coverings, it may speak with different accents and hold widely differing political views, but it always centers around God, His Torah given at Sinai and His commandments; in America you can find something claiming to be Judaism that has no God, no Divine Torah and no commandments, and a whole range of options in flagrant violation of the most explicit commandments and still claiming the name of Judaism.

Fourth, *"Buddhism espouses a kind of detachment from forms of identity... that would lead to this kind of suffering:"* What are we to do about this: cease being Jews? Is the problem our identity? Must the victim cease to manifest his very identity in order to end the suffering of being a victim? Surely it is the *aggressor* who needs to let go of attachments and problematic identification; the detachment that Buddhism teaches needs to be practised by the victimizers, not the victims. Incidentally, as you are well aware, even the most strenuous efforts to assimilate into a host culture, the most strenuous efforts to lose identity, did not dissolve the problem of our victimhood when anti-Semitic storms raged. Surely the detachment that is needed is not from *identity* but from aggression and malicious behavior, from bigotry and hatred.

Fifth, *"Buddhism espouses a kind of detachment from... places:"* I must be misinformed here; is Tibet not important to the Tibetan Buddhists in Indian exile? The Dalai Lama constantly expresses distress over this issue; I have even seen him quoted discussing under which circumstances violence might be justified to correct it. He talks and writes of the Tibetan homeland frequently. Am I missing something?

Maybe you mean he is not *attached* to his homeland; he loves it and thinks it would be a good idea for his people to live there unpersecuted and at peace, but he is not attached to that idea in a clinging, grasping way. If that is what you mean, I am with you. Let us live in Israel that way too, without tens of millions of neighbors focused on our annihilation, and we can work on the grasping problem.

Sixth, *"This is what comes of a religion that clings to ancient ideas, to myths and to lands."* Is an idea invalid because it is ancient? Buddhism certainly values ancient ideas, does it not? And who is clinging to myths? The wisdom of Torah is no mythology, as we have discussed previously. And as for clinging to a land, I would say we have had far too little opportunity to cling to our land over the centuries; we have longed for it throughout history, that is true; in that sense we have clung. Is our longing for the land of Israel our problem?

Where *else* have we had lasting peace and refuge? Which of our long exiles has allowed us the luxury of detachment?

Seventh, " *Show me a country torn apart by Buddhist strife:"* Israel is not torn apart by *Jewish* strife, but rather by enmity to Jews and Judaism. The enemies from without would certainly like to tear it apart. And internal strife is not a function of the country's Judaism, though it may well be due to a lack of it. A country based on Torah is not a country torn apart; when King Solomon ruled and the national law was Torah, an idyllic peace reigned. And it was an international peace; the world's leaders came to Jerusalem to pay respect and to learn from that greatest of sages. The country and the people experienced an almost messianic peace. Something similar can be said of King Hezkiyahu's period. When Israel is based on Torah, when all its functions are predicated on Torah values and practice, it will not be torn apart at all. That in fact *is* our messianic vision.

You know, David, there is really something bizarre about this discussion. Is our victimization really something to agonize over in this sense – is the question really whether we are right to feel it or not? I think there may even be some danger in forgetting exactly where we stand.

How far back do we have to go to gain some clarity – perhaps 1948 will do; that is still within living memory. Let me remind you: the country then consisted of settlers who had been draining malarial swamps over the previous few decades, motley new arrivals from many countries, and some thousands of exhausted refugees from a holocaust that had destroyed a third of the entire nation – not killed in a military conflict but gassed like so many roaches. A generation of orphaned children were still crying themselves to sleep at night on the date that an international fiat declared their residence there legal and independent. On that day, on the same day that the hope flickered to life of becoming a haven again for its people after millennia of dispossessed exile, the organized armies of all its neighbors attacked in a fervent effort to annihilate that sliver of a homeland and all its residents. On its first day, they attacked; the country had nothing that could seriously be called an army, much of it was unarmed. People I know personally fought there as teenagers; they used First World War vintage rifles.

Imagine attacking people who had just survived the horror of a genocide, orphans of parents who had been erased in their millions by the countries of their own citizenship for no crime, virtually undefended traumatized refugees who had only just found a tentative foothold in a home from which they had been separated for centuries of longing. Have they no shame? Is their urgent hatred so deep that it annuls even the last vestige of shame? How do you understand that, David? Would you not imagine they would wait a couple of days before marching in to snuff out the last child?

How far do we have to travel to see beyond a modern complacency that can worry about whether or not we are right to feel victimhood? Where do we have to go? It is probably easier to list the places that are *not* tainted. Spain six centuries ago? Is that too distant? Was that not adequately civilized? Mid-twentieth century Germany? Was that civilized, genteel enough? How far do we have to go? Or how near?

Joy

"When one experiences emptiness, when one frees oneself from delusions and attachments, one experiences a profound upwelling of compassion for all sentient beings. This egalitarian openness is a major avenue leading to the elimination of suffering. Even if you aren't enlightened, this is a joyful experience. Joy is not the major aim of Buddhism. Understanding is. But the two are closely related.

Where is the joy in Judaism?"

David,
The way you have put your question implies that Judaism does not encompass freeing oneself from delusions or experiencing profound compassion. If you know that these lead surely to joy, and you proceed to ask: "Where is the joy in Judaism?" you must be assuming that Judaism lacks those sure avenues to joy. But of course those are elements of Judaism. Of course we aim for freedom from delusions and a deep compassion. Why would anyone assume otherwise? Surely these are basic elements of the human path even before the religious path begins; as I have attempted to show already, what we call *derech eretz,* "the way" of the world.

You are bound to reply that you know Judaism teaches those things; the problem you mean to identify is that you do not perceive *Jews* manifesting those qualities (and quite probably they do not manifest real joy either, as far as you can see). The Buddhists you know certainly manifest these things; but we have been through this before

– you must look to the true exponents of Torah if you seek living Torah. And among them you will find joy; or rather, a deep serenity that is not shaken by the problems of life or its suffering.

What is the proper place of joy in Torah thinking and practice? Are we meant to strive for joy? Is happiness a mitzva, a commandment? What is the path that leads to joy in a world of ordeals?

Is real joy possible in a sad world? How can you be happy while you know that there are people suffering? Should you forget their pain so that you can enjoy yourself? What about your own pain – are you meant to experience joy in the midst of suffering? Is that possible?

Let us work through these questions in some detail. I hope a clear picture will emerge, and I think you may be surprised by it.

There is no direct commandment to be happy; it is not one of the 613 formal commandments of the Torah. Yet we find statements in the Torah and in the words of the Sages indicating that we should be happy. What sort of obligation is this? Why is it not expressed as a commandment if it is worth striving for?

"Serve God with joy." Here it would seem that joy is an obligation. When the Torah describes the curses that will befall the Jewish people when we fail to live up to our obligations, after listing the brutalities that we will suffer, it states the reason for these horrors: "Because you did not serve Hashem (the Name) your God with joy..." It appears, incredibly, that the reason for our suffering throughout history is that we failed to be joyous – is this possible? Is *that* the problem – lack of joy?

And how do you achieve joy in a world full of suffering without becoming insensitive to that suffering? How much suffering does it take to dampen your ability to experience joy? Surely, if you are aware of even one person who is in pain you should be unable to rejoice. And if you manage to forget the world's pain, surely that is a great insensitivity. Yet how can you be happy if you do *not* forget –

surely rejoicing while you are aware of someone's pain is even more insensitive?

The world's approach to this problem is simply to forget, to become unaware, at least temporarily to block out the awareness of human suffering and sadness and have a good time despite it.

But that is not Judaism. Judaism requires and develops awareness, not forgetfulness. We strive for a superconscious awareness. We do not aim to forget anything, and we do not forget that the world is full of pain.

Yet more difficult, the Torah sources that speak about the obligation to be happy do not distinguish between those who are comfortable and those who are in pain. It seems that *everyone* is required to be happy, *always*. Surely this is downright impossible – what about the mitzva of mourning, for example? How can joy be relevant in the face of a situation that demands the response of mourning?

The great Chazon Ish, Torah leader of the previous generation, makes a statement in one of his letters that seems so extreme it appears impossible to understand. Loosely translated, he states: "For one who knows the light of truth, there is no sadness in the world." No sadness in the world? How can anyone make such an assertion? The Chazon Ish himself lived through the agony of the Second World War; he had his own personal tragedies. How can a man say such things?

In the answer to these questions lies a central element of Torah teaching and one of the secrets of life.

We need a deeper definition of joy than the world's idea of forgetting suffering. Real joy does not reside there. Let us reach further.

Real joy is what you experience when you are doing what you should be doing. Joy is the *neshama's* (soul's) response to doing what it should be doing. Our vision of joy has nothing to do with forgetfulness or the ignoring of suffering; it has far more to do with the mature appreciation of a life developing correctly.

When you are moving clearly along your unique path to your unique destination, you experience real joy. When you are moving along the path that leads to *yourself,* to the deep discovery of who you are; when you are building the essence of your own being, expressing your destiny in the world, *creating yourself and making your contribution to the broader reality,* a deep happiness wells up. The journey does not cause joy – *the joy is the journey itself.*

Note that the expression on the face may not be a smile. The face may reflect pain, may be tear-stained and taut with strain; but if the journey is proceeding, if you are aware that you are building what you must build your heart will be singing within you despite the pain of your body and the tears on your face.

And more than this: your heart will be singing *because of the pain.* This needs explanation; let us think into it carefully.

The journey of life is always made against resistance. Life is work, and work is always performed against resistance. When you strain against ordeals and difficulties and move ahead, when you perceive that you are winning the battle and moving, building, your deepest essence experiences a joy even while your body is aching. That happiness is generated by the experience of moving ahead against resistance, building when the building is difficult. Things that come easy give only a superficial happiness; if no work is invested there can be very little depth of satisfaction.

One or two practical examples will make this clear.

Imagine you are carrying rocks and heavy logs and assembling them in the heat of the day. You are building something important and you have limited time. You sweat and shake with effort as you labor to complete your task, working against time and the limits of your physical abilities.

What do you experience as you see the result taking shape? What emotion fills you as you realize that you will complete your task in time? What deep and rich feeling swells within despite your raw hands, shaking limbs and grime-streaked face, despite the gasps of exertion and the tears of effort?

There is no doubt that the inner experience is joy. The fact that the outer expression is pain is irrelevant; on the contrary, if the pain is a measure of the effort, if the pain is felt because you are giving all to do what you must do, that pain is the measure of the joy. In fact, it is the joy itself.

Words are inadequate to express the depth of what is happening here, but if you have ever really struggled and suffered to build, you will know exactly what is meant.

And if you have never struggled and suffered to build anything, you have not lived.

Consider another illustration. Imagine a newcomer to civilized society who takes a tour of mankind's activities. Let us suppose that the first place our visitor inspects is a modern gymnasium. Let us say that our visitor peeps through the keyhole and witnesses a young man exercising on a machine or lifting extremely heavy weights. On the young man's face is an expression of agony; sweat is pouring from him. His body is racked by tremors of exertion and he appears close to the limit of human endurance.

There can be little doubt that our visitor would conclude that the young man is being tortured. He would immediately decide that just beyond his range of vision there must stand a menacing aggressor with a weapon trained on this unfortunate victim who is being cruelly worked to exhaustion.

But the truth is that the young man is working voluntarily. No one is forcing him. In fact, he is *paying* for the privilege of being able to work thus. And more than that: *he is loving every moment!* And anyone who has ever engaged in that sort of effort knows that *the pain is the pleasure.*

The pain is the pleasure because it is the pain that is building what he wants to build. The pain is the measure of the effort; the effort is the exact measure of what is being built. Without the pain, there can be no building. Without the straining against resistance there can be no progress.

Let us go further. What is the deep reason that effort is pleasurable when it is exerted in building? Why is the human psyche constructed in such a way that we enjoy laboring to build, working to solve a deep problem, forging through obstacles towards a goal?

To understand this, notice that the depth of the pleasure in the intensity of the effort lies in the anticipation of the result. The more one looks forward to the joy of the end-point, the more one enjoys the labor of getting there. It is the looking forward to what is being built, the vision of the end-point, that fuels the effort. The dream of achieving the result provides the pleasure within the pain of the journey.

You can see this clearly by considering its opposite: imagine you are forced to labor intensely on something that is to be destroyed before it is completed – that would be torture. (Note that Torah prohibits the imposition of unproductive labor on a worker.) If you knew that your effort would achieve no result at all, that effort would become sheer pain. The sweetness of the journey lies in the anticipation of reaching the destination; in every bit of effort, in every moment of exertion, lies the awareness that a part of the result has been built, and that is its joy. In fact, in many experiences in life the anticipation is more pleasurable than the result.

(It is important to see that deep faith is an indispensable element in sensing life's joy. Life's closures of opportunity cause pain, the passage of time itself represents life's ebbing; awareness of this passing must bring pain. But real faith transmutes this: the knowledge that as each precious moment passes and dies, as each relationship ends as all must, each of these transiences is being exported to an eternal zone; each event and experience is being transmuted into its perfect version in eternity. Nothing in fact dies, rather each thing travels away from us, but each travels to its point of essence and waits there for an ultimate reunion that we call resurrection. It is difficult to conceive of a genuinely joyous life without this knowledge – how can real joy be generated when all things pass? No moment can be sustained. One who lives in faith knows that nothing dies in essence; death is a deep separation, but not more than that.)

So the work derives its happiness from the expectation of the end-point.

And paradoxically, the end-point derives its happiness from the work. If you think about this deeply you will realize that the real satisfaction of the result lies in the fact that your work built it. A result without effort, a gift received free, means far less than a result that you labored to achieve. The depth of your joy at the journey's end lies in the effort you invested to reach that end. Standing on a high mountain's peak is exhilarating not only because of the view; the exhilaration derives in no small measure from the effort of the ascent.

Why is the world built this way? What can we learn about the nature of reality from this understanding of the relationship between work and result, journey and destination?

The Torah concept is that life is movement, a journey to a destination. The next world is the destination, and the journey has meaning only because there is a destination. I have pointed this out already; remember that in Torah terms the destination is bound up with the journey, it is nothing other than a real and timeless experience of the journey, the joy of experiencing the reality that the journey was building as it happened. If life is grasped as the building of an eternal result, the difficulties of life take on a new aspect. In fact, it is those very difficulties that build the result most significantly.

Our conception of that result is that it is pure pleasure. The Torah idea of the next world is that it is a dimension of pleasure, the pleasure that is exactly the experience of self in relation to Source, suffused with the knowledge that the self was invested in building that experience and that relationship.

The next world is a state in which you simply experience yourself clearly. No illusions, no facades. If you have built correctly, achieved your potential through the work of a life lived in resonance with objective reality, the result is the ecstasy of being exactly what you should be and knowing that you are the cause of that state. Nothing could be a deeper happiness: the happiness of real being.

(Conversely, the pain of the next world is the experience, the knowledge, that you could have built your realized self and failed. If the opportunity of life has been wasted, the pain must be immense. It is nothing other than the pain of a self which might have been, should have been, and was not. The mystical sources describe it as the pain of not-being.)

Life is temporary, the result is eternal. The journey is transitory, the destination is permanent. That is why any work in the world that produces a result contains the potential for a feeling of joy: it is a small sample of the joy of life itself; a small taste of the transitory translated into the permanent.

Since everything in this world is a reflection of the higher reality that creates it, every experience in the world contains a spark of that higher dimension. We feel a surge of joy when we build something in this world because in every small achievement here lies a seed of eternity. In every small experience of transforming effort into hard-won result lies the exhilaration of the ultimate achievement of transforming all of life and its effort into an eternal result.

That is why the pleasure experienced in the work itself derives from the anticipation of the result, and the pleasure of the result derives from the satisfaction of the work done to get there. That is exactly the pattern of life: the work of life draws inspiration from the knowledge that every moment of difficulty here will live forever in the next world, and the pleasure of the next world is nothing other than the summation of all the moments of exertion of the life that built it. This is deep, David; there is not much else that is worth the effort invested to understand as much as this is.

In mystical Torah texts this is expressed as: "The taste of the tree is like the taste of the fruit." The idea is that this world is a tree (the Hebrew word for tree, *etz,* is the root that means actuality, the core or essence of a thing, as in *etzem* – this is why the original Garden is a place of "trees"), and the next world is the fruit. The tree is dry, hard, woody, tasteless; it produces a succulent fruit. But the revelation of the next world is that the tree has the taste of the fruit – the tree itself is succulent, delicious. In other words *the fruit is the tree.* The next world is not the separate and divorced result of this world, it *is this world* correctly revealed. Words are very clumsy here; I hope you follow me.

Can we now answer the questions we posed?

"Serve God with joy." Does this mean that happiness is an end in itself? The verse is clear – it does not state "Be happy." It states *"Serve* God with joy." *That* is the aim: serving, working to build, and in that serving the proper mode is joy. If you serve as you should, the joy is guaranteed. If you take care of the work, the happiness takes care of itself.

"Because you did not serve Hashem your God with joy..." The reason for our suffering throughout history is not that we failed to be joyous. The problem is not that part of the verse; it is the *beginning* of the verse, that is the key: "Because you did not *serve* with joy..." Defaulting on the service, the effort of the journey, that is the problem. And if there is no work, there is no joy.

Happiness is not the goal, but it is *the assured result* of moving towards the goal. Joy is properly to be seen as part of the means, not the end.

For one who knows this secret deeply and lives it, indeed "there is no sadness in the world." Note that we mean sadness in the sense of depression; that is never appropriate. Pain, mourning, weeping – those are appropriate at various times, but the despairing, hopeless, end-of-the-road darkness of mind that we term depression is not appropriate. As long as there is life, the road leads on. Depression, the "no-road" response, is a spiritual error.

Let us study the nature of depression more closely; I think we can derive a significant insight into our subject. (I do not mean to consider organic or "medical" states of depression here; that is outside the scope of our immediate discussion. I am referring here to functional life-depression, the experience of those whose lives seem pointless and empty when there is often no obvious reason for that response.)

A central feature of the sensation of depression is the feeling of hopelessness, the feeling of no movement towards any goal, the feeling of the impossibility of reaching any goal. And the cause of depression is exactly that: *absence of movement towards a goal.* When the soul senses that life is sliding by and no meaningful progress is taking place, no real development is occurring, there is a sense of stagnation, of despair. Happiness is the response of the inner being to its journey through life, the response of the soul to its own development – depression is the response of the soul to stagnation, to motionlessness and the absence of development.

When the soul senses that the journey has come to a halt, that life is moving by but going nowhere, depression is the response. If the journey is life itself, every step on that journey is essential and priceless (you cannot get to a destination unless you walk the *entire* road that leads there), and when time is passing but the journey is not progressing the soul feels the cold hand of death. Depression is no less than a minor experience of death itself; that is exactly why it is so painful.

A depressed person may not know that this is the cause of the problem, but the soul knows. It is weeping, crying out to move on, to move actively and surely, and it is being obstructed. It is being held back from the most important task that there is, the task of building eternity in a medium of fluid transience. The response of the obstructed soul is a feeling of deep pain, of life and its opportunity lost. It is quite possibly the deepest pain there is.

What is the correct approach to depression? If the problem is lack of meaningful movement, the solution is to *get moving*. When the soul feels its own movement it will forget all sadness; the depression will end.

You cannot feel depressed when you know you are moving correctly towards a correct goal. You may feel pain, you may feel agony; your face may show strain and your eyes may fill with tears, but if you are winning the battle and moving ahead you cannot be *depressed.*

Often it is necessary to start the movement externally: getting the body moving may be necessary before the soul can be roused. Judaism teaches that the "external awakens the internal;" experiences and actions of the body stimulate inner experience. It may be necessary to begin with physical motion so that the outer can begin to drive inward and affect the soul, but the idea remains: cure stagnation with movement, passive misery with activity. Whether the activity is vigorous bodily exercise or exacting work for the hands (or best of all, active work in giving, doing something to benefit someone else) the principle is to convert stagnation into action.

One who is laboring to build and is aware that the result is taking shape as it should *cannot be depressed* no matter how hard the work.

I must point out that there is an alternative to depression as a response to lack of life movement, and it is perhaps even more dangerous. It is possible to satisfy the deep need to build by building trivial things; to divert the drive to build into superficiality. This escape can provide a sense of work transformed into result which is *enough to keep a person from the real task* of life without the warning sign of a sense of emptiness or depression.

People will build collections of objects or throw themselves into projects that are meaningless because the total commitment and extreme, focused effort give a sense of purpose and movement; the fact that the purpose is irrelevant or foolish is easily ignored.

Some people build collections of paintings, some build collections of beer cans. Some devote themselves to sporting achievement, some to business. Some build muscle, some build empires. All of these have the potential to appease the urge to produce, to move, to build; at least for a while, and sometimes for a lifetime.

But very often they are simply superficial substitutes for the real work of building the self and the world correctly. Building things in this world may be necessary and worthy, but when the building here becomes a substitute for the building of eternity, that is a tragedy. This world and its achievements must always be the vehicle for the real journey. Sublimation of the deepest drive of the soul into a beer can collection made for its own sake is too tragic for words.

(You will notice that Jews tend to do these things seriously. There is in the Jewish psyche a certain intensity, a need and an ability to focus and dedicate energy that leads us to take what we do very seriously. Mark Twain referred to the "aggressive mind" of the Jew; this is deeply part of our nature. When a Jew does something, as a very general rule he does it intensely, whatever it may be. That is part of the reason for the contribution Jews have made to the advancement of every society they have inhabited. I am certain that when Jews explore Buddhism they do so intensely; is that your experience? I would not be surprised to find that even if Buddhism urges its adherents to de-intensify, to give up a sense of drive, Jews will try to do even that with drive and intensity!)

The stagnant soul has only two options: expression of its stagnation as depression, or conversion of its stagnation into movement. That movement may be genuine spiritual progress or it may be deflected into movement towards the trivial, towards no real destination. Depression may, if handled with mature insight, lead to a correct diagnosis of its underlying existential cause and from there to its cure; a lifetime spent furiously building trivial things may never realize its own futility.

There is another closely related aspect of this subject: the joy of experiencing destination itself. I suspect this may have relevance for Jews in Buddhism. There is a powerful drive to experience the joy of that end-point, to live in that rarefied zone of next-worldly ecstasy, that state of being-in-itself. One of the proper expressions of this experience is in the mitzva of Shabbat: the experience of a day that is a premonition of the world to come. Shabbat is experienced by desisting from acts of creation, as I have pointed out; this observance gives us a taste of the state of pure being that is existence in the next world where no creation is possible; where nothing is becoming, all is being.

Objectless meditation may give an experience of that state, but it must not be overused. The joy of intrinsic being, the joy of the pure now, is felt in meditation, but my guess is that many Jews doing this will reach a saturation point where a gnawing anxiety begins to intrude. This is because the Jewish soul knows deeply that this world is for more than end-in-itself experience. Shabbat cannot be lived daily. I imagine that Jews who experience this may interpret it as a difficulty inherent in their meditation; perhaps they will persevere, and perhaps even with success, but the problem will refuse to go away entirely. It is a Jewish characteristic to need to feel the journey's progress.

Meditation

"Most Jews are drawn to Buddhism because it is, by its very nature, quiet, deliberate, even solitary. It is inwardly focused, calm, serene. No minyans, no noisy shuls, no scolding rabbis. Is there such a thing as Jewish meditation?"

David,

The mitzva of *tefilla,* prayer, most intensely expresses what you know as meditation. There are other forms, too, such as the preparation for prayer, that more closely approximate what you call objectless meditation (the early *chassidim* – masters who transcended mere righteousness – used to spend an hour in preparatory meditation divesting the consciousness of bodily attachments before each of the three daily prayer-meditations in addition to the hour of prayer itself, and an hour in "coming-down" meditation afterwards; many hours daily engaged in this exercise). But since prayer is the concentrated focus of this idea in Judaism, this is the place to begin.

Prayer is probably as misunderstood as any aspect of Judaism today. Let us look into this mitzva and understand its meditational heart.

First, let me raise a few basic questions about prayer.

There are aspects of prayer that defy explanation. Our prayers are phrased as requests: we ask for our needs and the needs of the world; this is an essential element. The difficulty is this: how can we hope to achieve anything by asking? Even a child should be bothered by this question: surely God knows what we need before we ask, and surely a loving father would give his children what they need even if they do not ask? And conversely, surely He would not grant a request if the consequences would be harmful. So what difference can asking possibly make?

Put more sharply, how can we hope to change His mind? If we could effect some change, somehow, that would be nothing less than miraculous in the deepest sense.

Are we really expected to pour out our hearts in deeply-felt pleading while knowing that our pleas can have no effect?

Why are our prayers expressed as requests at all? If prayer is a deep meditation, as I am suggesting to you, personal requests would seem an inappropriate medium; surely depersonalized concentration would be better?

And if prayer is *service*, asking for our needs seems quite the opposite: how does focusing on my needs constitute service? Service would seem to be about giving, not needing and receiving. In fact, one of the deep derivations of prayer in Torah is rooted in the idea of sacrifice. How is this consistent with requests? Sacrifice means a giving of self, not a taking.

There are other paradoxical aspects of prayer. The word *tefilla,* prayer, is based on a root which has two contradictory meanings. It has the connotation of the hope of highly improbable consequences, great kindness being expressed against all odds, as it says *"Re'o panecha lo pillalti* - I could not have hoped to see your face again," the words of Jacob's wonder at seeing Joseph after many years of separation during which their reunion would have seemed possible only by miracle. Yet the same root means strict, deserved justice in the narrow legal sense – exactly the opposite of unexpected bounty. How are these conflicting elements contained in prayer?

And a deeper problem: the Talmud states quite plainly that God prays. God Himself, the source of all reality, praying? We are forced to ask incredulously: to whom? And what exactly does He "ask" for? How is it possible to understand this statement at all?

Let us begin with the problem of somehow changing God, an obvious impossibility. The key is to understand that prayer is *not* directed at changing God at all; it is directed at changing *you*. The idea is that the work of *tefilla* (prayer is known as the *work* of the heart) is work on the self. A *tefilla* that does not change you is a failure. Work on the personality means making changes; some refinement, some elevation must occur. The form of the verb "to pray," *hitpallel,* is reflexive; something is being done to the self that is praying.

The reason we can hope to achieve a result through *tefilla,* to make some change in the world or our situation in it, is this: you certainly cannot convince God that you need some particular thing if He knows otherwise. But *you can change yourself to the point that the object of your request has a different meaning.* If a person wants wealth, for example, and is being refused that request *because it would not be good for him* (wealth can be a serious problem no less than poverty, as you must have noticed), no amount of pleading will change that. But working on the self until one reaches a refinement, an insight into the purpose of life and the correct perspective on wealth, could result in a situation where that gift may now be *good* for the one who is asking. You *can* change the dispensation granted to you – by changing yourself. A new dispensation now becomes appropriate. So you see that *tefilla* is not only a meditation in the conventional sense; it is most certainly intended to produce results too. Of course it is immediately apparent that the work of *tefilla* is not simply asking for things; it must be very hard and sincere work indeed to change oneself genuinely.

The change in self that prayer effects is layered. First, the act of asking itself begins the process of placing the self in correct relationship with the giver: you ask for a thing only from that which you understand to be the valid source of that thing. When you walk into a store and ask for a certain article you are asserting your belief that they sell that article there. A father may be ready and willing to give his child some particular thing, but he may be withholding it because his prime objective lies within the relationship between himself and his child – if the child were consciously to acknowledge his father as the giver, turn towards him in that way, that may be all the father is waiting for. Asking transmutes the self-contained, self-reliant individual into an empty vessel facing the source that must fill it.

A spoiled child may not be given what the father *longs* to give because the father can see that such a gift will exacerbate the child's immature sense of independence. When the child changes, develops, to the point where the father can see that the gift will be appreciated, he will give it immediately. The child has not changed the father, he has changed himself.

Further, apart from turning the self to face in the correct direction, the acknowledgement of a need, a present lack, begins the process of developing correct perspective *within* the self. The very act of asking teaches the intrinsic incompleteness of the self. The undeveloped childish grasp is a sense of self-contained perfection, of completeness; the Talmud demonstrates that the unborn fetus does not yet have a *yetzer ha'ra* – an "evil inclination," or lower self – because if it did it would kick its way out of the mother, absolutely sure that its development is complete. At birth, that egocentric grasp of self begins. In other words, a central element of the immature, lower self is a complacent sense of ripeness. Maturity requires an awareness of genuine deficiency, an objective awareness of the lack that further growth will fill. A genuine student of the spirit knows that his path leads continually to the blossoming of those latent areas of self that begin incomplete and find their completion with work and experience.

You can see that this is only another expression of our constant theme of ego clarification. False ego is always an inaccurate sense of completeness or perfection. Genuine humility recognizes the areas of growth still to be attained.

(The aim is to reach a consciousness devoid of ego and illusion. In fact, ego is destroyed *by* destroying illusion: when reality is objectively perceived there can be no false ego. If you know exactly who you are with no hint of fantasy, if you take no undue credit for what you are, you have risen above the inflation of self that is ego. The pride of ego is all illusion; one who knows himself objectively has no false pride. A genuine greatness objectively grasped is not ego; it is simply the grasp of fact. A genuine humility, too, objectively grasped, is not false humility – the Talmud tells of the search for a genuinely humble individual that ended successfully when such an individual stepped forward to announce that he was extremely humble. There is no contradiction here; he had reached a certain level in that quality of character and he saw that fact objectively. Real humility, in fact, *requires* real greatness: one who is genuinely nothing and says he is nothing is not humble – he is simply right!)

Dispelling illusion is the method of dissipating ego. The road to character development is the road of clear thinking and clear perception. The Jewish tools of clarifying perception are Torah study and prayer: Torah as the rigorous and definitive exercise of training objective thinking; prayer as the exercise of driving that objective thinking and perceiving deep within the self. (A Torah teacher is essential; reaching pure objectivity without a master is beyond the capacity of most students. The relationship between master and disciple is itself a major Torah theme.)

Prayer is a deep meditation even before it begins. It requires a complete clearing of the mind in objective humility. Classic Torah sources say that this is its essence; the coming to stand face to face with God. (And that is its joy. I vividly remember my teacher, in a very rare moment of personal expression, referring to the sublime joy of this experience. You can add this as another layer to our discussion of your "Where is the joy in Judaism?" question.)

But there is a deeper change we are seeking to effect in the meditation of prayer. A real change in the personality must be a change in *ratzon*, root desire or motivation. Only a change in the root can be meaningful, all else is only technical re-arranging of the superficial. How do you change your *ratzon?* How do you "bring in" a new desire? This issue is pivotal.

Note that we are not using the idea of desire as you define it in Buddhist terms; we do not mean the lower cravings that originate in the body and the emotions. Here we are referring to the root of all thought and motivation, the point of origin of any inner movement. The word "will" or "volition" may be better. The word *ratzon* is numerically equivalent to *makor*, the word for source (and also to the word for "His Name," the ultimate source). This is the root of the inner being, the interface between what lies above conscious awareness and consciousness itself. All inner movement begins here. Before any intelligent process can begin, it must be motivated, willed. *Ratzon* is the real source.

If you wish to know yourself at root, find your deepest *ratzon*. The *mussar* exercise is this: ask yourself what you really want, and patiently recognize the image that comes to your mind. (It may be superficial, even humiliatingly so, but this is not the time to be squeamish.) Then ask yourself *why* you want that thing. You will discover the underlying deeper reason for that desire – if I had *that*, I could do (or be).... whatever it is. Now ask yourself why you want *that* deeper level. If you persist with fearless and brutal honesty, sooner or later (and it is usually sooner) you will find a thing or a state that you want for no other reason than that you simply want it. No deeper motivation fuels it, no reason for that desire exists outside of itself. *That is you.*

If *ratzon* is source, and if source is essence, then you have discovered your essence in terms of all that moves you. This exercise is a deep and difficult meditation, and it lies at the core of prayer.

The first phase of prayer is to reach the *ratzon*, to ascend in consciousness until one penetrates into the very core of one's personality. To face one's own root desire, that distilled essence from which all the rest of one's inner life and outer behavior flows, to face it honestly and unafraid, is an absolute requirement for genuine change. This is a very high meditation indeed, and it requires total detachment from the physical world (see the Nefesh Hachaim for a definitive exposition).

Now the question becomes: when you reach that depth, how do you change it? How do you go to a source that is above awareness? How do you change the source? That is who you are. The image of trying to lift yourself by pulling on the roots of your own hair comes to mind. How do you create a new desire? How do you sincerely come to want that which is higher, more refined, if you do not want it now? Simply to *say* that you want something else would be a lie; it must be felt, known, more deeply than anything else.

You cannot cause a new *ratzon* to manifest. By definition, the root cause cannot be an effect of some other cause. The will itself cannot be willed to change. No, *you* cannot do it; it can only come as a gift. A change of the deepest essence of the self, an elevation of that essence, is a gift. It must come from Above the self. This is central to understanding the Torah path; the climb to the top is work, going beyond that top is a gift. It comes from outside the self – a new level, a new sensitivity; that is the ultimate gift, *that* is the answer to prayer.

(Although one cannot voluntarily create a new desire, there is one desire that can be felt powerfully and naturally: the desire to change the root. One *can* honestly say: I *want* a higher *ratzon*, I *want* to feel a higher desire. The *desire for the desire* is certainly accessible. One should pour one's heart out in the request to be elevated.)

How do you merit this gift? In order for that *shefa*, that flow, to fill the soul one must become a vessel for it. The flow is there; the question is only where are the vessels? His desire to give is maximal and permanent, the question is, where are we? A hint lies in the blessing brought about by Elisha for the poor woman: Elisha instructed her to bring vessels, and oil flowed miraculously to fill the vessels – *until there were no more vessels*. He did not produce the vessels for her; that was her task. And although the vessels were filled miraculously, the miracle was limited to the vessels available. There is no problem with the oil; the limitation is only in the vessels.

What does it mean to become a vessel? How exactly is this done? The mystical idea is that the highest level of the personality is crystal-clear and transparent, but the lower self clouds it. (Spiritual beauty is expressed as transparency, the Higher light shines through. When one sees a *tzaddik,* a righteous and holy individual, one is perceiving something of his Source; the limited human dimension has been clarified and a higher reality becomes visible. In fact the opposite of beauty, ugliness, is *chi'ur* in Hebrew, comprising the same root letters as *achur*, opaque.)

You cannot generate a new *ratzon;* all you can do is sacrifice the old. You can hollow out the present vessel. You can annul the lower self and become open for a higher gift.

There is a parallel in the realm of thought: concentration applied to solve a problem does *not* mean focusing on the solution – you do not *have* the solution to focus on yet. Concentration simply means clearing the mind of extraneous thoughts and mental "noise," clearing a space in the mind – and the solution *appears.* An idea is not created – it happens. In Yiddish an "idea" is an *"einfal"*: it *falls in.* (There is a humility in that term, a recognition that a new insight comes from outside as a gift, that the word "idea" can never convey.)

The greatest man who ever lived, Moses, was also the humblest; no accident – his humility was the *reason* for his greatness. When the vessel of the self is emptied, God can fill it. Our work is not to cause the light to shine, only to stop obstructing it. In the words of one of my revered Torah teachers: "The world is full of light except where we cast the shadows."

The spiritual path is always a paradox. Real honor finds only those who flee from it (really flee: a man once complained to the Chazon Ish that he had fled from honor all his life and it had still not found him! The Chazon Ish gently chided him: "You have been too busy looking over your shoulder!") Real content is found only in those who are really empty.

Put in *ratzon* terms, this clarifying process means *yielding* all one's will to the higher will. This is the meaning of "Make His will your will," want what He wants. (As we have already noted, this does *not* mean becoming a passive, colorless individual; on the contrary, it means *passionately* and *personally* wanting what He wants.) This level is given as a gift exactly to the degree that one gains control over one's own drives and interests.

So the meditation and the work of prayer is to identify one's deepest core and then to yield it. "This is who I am. This is *everything* that I am; all meaning in my life is concentrated here, in my deepest desire. Take it; I give myself to You."

The paradox of *tefilla* requires unique work: building and simultaneously yielding the *ratzon*. The desires should be richly felt and simultaneously sublimated into a higher service. This is the deep reason that prayer is composed of requests, desires expressed. That is exactly the medium of prayer; prayer is the work of changing desires. The work of prayer is work on *ratzon*.

The Nefesh Hachaim explains this: our prayers are requests because we are working on *ratzon*. When we ask, we should be asking for those things for God, not for us. We *use* our desire, but for Him. Give us wisdom – to understand You. Give us health – to perform Your mitzvot. And so on. An exercise in self-development, using the potentially selfish motivations, sublimating those very motivations to a higher purpose. Of course some thought will show that it has to be this way: standing before God with a list of personal requests for completely selfish reasons would be sheer *chutzpa,* not service.

The Nefesh Hachaim points out that we learn many aspects of this subject from the prayer that the childless Chana offered when she came to the Sanctuary to pray for a child. We are told that Chana prayed powerfully, even somehow going beyond the apparent limits of what should be said. The Beis Halevi explains that she went so far as to threaten extreme action: she told God that if He refused her request for a child she would seclude herself with a man other than her husband and cause herself to be subjected to the test of the *sotah* (woman suspected of unfaithfulness) in which the Divine name is erased in water. When the suspected *sotah* drinks the water, if she is guilty of infidelity, she suffers a miserable end, but if she is innocent she becomes pregnant by her husband – a promise of the Torah.

Chana used this stratagem: "God, I intend to do this. Since I shall be innocent, You will *have* to give me a child – You have promised thus in Your Torah, and You will never make Your Torah untrue!" Forcing the Divine hand! A sharp prayer indeed.

But the meaning is clear, as the Nefesh Hachaim explains: Chana was motivated only for God's honor and glory. We are dealing with one of the greatest women who ever lived, great enough to become the mother of Samuel and to teach the Jewish people the depth of what prayer means for all time. You cannot think of forcing the Divine hand if your intention is no larger than your own unclarified immature desire; *chutzpa* would be too mild a word for that. But if *all you are* is His, the meaning of your desire is entirely different. Chana's desire, her desire as a woman for a child, was entirely one with her desire to serve God. The intensity of her prayer was this: by undergoing the test of the *sotah* I shall definitely have a child. But I am asking You for a child without having to go through that because *that would mean erasing Your name.* Allow me the inevitable result without that desecration of Your honor! And we see her sincerity: she dedicated to God the child she was granted, from the earliest possible age – she presented her son Samuel to the Sanctuary to be raised in God's service for the rest of his life. Her very *desire* for this child was dedicated to God; she wanted a son *for His sake* – she sublimated her personal and natural desire to be a mother to the service of God. Note again, the approach is not the stilling, the killing of natural desire but its amplification and elevation.

Perhaps now we can understand the paradox of the root of the word *tefilla:* the strict line of destiny, yet combined with the almost incomprehensible kindness of unexpected results. God wants to give, *intends* to give, but He waits for our *tefilla.* He waits for us to make our *ratzon* His *ratzon.* He makes His desire to give dependent on our desire to receive. When we *ask,* He reveals what must be. The result occurs *only* because we ask, and yet it is a revelation of that which must be.

Let us go back further in Torah, to the beginning. The Midrashic sources say that when Adam was created, he did not see a garden. The foliage of the garden was not yet present; growth had stopped at the surface of the ground because there was no rain. And there was no rain because "There was no man to work the land;" "work" here is a reference to the work of the heart – prayer. Since there was no one to pray, there was no rain. Despite the fact that the rain is waiting, poised, destined, a necessary part of Creation, it *will not be* if man does not express his desire for it. Adam must ask for rain. And when he does ask for it, the garden is revealed *as it had to be.* This is the paradox of prayer – it achieves what was destined; it reveals what was meant to be but would have remained hidden without it. It is both natural and miraculous.

Rain is one of the few things in Creation that God Himself causes directly, not through any intermediary. (The Talmud states that He holds three keys "personally:" the keys to rain, birth and resurrection.) The profound teaching here is that the response to prayer is the deepest response imaginable – the activation of an infinite-finite partnership. At the very beginning of Creation, the essential nature of this mitzva is taught. Not a nicety, an option, but an absolute requirement within the root of reality. The result is a harmony of Divine and human will that builds the world, quite literally.

Can we now approach the statement that God prays? We have defined prayer in essence as a change in will. The Talmud states that His prayer is: "May it be My will to arise from the throne of justice and move to the throne of mercy." May it be *My will.* We are being taught here that an act of prayer is an act of changing will.

I hope this begins to identify some common misconceptions in the subject of prayer.

Prayer is a carefully constructed meditation designed to clarify the personality, to polish it to the point of transparency. It is a breakthrough into the root of the personality to connect with the Root of the world. That connection is made in the work of conquering the lower desires and drives. By *becoming* that desire to manifest His desire. And who better to learn from than David, who comes to the world to teach absolute ego-emptiness, to reveal God's kingship in the world through his own kingship. David, in dedication of every fiber of his being to God, says of himself: *"Va'ani tefilla"* – not "I pray," but "I *am* prayer."

Complexity and Simplicity

Akiva,
I've learned a great deal from you about prayer.

My initial reaction is that you have found a fundamental spring of spiritual strength that most Jews have not tapped into, and that many Jews who go looking in Buddhism would never have found in Judaism.

The pared-down forms of Buddhism popular in the West are presented in simple terms; this is attractive to Jews who are put off by what they perceive as the inaccessibility of God and the hopeless intricacy of Jewish modes of prayer and worship.

The questions that arise now are:

Why was prayer never presented to me this way before? Why is it not taught this way?

Why does there seem, in fact, to be resistance to understanding prayer in this way, among rabbis as well as fellow congregants?

It sounds so great. How do I do it?

David,

Firstly, regarding the "inaccessibility of God:" if this is why Jews look to a system that does not relate to God, that is not logical – if Buddhism teaches the central importance of accessing reality, then by its own teachings reality must be probed and faced, despite any difficulty. If you lose an object in a dark place, that is where you must seek it – going off to a place where the light is better will not help! (The wise, of course, will *bring* a light to aid the search.)

Deep inner effort is obviously not foreign to Buddhism. Jews cannot seriously be going there to escape that.

Secondly, regarding the "intricacy of Jewish modes of prayer and worship:" the structure of prayer comprises a simple core surrounded by concentric layers of complexity and intricacy. I have pointed out already that Torah reflects the world exactly (or more accurately, the world reflects Torah exactly). Therefore all aspects of Torah will have complexity, intricacy and detail. That is how the world is. The point is not to seek simplicity because it is easier; the point is, what is reality like? If it is complex, deal with it; do not redefine it and escape it. (That is not the Buddhist approach to reality, either.) The Jewish path (and the path of all wisdom) is to see the exquisitely ordered complexity and cut through to its utterly simple core.

So what is the problem with intricacy? When a subject is mastered, it becomes simple. I remember the overwhelming complexity and never-ending detail that faced me when I began my medical education; anatomy at ever deeper levels, details within details – how would I ever gain any mastery? But the further I went the more I saw that the skill needed lies far more in the grasp of the unifying principles than in mastery of the details. The power of the professional is in the grasp of principles. The greatest teachers (in Judaism no less than my great teachers in medicine) show how to cut through to the core and the essence, how to find the pure and simple beneath the detail. And then you begin to see how organized and beautiful (and necessary) is the detail.

You have identified the problem of dealing with intricacy in the field of prayer. Let me point out to you that in Judaism the basic training for life and thought is located in the effort of Torah learning. That effort is exactly the exercise of learning to see simplicity underlying complexity. Talmudic learning is the science and art of teasing apart intricate details to discover the unifying principles.

We are driving for simplicity; in perception and in living. Perhaps the most important tool of the mind and heart is to learn to identify what is essence and what is not. Prayer is no different.

You ask why prayer was never presented to you in depth. David, I am afraid it depends on the company you keep. We have already lamented the fact that many in this generation, including some who teach and lead, have never had any real connection with Torah. What passes for Judaism on the modern scene, as you know, is virtually whatever you want; in most cases Jews would be nearer the mark in Buddhism. But if you move in the right circles you will find the depth. It takes effort, but it is available. You know that in Chicago you can find Torah-true Jews; seek them out, ask them to learn with you. (They are easily identified – they are the ones universally regarded as wrong. If there is one thing non-Torah Judaism agrees on today it is that those who are loyal to real Torah are definitely mistaken. So you should not have too much trouble finding them; look for those who are regarded as so Orthodox that they could not possibly have anything meaningful to contribute.)

And watch them carefully; watch them pray. If there is talking (*any* talking) during the service, if the prayers are mumbled and rushed, if there is not a palpable concentration and sanctity throughout the entire service, you are in the wrong place.

Go to a major yeshiva and watch the students and their teachers; speak to them, learn with them. Visit *any* large yeshiva in Israel next time you are there, particularly during a service.

As for your own effort to master the art of prayer: study the Nefesh Hachaim, for a start. Note carefully what he says about divesting the mind of its bodily attachments; your background in meditation will prove most useful. Next, learn to focus on each word at the simplest level of meaning; that is always the basis, and it is a major challenge. Maintaining perfect concentration on even the first few of the nineteen sections of the *amida* is a serious achievement; as proficiency develops, include more. In general, remember that you are playing a masterpiece; your prayer book is the score, but the music must be yours.

There are other meditative expressions in Judaism, too. You mention "walking meditation;" I assume that is not simply meditating while walking, but rather that the walking is part of the meditation itself. In Judaism, dance can be a meditative exercise. You are probably aware that in the world of the yeshiva, we dance in circles. There is a deep reason for this. The circle can represent a lower state: a circle is all repetition; it has no point of newness, no singularity. Deep Torah sources point out that a circle is the only conceivable shape that has no distinctive point; *all* of a circle is the same. Describing the very smallest arc already predicts the entire circle; there is no unique point, and travelling in a circle means endless repetition, which is spiritual death. There is no point of beginning to a circle, nothing new about any of it. It is totally self-contained, locked in on itself entirely.

In the written Torah, this shape is represented by the letter *samech,* which is in fact a circle. The Midrash makes the striking observation that in the entire description of the Creation in the Torah, there is no *samech.* The beginning, that part of the Torah that is all singularity and not continuation, has no *samech.* (Try writing a few pages of English prose without an "o"!)

Now the idea of dancing in a circle is the redemption, or elevation, of this shape. As we move round, again and again in repetition, we are seeking to infuse the seemingly irredeemable world of habit and tired unconsciousness with *chiddush,* newness. (This is true of the cycle of the Jewish year, or the week too, for that matter.) Each time round is a repetition, but it is also an elevation. On one plane, the pattern is a circle, it is all repetition; but on another plane, it is a spiral – each revolution is higher than the previous one.

In the very act of exact repetition we discover a new taste, a new creative expression in each revisitation of a point we may think we know already. Looked at from above, there is only a circle, but looked at from the side, each ring moves up and each one is entirely new. Each revolution brings us back to the same point in one sense, but in a deeper sense that point has never been reached before. Physical eyes see a circle, but spiritual eyes see a spiral.

In the last generation, before the era in which amplified music destroyed any vestige of sanctity that there might have been in the dancing, the custom at a wedding was to dance to only one or at most two *nigunim* (melodies) all night. The words were the sublime words of a Torah verse or phrase, and each repetition was a meditative experience of climbing higher in the understanding and experiencing of the unlimited meanings in those words. Often the *nigun* was wordless, and for those whose minds were all Torah, it was a higher meditation yet. (That was before the age that is bored by repetition and demands constant cheap stimulation, of course, and today you will have to search harder to discover those enclaves where the dancing is still pure.) This is how we dance at a wedding, and this is how we dance on Simchat Torah, the festival of rejoicing with the Torah.

There are other meditations in Torah, too. Music itself is a source of meditative elevation – when the prophet needed to climb to a state of prophecy, he called for music. The verse says: *"v'haya k'nagen hamenagen..."* usually translated as: "When the musician played..." meaning that the prophet was able to reach the height of meditation that is prophecy when he heard the music. But a more sensitive translation is: "When the musician *became* the music..."

The Hebrew word *nigun,* melody, begins and ends with the same letter; Hebrew words with that characteristic imply a cycle, a process that in some way revisits itself. The word for a song, *shir,* also means a ring or circle. The Sfat Emet points out that the letters of that word are also those of *yashar,* meaning straight – the song goes round, it describes a circle, always returning on itself, but it also leads straight to a higher destination, a place entirely outside of itself.

The One and the Many

David,
You say that one of the goals of meditation is to experience the interconnectedness of all things in the Universe, the oneness of reality. In Judaism this takes the form of a mitzva, the meditation of *"Shma."* What is the depth that lies behind the recitation of *"Shma Yisrael..."*? What exactly do we mean when we begin and end every day with "Hear O Israel... God is One"?

The mitzva of declaring *"Shma Yisrael..."* is the building of oneness in consciousness and in the world.

The daily recitation of *Shma* is preceded by God's love for us – this is the subject of the preceding blessing, and it is followed by our mitzva to love God – that is the subject of the first verse after the declaration of *Shma*. Now love is exactly a building of one from more than one; two becoming one is love itself. So the process of which *Shma* forms the center is the building of oneness from parts.

The intention in saying these words is exactly to perceive the oneness of all things, and the unity of all things with their Source. In saying the word *echad* – One, the meditation is to focus on the intensity of oneness to the point that nothing else exists, not even the one who is saying the word. In that moment there should be a meshing of the speaker, the word, its meaning and the Source. The deeper texts refer to this as concentrating on the idea of: "There is nothing besides Him." *Nothing*.

Let me select just one aspect of this mitzva in order to point a direction for further thought.

The word *Shma* is translated as "Hear," but its deep literal meaning is "gather together into one," as the verse states *"Va 'yeshama Shaul... –* And Saul gathered... (the nation)."* That is remarkable – our statement of God's Oneness requires a "hearing" which is itself an act of gathering elements, of generating unity. What lies beneath the surface here? In fact, why does the *Shma* begin with the instruction to hear at all – do you think for a moment that it is a call to attention, a warning that what follows needs to be heard? The inference would be that *this* needs to be heard, but the rest of the Torah does not! Nothing in Torah is incidental; it must *all* be heard, that is fundamental. So why does the Torah particularly mandate hearing *this*?

In order to understand this key concept, we shall need to examine the phenomenon of hearing in the physical world to perceive its higher meaning. The kabbalistic sources compare seeing and hearing – let me present part of the more accessible aspect of that analysis.

Seeing happens in the light; what is seen is clear. In Hebrew the word for "seeing" is the same word as "proof," what is seen is undeniable. Deeper than this, the elements of a scene are all perceived at once, seeing is an instant mode, all is seen *together.* Also, the scene is external, it is seen "outside" of the self.

But the faculty of hearing is diametrically opposed to this. It happens in the dark. What is heard is not heard at once: the elements of sound are heard *in sequence,* over time, and they must be assembled by the listener. Hearing is internal, what is heard depends on how the listener assembles those elements. You cannot hear all the syllables of a sentence, or even one word, together – that would be noise. You must hear one syllable, by itself meaningless, then the next. By the time you hear the second, the first has faded into memory. When the third is heard, the second has faded. And so on. When the entire sentence is completed, the elements are combined *within the listener* and understood. A dark and subjective process indeed. In a world of seeing, only truth exists. In a world of hearing, faith has a place.

The mystics explain that seeing is "higher" than hearing; the next world is seen, in this world one must hear. This is a world of *process,* of *movement towards.* I have pointed out before that the Hebrew word for the earth is based on the root that means to run or move; the name for Heaven is based on the word meaning "there." This world is all movement towards; the higher dimension is all destination. This world moves through time since it is all process, the next world is beyond time because all is one there. In that world there is truly "only the moment."

This idea is a key that opens some difficult areas. If one understands that what is *heard* in this world is *seen* in the world of revelation, perplexing verses become accessible. "And all flesh shall *see* together that God's mouth has spoken." Surely it should state that all flesh shall *hear*. One does not see speech! But in that world of revelation, one certainly does. What is *heard* now will be *seen* then. (And even the "flesh," the lowest component of the human dimension, will see. And of course "together" – unity is the precondition.)

A more striking example: describing the Sinai experience, the Torah states explicitly that the Divine *shofar* sounds at Sinai were *seen:* the people "saw the sounds." What is the meaning here? We can approach this remarkable description with our principle: at Sinai, God appeared; the higher world was manifest here in this world – this world melted into the higher existence. That is why the Talmud states that all the people present *died* when God spoke and had to be revived; they entered the higher world as it became manifest. And that is why the Midrash states that when God appeared nothing in the world moved – of course not: when the higher world manifests, when the domain of end-point is revealed, *nothing can possibly move,* there is nowhere to go. Everything is already *there.*

The world of time and process makes hearing relevant; sequential components are assembled into meaning. But in the higher world *hearing is not possible* in the way that it is here; there is no sequence of events one following the next, all *is* at once, all moments exist together. *The modality there is seeing.* And therefore when He brought His Presence into contact with the finite world, when this world was elevated to the level of the next at that indescribable moment at Sinai, seeing became the primary mode – the *shofar* sounds were seen.

Remember that a prophet is a "seer," his mode is vision. The prophet sees, the wise must hear. When the Zohar, the central kabbalistic source-work, reveals a concept, it begins with the phrase: *"ta chazi"* – "Come and see." When the Babylonian Talmud, the repository of the Oral Law whose mode is logical analysis, introduces a concept, it begins with: *"ta shma"* – "Come and hear."

"Shma Yisrael;" that is our meditation of reconstructing oneness. "Hear O Israel" is not a call to those who are not paying attention; it is a deep instruction. Hearing correctly is the work of assembling the fragments of perception into a coherent unity.

The meditation of *Shma* brings into consciousness the central paradox of Jewish mystical thinking; the knowledge of "two that are one" that does not negate the twoness. The effort is to understand a multiplicity that is one, not a simple oneness. This paradox runs through all of Torah; in learning there is a concept known as *"elu v'elu..."* in which two quite different meanings of a source are understood to be true, even when the two are apparently mutually exclusive.

In depth, this paradox is at the root of Torah. It is behind the impossible combination of *din* and *rachamim,* the quality of strict justice which admits no leniency and yet is tempered with leniency, and it is the basis of the impossible co-existence of Divine foreknowledge and human free will. These are subjects that need full analysis; I mention them only to point out the centrality of the concept of "two that are one" in Torah.

Silence

Akiva,

Shunryu Suzuki laid the groundwork by trying to sweep away preconceived notions both of what religion should be and what Zen is. He was rigorously simple in his discipline and in his teachings, and as a spiritual descendant of Eihei Dogen, he taught that "zazen," or seated, objectless meditation, was the very heart of Zen practice, and that in order to prepare the ground for this practice, much mental sweeping had to be done.

The very definitions of knowledge and belief in Buddhism differ profoundly from Judaism in some regards. There is, of course, a great deal of textual study available in Buddhism, but much Western practice consists of meditation, instruction on meditation, and reading about meditation.

Because reality is viewed not as a fixed set of events or things but as a constantly unfolding, shifting set of interacting things and beings, which themselves have no inherent fixed identity, *knowledge is seen as something residing beyond intellect and mental memory as a deep, extra-verbal awareness. This makes the intellect a troublesome tool, because it can become fixed onto ideas, concepts or facts that wind up encouraging attachment.*

Buddhist knowledge blossoms in meditation, a non-verbal, pre-verbal field in which one learns to learn in a realm beyond logic and words.

This surmounts the dualistic nature of language and speech and engages a part of ourselves that comprehends Source. The challenge then is to transmit this knowledge in writing, which uses the very forms that cannot encompass that knowledge. *This perhaps explains the use of koans and the predilection for paradox in Buddhism: these forms fertilize the mental ground for understanding that one must use words to get* beyond *words.*

In one of his first and perhaps most famous teachings, the Buddha, seated among a group of his followers, wordlessly held up a flower. When he saw one of his disciples, named Mahakashyapa, break into a huge grin, he knew that this man immediately apprehended all that he could have hoped to communicate. Mahakashyapa at that moment was entrusted by the Buddha to be his "dharma heir," or successor. This single incident is considered the seed of the beginning of Zen Buddhism.

David,
You say that Buddhism identifies words as inadequate at best. This is a basic Torah idea; in Torah thinking, silence is an essential exercise for developing inner knowledge. We aim to enter the area of inner knowledge and to *stay there*, that is, to come down into life and its daily activities with that level of pure consciousness intact and functioning. The mode that trains this faculty is silence.

Years ago, I commented to my teacher that the most important thing he ever taught us was awareness of this issue; that the gift of opening the mind to its deep ability to know beyond words is the most important faculty in Torah. He responded with perfect silence.

There is no question that this is the most important aspect of mind to develop; without this, nothing has value. Yet despite its centrality, it is probably the field least taught and known in the modern era, and you can see why: if it is beyond words, how do you teach it? The Talmud says that the master may give the disciple only general guidance in this zone, he may not teach its details. The correct understanding of this warning is not simply that there is a prohibition in teaching the esoteric wisdom of Torah explicitly (although that may be true, too); the depth is that the master may not say these things because he *cannot* – this is the area beyond words, and any words said here could only be false. The master must "push the disciple over the edge;" when he "falls in" he will understand. The mystics say that when you learn something spiritually true you do not have a sense of learning that thing, you have a sense of *recognizing* it.

The Torah term for kabbalistic teaching is "secret." It is a beginner's error to think that this means secret in the sense of information that no-one has told you yet; that is not *intrinsically* secret, that is *accidentally* secret: when someone tells you, it will no longer be secret. That is utterly wrong; Torah terms are always intrinsically true, not accidentally true. The reason that this area is called secret is not because no one has told you, but because no one *could* tell you; there are no words to tell it with. It is *always* secret, even when you know it.

Meditation opens this faculty directly; this is no doubt one of the reasons it is so fascinating to the Western mind. Western thinking is extremely limited in this area; Western thought is the legacy of Greece, it is all explicit and empirical. The West is uncomfortable with non-empirical, experiential thought. Western thinkers are trained to be doggedly skeptical about anything that cannot be tested in the laboratory or argued through in mathematically logical terms. And of course, things that inhabit the world of spirit are not directly amenable to that process – you will recall our discussion of faith and the limits of knowledge. Westerners who are open to the experience respond deeply when they glimpse their own inner world, when they make contact with this fresh and immediate mode of knowing.

This is the basic mode in Torah. This way of thinking (or knowing) should underlie all our mental activity. The fact that Westerners and Western Jews do not know this is exactly the victory of the Greeks over us – they taught the world to work in empirical, measurable, expressible terms and to doubt and disparage the reality of the transcendent. But as Jews we *live* in it. Now you see Jews enthusiastic about meditation – moved at discovering the higher mode because it is a new and amazing thing for them; but it is the beginning of the process of real Torah development.

Let us look briefly into the Torah theory of knowledge in order to approach this inner faculty more closely.

The mind comprises an outer, more earthbound layer, and an inner, more elevated core. Concerning the inner knowledge, the *da'at*, the Talmud states: "He who has it has everything; he who does not have it, what does he have?"

This faculty is capable of deciding correctly even when the sides of a question appear evenly weighted: it is that unique ability of a person great in Torah to define the correct course of action even when the options seem balanced; it goes far beyond the merely arithmetical.

Many words and much clumsy explanation are needed to convey it, yet when it is grasped, it is fundamental and obvious. A crude analogy would be teaching an art or a skill: no amount of words can convey the nuances of style that add up to that skill. But the instructor talks and demonstrates in order that the student gets *close enough* so that he eventually gets the idea almost accidentally; when he has it, it is obvious and never lost. (Of course it will take him great effort to teach it to another student.) The very definition of this faculty is that words are irrelevant to it.

A useful way to approach this inner wisdom is by exclusion – to understand which parts of the mind are *not* included in it. The classic presentation of this idea is Rabbi Dessler's; he puts it like this:

There are two parts to the mind – the *mabat ha'chitzoni*, the "outer eye," and the *mabat ha'pnimi*, the "inner eye." The "outer eye" is easily defined: it is the part of the mind that grasps the world through the five senses, and it includes the rational or logical faculty. It deals with the finite, the measurable, the arithmetical, the logical. Anything that this faculty can grasp can be expressed in words, tested and proved. Perfect communication can be achieved between people at this level. Everything in the physical world is essentially accessible to this form of knowledge, and a machine can duplicate its functions (often more efficiently than the human).

The aspect of consciousness that is not included in this definition comprises the "inner eye," the deeper wisdom. It is intrinsic knowledge. It grasps things *as they are* and *because they are,* not because they can be measured or proved or expressed. No machine could ever contain this knowledge. Things known externally are simply registered; things known internally are not registered, they are the knowledge itself.

In Torah, knowledge means intimate communion, intimate marriage. The inner mind and its knowledge are inextricably bound. The mystics say that if you know something with the external mind and it proves to be false, it is simply deleted from the mind, but if something grasped by the inner mind proved to be false, *you would cease to exist.* (Think about it; what would you be if the consciousness of your own existence turned out to be false?)

The elements that are held in this knowledge are the most important: knowledge of one's own existence (this is the primary knowledge); knowledge of the present; knowledge of one's own free will; the grasp of meaning; the grasp of intrinsic right and wrong; and ultimately, this is the vessel of consciousness of a transcendent reality (recall that one of the Divine names is "I").

None of these critically important issues can be proved. And although you may know them most profoundly, they cannot easily be put into words.

How are these areas to be examined and refined if they cannot be proved or expressed? How can one begin to think about them? The answer is this: just as the external mind must be used to grasp those things that are accessible to it, so too the inner mind must be used for its own material. Using one of these modes for the material of the other is a recipe for failure.

In a classic illustration, Rabbi Dessler suggests that the external mind is like a camera. A camera can take a picture of anything in the world *except the camera itself.* The outer mind's logical, arithmetical, finite eye can never be focused on the inner zone. It must always be focused on the external world, and the intrinsic wholesome faculty of the inner mind must be used to grasp its own existence and facets.

I know that I exist *intrinsically,* axiomatically. I do *not need* any particular sensory input to be aware that I exist. I simply know it, most profoundly and powerfully. One who cannot feel, taste, hear, see or smell is most certainly not without consciousness of his own existence. The contents of this area are first principles. If proof is attempted, it collapses.

Meditation is a building of this faculty. Here too, the words are necessarily misleading. Some who teach meditation teach that one must "switch off the mind" to meditate. But "switching off" the mind is not meditation, it is unconsciousness! Relaxing perhaps, but not meditation. Meditation is a *"switching on"* of the mind. What is meant is to switch off the *external mind,* that is *exactly* the way to activate the inner mind. Since the two tend to conflict, the inner seeking to transcend and the outer seeking to hold in the finite, the battle must be stopped before inner knowledge can flourish.

A classic experience that frees the inner mind is abject terror. Fear suitably paralyzes the outer faculty and a rich experience of existence remains. Equally powerful is the ecstasy of being alive felt for a few moments after experiencing mortal danger. A sage once described the experience of being drawn under the waves in the ocean until he almost lost consciousness. At that desperate moment, he broke the surface and gasped a life-saving breath of air. "A breath of pure *da'at*," is the way he described the superconsciousness of being alive when that simple fact was critically held in the balance.

Although the modes of inner and outer wisdom are in conflict, they are bonded together. External facts are not simply registered in machine-like fashion; once they are registered they are also *grasped, understood,* as part of consciousness. External facts enter the external mind; thereafter the inner mind takes them in, bonds with them, *knows* them intimately.

You may grapple with a problem for hours and not see the solution, or sometimes even see the solution but not understand it, not *connect* with it. Typically, you give up in exhaustion and go to sleep. And often, you wake with "I've got it!" This happens because powerful logical thought may *shrink* the inner faculty; however, sleep *stills* the driving of the logical, the limited, and the inner can flourish. It is *because* you stop thinking about the problem that you understand it.

Wisdom requires both faculties: external information gleaned from interaction with the world and analyzed clearly by the calculating function of the brain, and the inner grasp of that information that no calculator could ever do. Information without understanding is not human. Understanding without information is impossible – bonding must occur *to something.* This is the meaning of the Mishna: "If there is no *da'at* (inner knowledge) there is no *bina* (logical, analytical knowledge); if there is no *bina* there is no *da'at.*" This formulation means that each has value when they are together.

In a culture that spews out words constantly, the only way to develop depth is by learning how to be silent. As you have said, words, no matter how perfectly chosen and eloquent, are only fragments of meaning. The most significant moments demand silence; words would intrude then, reduce the moment to a parody of itself. Real communication is possible only with one who has his or her own inner knowledge; when two people have such an understanding, they can communicate. If words are needed, there will probably be a lack of communication. And if many words are needed, the attempt is probably hopeless.

A well-known anecdote is repeated in the yeshiva world concerning two of the last generation's Torah leaders. One arrived to visit the other during the festival of Succot, they met in the *succah,* exchanged greetings and sat in complete silence for the entire duration of the visit; and those who were present describe the intensity of the communication that took place.

The Maharal explains that Moses could not speak well because of this problem. The conventional understanding is that he suffered from a speech defect, an imperfection. But the opposite is true: he could not speak well because of his *perfection.* He was living at a level where things are grasped as they are, grasped by pure *da'at.* Things grasped thus could never be shrunk into words. Moses knew things as they are, far beyond the level of the words that may attempt to describe them. To do so would be to reduce Divine knowledge to a finite level. Then, after the *miracle* of the giving of the Torah at Sinai *which was exactly that:* a condensing of the Divine word somehow, miraculously, into the words of Torah, Moses spoke normally (as the verse states: "These are the words which *Moses spoke"*).

A potent illustration of the constricting effect of speech is found in the Talmud's description of the process of birth. The fetus learns Torah with an angel; during the months of pregnancy the unborn child learns the wisdom of the entire Torah. When the child begins the process of transition into the world, he receives a blow on the mouth and forgets all that he knew. This is strange: why a blow on the mouth? Surely a blow on the head would be more appropriate? The Maharal explains that the blow on the mouth is the *gift of speech.* A blow, mystically, is always a challenge to grow, to develop a new faculty or level, and *on the mouth* because that is the organ of speech. As the child gains the nucleus of the ability to formulate finite words, he begins to lose the clear, intimate higher knowledge. Not just simultaneously with acquiring the gift of speech, but *because* of the gift of speech – being articulate means being able to shrink things into definite, bounded form; and that is exactly the opposite of being able to expand things into their unlimited essence. Only miracle can reconnect the two – miracle, or the work of silence.

When a great pain is experienced, it may be extremely difficult for the one who bears it to speak about the events that caused that pain or about the pain itself. Very many who survived the last century's European destruction did not speak about it subsequently. Many children and grandchildren of those survivors will tell you that their parents or grandparents would never speak about their experience. It is usually understood that their silence is due to the fact that the experience was so painful; the victim does not wish to re-open that area of his or her life because the pain would be too great. That part of the person's life has been closed and must be kept closed.

But that is not the reason for their silence. There is something much deeper here. The reason that those people remain silent about their experience is *because it cannot be put into words* – it is too deep for words. No words could ever convey the enormity of what happened; it is beyond human ability to express. The horror transcends human grasp, therefore it cannot be expressed. Those people are not silent because they do not wish to talk about what happened, they are silent because *they cannot talk about it.*

Any amount of talking would shrink the experience to the proportions of the words used to describe it, and that would be a gross misrepresentation of the depth of the experience itself. Only silence is appropriate; only silence can begin to be an appropriate vessel for things that are inexpressible.

This idea has a reverse expression, too: the therapy for one suffering a pain too great to bear may be to talk about it. For one who has been through a traumatic experience that is causing ongoing anguish, speaking it out may help. The sheer enormity of the anguish, the very fact that it seems greater than that which could possibly be survived, is a central part of the suffering; that is exactly why it feels overwhelming. If a sensitive listener draws that person into discussing the trauma, if the pain is expressed in words, it may begin to shrink to the proportions of the words. What was beyond expression has been expressed; what was beyond measure has been given some semblance of measure.

In spiritual learning, if you understand something deep and particularly meaningful and you speak it out immediately, you risk losing it. If it is still fresh and new, if it has not yet made total contact with the inner being, if it is still alive with all its inexpressible depth and you put it into words, you are in danger of losing that depth.

Rabbi Simcha Zissel Ziv, a master of the *mussar* movement, once waited twenty-five years before sharing a particular insight with his students because he wanted to be sure that it had made genuine contact with his own mind and consciousness before he dared shrink it into words. He knew that you must wait until the experience of novelty has settled, until the idea has done its work of affecting the inner being, before you dare to speak it out.

We are in real danger of losing the ability to think beyond words; too often we actually think in dialogue – saying something to ourselves, listening to the words we have said, replying in words. But that is a desperately low level of thinking and understanding.

Silence develops the deep well of the personality; it is an obligation, not a luxury. There must always be more than can be expressed. No matter how much is revealed, there must be infinitely more. Someone who describes himself fully during his first conversation with you must be very superficial indeed. A real relationship is one with a person who has a depth that cannot be expressed, certainly not in a few minutes of talking. As you get to know such a person you begin to discover that there is far more than you realized at first, and as your relationship deepens you continually discover more. At every level you find more than you knew previously, and the relationship is an endless process of discovery. Human essence lies in the unrevealed dimension; one who lives entirely in the revealed, within the confines of words, has forgotten this basic idea.

There is an incident in King David's life that illustrates this. When he brought the Holy Ark up to Jerusalem, the verses describe King David dancing before it in joy and ecstasy in the most expressive way.

When he approaches his home, his wife Michal, daughter of Saul, objects and chastises him for conducting himself in such unbecoming fashion in public. She accuses him of having been immodestly exposed in the eyes of the maidservants and the people, *"k'echad ha'reikim"*– "like one of the empty fellows." David responds by explaining that for God's honor his own is not to be considered; he tells her that he would like to do even more: in the eyes of those same maidservants "I will be even lighter than this." The subsequent verses indicate that because of her improper criticism, Michal had no child until the day of her death; a close reading of the text indicates that in fact she died in childbirth.

What is the meaning of this exchange? What exactly was Michal's concern? What was David's reply? Was she concerned because he revealed himself bodily, physically – perhaps his ankles? His knees? All Torah has unlimited depth; what is beneath the surface here?

David was not revealing his ankles; that was not the problem. He was revealing his *neshama,* his soul. Dance is a particularly powerful expression of internality; one can tell if a man has depth from the way he walks, all the more so from dance. David's dance must have been pure spiritual fire. David's dancing revealed so much that Michal felt he had emptied himself entirely, exposed his entire soul in those Jerusalem streets – *k'echad ha'reikim,* like one of the *empty* fellows. She felt that he had emptied himself entirely, *and that is never allowed.* There is a deep obligation, the deepest obligation, to retain far more depth than one reveals. If all has been made explicit, where is the connection to the inexhaustible well of the spirit?

One who is entirely expressed is entirely within the world; he has lost his connection to the endless.

Michal was a woman great beyond our grasp, and she felt she had seen to the very depth of David's soul. But David's reply is: "I shall go further than this" – in other words: "Do you think that what you saw revealed is *all there is?* There is *far more* unrevealed than what you perceived! I have not forgotten that obligation of nurturing depth that concerns you. But you have misjudged my depth." That is how surely it was hidden; that is how deep it was.

(Perhaps we can speculate on the reason that her death occurred in childbirth: at her sublime level, she had accused David of emptying himself, of disconnecting himself from the source of life by revealing all of his soul in the world. The measure-for-measure result of that error was that in bringing a life to the world *she* was emptied of life; she was able to reveal a soul in the world only at the cost of detaching from the source of life. Her entire life was poured into the child; none remained.)

Suffering

"Buddhism aims to eliminate suffering. Judaism seems to see suffering as integral to growth. Yom Kippur, one could say, positively enshrines suffering – ennobling the very thing Buddhism seeks to extirpate! There is a fundamental gap here."

David,

Joy is the purpose of the Creation. In Jewish living, we are looking forward not just to the termination of suffering, but to absolute joy. You must be aware of the prophet's vision of the Messianic era in which each of us will sit "under his vine and under his fig tree." Why those two fruits in particular? No detail in Torah is accidental. The uniqueness of the fig is that it has no inedible parts, no skin or pips, unlike other fruit; it is all taste. This is the symbol of unadulterated pleasure. (Grapes and wine always refer to the deeper wisdom.) Our vision of the next world is one of pure joy; this world is the opportunity to earn that state, and as we saw in our discussion of happiness, it is possible to feel some of that joy within the work of this world. Part of the meditation of self-awareness in *mussar* is to experience the next-world self even while in this one; people of spiritual greatness know and feel that world as they live.

In Chassidic circles the story of Rabbi Mendel of Tzefat is told. Rabbi Mendel was an exemplary *tzaddik* who lived in Tzefat more than a century ago. One day his wife came home from the town market and told her husband that people were saying that the Messiah had arrived – someone was blowing a shofar and excitement was building. Rabbi Mendel arose from his volume of Talmud, went to the window, put his head out, paused, and returned to his learning, saying: "No, the Messiah has not come – nothing has changed." He could sense that the air was unchanged; the Messiah could not have come. Now the Chassidim ask this question: why did he have to put his head out of the window? Why could he not simply sense the atmosphere where he sat? They answer: because where he was, in his home, in his own private inner domain, there could be no change – that domain was already on the Messianic level and no change would be palpable there.

"Yom Kippur, one could say, positively enshrines suffering as a noble institution..."

This is an error. Yom Kippur is not about suffering; it is a disciplining of the body so that the soul can fly. Remember that it is a *festival.* Abstaining from the five areas of bodily pleasure as we do on Yom Kippur is a temporary asceticism to free the soul. We fast to allow the soul to distract itself from its bodily envelope to an unusual degree for one day. Note that this is rare: the normative Torah way is to engage the physical, not to abjure it, as we have discussed at length – the Jewish path to soul elevation leads through the physical. On other festivals we give wings to the soul by expressing the physical – eating and drinking; on Yom Kippur we do the opposite. For one day in the year we become ascetic and celibate; we enter the monastic, if you like, and immerse ourselves in a night and day of virtually uninterrupted meditation. Even today in our relatively weak generation, some still practice the custom of *standing* in the meditation of *tefilla* (prayer) and *teshuva* (repentance) throughout the entire night and day, more than twenty-four hours of focused concentration.

Tisha b'Av (the Ninth of Av) is a fast in sadness, that is a suffering. We remember the eras of destruction and lament our failures. The suffering of the body sets the tone for repentance. Yom Kippur, too is for the work of repentance, but it is a day of joy; it is a day of atonement when the scars of sin are healed – what could be more joyous? In the yeshiva world they put it this way: "On Tisha b'Av, who could eat? On Yom Kippur, who needs to?"

On Yom Kippur we are sustained in a different way. My teacher once said (in Yiddish it sounds better): "On Yom Kippur we eat the fast...."

You may know that there are five levels to the soul; five layers that make contact with the body through the lowest of the five. On Yom Kippur we are lifted out of the body in all five dimensions; hence the five types of abstinence or detachment that we practice on that day.

Let me give just a beginning of insight into the lowest: we do not wear leather shoes. What does this mean? What does it achieve? You are aware by now that every detail of a mitzva reflects depth; what is reflected here?

You will notice that whenever a complete transcendence is experienced, it is facilitated by removing the shoes. The key is this: the shoes are to the body what the body is to the soul. Just as the shoes carry the body over rough ground, the body carries the soul through the world. Just as only the very lowest part of the body, the foot, engages the shoe, only the very lowest part of the soul (called the *nefesh*) engages the body – the rest of the soul's layers remain "above" or outside the body. Recall that the feet are the lowest parts in the deeper sense – the serpent's bite is on the heel; the heel is dead even in life, states the Talmud. Leather shoes have laws in common with a corpse – the hands must be washed after touching them.

When the priests serve in the Temple, they wear no shoes. Moses must remove his shoes when God speaks to him. A mourner may not wear shoes – he is expressing empathy with a soul that has left its body; the action that reflects this most closely is the removal of shoes. Contact with the higher world that necessitates detachment from the lower world is expressed by the removal of shoes. I am sure you can work out the depth behind the startling statement of the Talmud that one who has no shoes is as if dead and buried.

This also gives an insight into the mitzva of *chalitza* – the mitzva fulfilled by a widow who cannot marry her brother-in-law in the process of *yibum,* or levirate marriage, in which she removes his shoe. When a man dies childless, the Torah mandates that his wife marry his brother; if the brother will not marry her, she must remove his shoe to dissolve the obligation. What is happening here? The deeper understanding is that such a marriage brings down a reincarnation of the deceased brother; the widow marries the living brother, a spark of the same root soul, to bring a child into the world for her late husband. This child is in fact an incarnation of the deceased; you will recall that when Tamar married Er who died childless, she went on to marry Onan, his brother, in fulfilment of this mitzva. But he too died childless, and she then married Judah their father (going to the family root for the same reason). The deeper commentaries deal with the obvious problem – if there were *two* previous childless husbands, which would be incarnated? And as I am sure you are aware, Tamar gave birth to twins (Peretz and Zerach).

But if her brother-in-law refuses to marry her, she removes his shoe. She is saying to him in very clear Torah terms: "You are refusing to marry me and bring down a child for your brother; you are keeping a body and soul apart." What clearer image could there be to express this than the separating of foot and shoe?

So when we remove our shoes on Yom Kippur we are separating body from soul at a certain level, we rise out of the constraints of the physical. That is the reason for the joy of Yom Kippur; it is an affliction of the body for the freeing of the soul.

"Buddhism aims to eliminate suffering."

From a Jewish perspective, this is not the primary aim. We see the elimination of suffering as the result of a perfected world; a consequence more than a goal.

Avoiding suffering may be inadequate as an absolute goal. You can see that there are many ways to avoid suffering that are not intrinsically good. By avoiding certain distressing situations we may avoid suffering, but these means may be wrong. The point is this: we need to eradicate suffering at root, not at the level of a symptom. Therefore the aim must be a perfect world, not primarily the avoidance of suffering. The absence of suffering that is the assured result of human perfection will be the real and good state.

We do not seek to avoid suffering as our primary, overarching goal; rather we seek spiritual perfection. That will lead to the absence of suffering as a consequence. So we set before our eyes the goal of fulfilling our obligations. The result will include a sure end to suffering, but that is not our first concern.

I would suggest an analogy from the practice of medicine: the physician's goal is not always properly the alleviation of suffering as a primary act. In fact, more than occasionally he must *inflict* some degree of suffering in order to achieve health – a deeper and more lasting freedom from suffering.

Suffering must be eliminated by reaching for a state of balance in the world, not by focusing on the elimination of suffering as primary. The wise physician seeks to diagnose and treat the real pathology, not the symptom. Of course he is sensitive to the symptoms and of course he will alleviate their distress if he can, but that is not his primary aim. And if he must choose between defeating the symptom or the disease, he will choose the latter, and even at the cost of the former.

Does this mean that Judaism "enshrines suffering?" Of course not. Now if Buddhism seeks to end suffering by bringing about a spiritual balance in the world, we need have no argument. The argument will be over what is the correct way to that balance, and we have discussed some of that already.

Four Questions

David,

In the light of what we have shared thus far in our journey, I have some questions for you. I do not mean to enter a debate; our goal throughout this correspondence has been to say something meaningful about Judaism in response to a Buddhist experience, not to debate the two and not to attempt a critique of Buddhism. I raise these particular points for your consideration because I think they will bring out essential features of Judaism in contrast to Buddhism.

1. I would like to know why Buddhism omits certain elements that are fundamental in Judaism. Two that come to mind are honoring parents and the field that corresponds to positive commandments in general.

Honoring parents is one of the Ten Commandments, as you know. I notice that it is not one of the basic Buddhist precepts (although I am sure it is included somewhere in Buddhist morality). Why is this fundamental in Judaism but not in Buddhism? I would like to probe this issue by suggesting an explanation.

Let us start by asking why honoring parents is fundamental in Judaism. And why is it listed in the *first* five of the Ten Commandments? The Ten Commandments are divided into two sections, the first five relating man to God (faith, the prohibition of idolatry, Shabbat...), the second five relating man to man (the prohibitions of killing, stealing, false testimony...) The problem is why honoring parents is included in the first five, those that mandate man's correct relationship with God. Surely honoring one's parents is simply another case of dealing correctly with people, in this case the particular people that are one's parents?

But there is a fundamental Torah message here. Beyond the obvious correctness in showing appropriate gratitude and honor to parents, there is something more. Relating to your parents turns you to focus on your point of origin, your source. The teaching here is to defer from yourself (the immature instinct) to the cause of your existence. Rooted here is a deep training to follow things to their source; your parents are your proximate cause and you need to learn to look to them in a training that sensitizes you to the source of things, to appreciate that all things emanate from a prior cause. Nothing in the world causes itself. The effort of looking to causes will train the mind to look to causes of those causes too, and ultimately the sensitized mind will trace all things back to their root Cause. When we honor parents we begin the process of reaching back to the original Parent. That is why honoring parents is one of the Ten Commandments, and that is why it is located in the first five, not the second. This, too, is why it is the *last* of the first five; it is the link between man-God and man-man relationships.

This has a clear parallel in *mussar*. In *mussar* teaching, gratitude is classed as a primary quality of good character. Why is this? In what way is gratitude more important than other refinements of character? The depth here is that gratitude is a training to see source. When I thank you, I acknowledge you as the source of the favor I have received from you. (The Hebrew word for "thanking" is the same as for "admitting" – thanking you is my *admission* that I am not the cause of this favor; you are.) One who feels no gratitude admits nothing outside of himself as his benefactor; one who feels gratitude is turned to the source of things. One who always turns to the source of things will find God. Gratitude is not just a refinement of character, it is a training in seeking God.

So the depth of the commandment to honor parents is deeply related to discovering God. Now could it be that Buddhism does not place this as fundamental exactly because it does not relate to God? Is this a deflection of the obligation to follow the path back to root and thence to Root, since Buddhism does not talk of an ultimate Root? If Buddhist consciousness relates only to present experience, it will have no place for tracing things beyond present experience in an effort to discover an ultimate cause. What do you say?

I notice that Buddhism does have an obligation to honor one's teacher. (In Torah there is a close link between the obligation of honoring parents and honoring one's Torah teacher.) Is this because venerating sages in Buddhism takes you back to the Buddha, but honoring parents takes you back to the first parents and thence surely to God – so this is absent in Buddhism?

2. I note that the Buddhist precepts are all phrased in the negative – do not kill, do not steal, do not lie, do not use intoxicants and so on. Are there *positive* precepts in Buddhism? This is a critical question, because in Jewish thinking it is the positive commandments that build the world.

The commandments are divided into positive (know God, give charity, take the *lulav*, eat *matza*...) and negative (do not kill, do not steal, do not eat certain foods, do not desecrate the Shabbat...) Now the negative commandments are a protection for the world; that is, they prevent damage to the fabric of reality – killing, stealing, eating forbidden foods, breaking Shabbat all cause enormous spiritual damage and these commandments proscribe causing such damage. But they do not build anything; this is fundamental to understand. Only the positive commandments build – each of them has a source in the spiritual world; each performance of one of these commandments "goes to its source" and brings down a flow of energy to the world. The positive commandments are manifestations of love, the negative commandments are manifestations of fear.

An analogy may be useful: in a love relationship, say a marriage, there are positive and negative obligations. The positive ones build the love (doing acts of kindness for the beloved, giving to the beloved), the negative ones simply prevent damage (not being unfaithful in any way, not harming the beloved). The *entire* purpose of the relationship lies in the positive, not the negative – no one marries in order not to be unfaithful! Each act of love builds the love; each act of abstinence from treachery hardly *builds* the love, all it does is protect what has been built. Try eliciting praise from your wife because you do not commit an act of betrayal!

This, incidentally, is the depth behind the halachic concept of *"aseh doche lo ta'aseh"* – a positive commandment renders null a simultaneous negative commandment when the two are in conflict (although punishment for the negative is ordinarily greater than for the failure to fulfill a positive). An example would be the affixing of woollen *tzitzit* (fringes) to a linen garment: ordinarily, combining wool and linen is forbidden, but fulfilling the positive mitzva of *tzitzit* renders the prohibition null when they are simultaneous. Again, the rationale is that the positive actions define the relationship, they are its reason and purpose. The negative are only protections. (The reason that *transgression* of a negative commandment is more serious than the omission of a positive is because *destroying* something good is generally worse than simply not having built it – an act of disloyalty in a relationship is far worse than the omission of an act that affirms loyalty.)

I hope this is clear. The negative commandments ensure an intact world, they guard it from breakdown. They are essential, *but they are not the reason we are here.* The negative commandments prevent us from doing harm, but that does not build the spiritual world. Desisting from damaging the world is fine and necessary, of course, but Torah is more than that. Torah effects connection of the world with its transcendent source; that is the path of the Jew. If Buddhism teaches the idea of not harming the human and the manifest world, that is fine, but it is not Torah. The Jewish people have another role, beyond the primary care that is necessary not to damage the world. We have another zone of operation, another mission. We represent another crew on this construction site.

The Torah posits a set of commandments for mankind in general; all of these are in fact negative commandments (the Buddhist precepts are generally close to these). A non-Jew is not required to take a *lulav* or to eat *matza*. But our *unique spiritual expression* lies in these commandments; to miss this is to miss our role and purpose.

3. Why does Buddhism focus on experience and yet talk, for example, of many lives? Do modern American Buddhists claim to experience their incarnations? How is reincarnation relevant to immediate

experience? Of course it is important; there is an entire body of Torah sources dealing with it. But my point is that this would seem to be an aspect of teaching that must be accepted, not experienced, by relative beginners. So why accept teaching beyond experience here and yet be opposed to that process elsewhere?

4. The law of karma – surely this concept implies a conscious Universe? How are all actions and their consequences brought full circle, particularly over many lifetimes, if the Universe is an unconscious, unthinking entity? It is axiomatic in Torah that all actions and events play themselves out to perfect balance in the fullness of time, but that is because the infinite Wisdom that is the soul of the Universe invests all actions and events with meaning and moral content. Is karma not really a moral thread, a theme of justice drawn through space and time? How can you invoke this idea within a non-sentient Universe? When you talk of karma have you not come back to God?

Akiva,
What do you know: I have answers to the Four Questions!

I sent your questions to a fellow student of mine at the Zen center who is now a Buddhist priest, and here's my attempt to interpret and augment her answers. (My comments follow a quote from hers in each case.)

1. Honoring parents:

"Practising the precepts helps keep the mind clear from complications and fetters and hindrances. In a deep sense practising the precepts is practising peace and liberation. It is not to become a good child or a good person or a good Buddhist; it is to actualize the true nature..."

A Buddhist wouldn't really understand the question of why honoring parents is not a primary precept: Buddhists would say that they honor all sentient beings. This is part of learning to see everyone as interrelated, and penetrating blood relationships and other attachments to see everyone as both unique and non-special at the same time.

This is best achieved by honoring everyone. This doesn't mean that you have no special relationships. It means you recognize that we all have a common source, and you do so by extending compassion in all directions.

A second reason, and one of my own inference, is that Buddhism urges a "devotion to the Way" so complete that one sheds all previous attachments in one's determination to find enlightenment. It's said that the Buddha himself fled his princely palace upon his first exposure to human suffering, and that on this quest to find true spiritual liberation, or enlightenment, he left his wife and children as well. (After achieving enlightenment he sent for them, and his wife became his first female disciple.)

Buddhism has a significant "home-leaver" tradition: those who enter monasteries or go on extended pilgrimages to Zen masters must shed attachments of all kinds. This is a reflection of the single-minded devotion with which Siddartha Gautama shed all earthly attachments in an effort to find and overcome the source of all suffering

(Honoring parents may not be a fundamental teaching in Buddhism, but it is there; for example there is this from the Maha Mangala Sutta: "Service to mother and father, support of wife and sons, and straightforward work – this is supreme good fortune." It is supreme good fortune because it is selfless service, the very foundation of a Buddhist life.)

2. The negative phrasing of Buddhist precepts:

"Restraint of the habitual, conditioned self is essential to seeing and knowing the true heart and restraint is doing good. As one restrains or lives the not committing harm one finds goodness. We are not the owners of good anything for there is no thing to own or get; it is more a way of discovery. By clearing the mind, by practising the precepts the mind clears, and we see the indescribable wondrous dharma."

I don't think the precepts are all negatively phrased. The Teaching of all Buddhas is one of the most highly regarded teachings across all schools of Buddhism:

Refrain from all evil,
Practise all that is good,
Purify your mind:
This is the teaching of all Buddhas.

This is positive in its nature. Similarly, the three pure precepts:

Embrace and Sustain Forms and Ceremonies
Embrace and Sustain All Good
Embrace and Sustain All Beings

and the Three Refuges, or Three Treasures:

I take refuge in buddha
I take refuge in dharma
I take refuge in sangha.

The Ten Grave Precepts are *phrased negatively. This is because a great deal of restraint and discipline is required in order to let distinctions fall away, and to live an upright life. This is what "restraint is doing good" means.*

A disciple of the Buddha does not kill
A disciple of the Buddha does not take what is not given
A disciple of the Buddha does not misuse sexuality
A disciple of the Buddha does not lie
A disciple of the Buddha does not intoxicate body or mind of self or others
A disciple of the Buddha does not speak of the faults of others
A disciple of the Buddha does not praise self at the expense of others
A disciple of the Buddha is not possessive of anything
A disciple of the Buddha does not harbor ill will
A disciple of the Buddha does not disparage the Three Treasures

3. You asked: "Why does Buddhism focus on experience and yet talk, for example, of many lives?"

"The three pure precepts are the source of all the laws of Buddha and like all phenomena arise in the moment, i.e. not committing harm is activity in time, not a fixed view. Deeds, words and thoughts are phenomena and abide by the laws of phenomena. All phenomena are created in our minds by imputation or concepts, all phenomena arise co-dependently and all phenomena are just this, just perfect, just now."

I believe what's being said here is that all of reality arises in the moment. Actions arise and fall away, but views are just views, and in being fixed are illusory. Views are staked out and clung to. So whether or not we believe in reincarnation is, on one level, irrelevant. More than that, harmful even to entertain because it then becomes a fixed belief, a hook on which to hang perceptions of reality, and that is to become fixed in a fluid Universe. What is being said is that whether or not we believe in something, all phenomena arise and fall away. Reincarnation is not an "accepted teaching," it is both an idea and a metaphor – the metaphor being our need to experience things over and over again until we attain the Way.

This addresses the Buddhist notion of karma. I do not know of Buddhists who experience past lives. I can tell you that karma is a kind of cause and effect: the cumulative effect of the momentum of our actions across time and space, the establishment of a pattern of existence that benefits or has the potential to harm ourselves and other beings. In the same way that a butterfly gently flapping its wings can contribute to the atmospheric conditions necessary to create a hurricane, so our actions reverberate over immeasurable spans of time and space in ways that are often too subtle for us to detect.

In the time of the historical personage that was the Buddha there was a strong belief in reincarnation. Buddha said that his enlightenment brought to him the realization that one progressed on the Path over many lifetimes, and that enlightenment and the end of suffering meant a cycling out of the realm of earthly existence. This was seen as a good thing, and this is why many attribute to Buddhism a kind of nihilist bent.

Whether or not one experiences a multitude of lifetimes, what one learns, on a scientific level, and what Buddhist practitioners in the earliest days understood, was that some aspect of us goes on: not just our actions, but our chemicals, our molecules remain, imprinted with the effects of our actions and the actions of others that have affected us. I believe you're right: you can't really experience a multitude of lifetimes. What you can experience is a vast perspective on the consequences of actions and attitudes, stretching from long before your existence to long after you're gone.

(It may be more accurate to say that Buddhism requires a constant, open and rigorous examination and verification of belief, than to say it rejects all belief. The Buddha did enjoin his followers not to accept anything whole cloth until they had verified it for themselves. This has led to the popular misconception that "Buddhists don't believe in anything.")

"So why accept teaching beyond experience here and yet be opposed to that process in Judaism?"

I don't and I'm not. I do, however, see the truth of teachings in both traditions on both a literal and a metaphorical level. For example, though I have trouble believing in the physical occurrence of, say the Ten Plagues, I have no trouble believing in their psychological and cultural equivalent. Historical accuracy matters less, one could argue, than the lessons drawn from the depiction of history.

4. The law of karma implying a conscious Universe:

I have not received an answer to this question, apart from a suggestion that we look together at a foundational text of contemporary Zen.

I believe what we have discussed already is relevant here as well – the "laws of Buddha" are not laws that Buddha handed down; they are the inherent Buddha nature in all things.

And finally, in general response, she says:

"Essentially... there is no measurement in the Buddha-Dharma; what could we use to do that? '...the sound that issues from the striking of emptiness is an endless and wondrous voice that resounds before and after the fall of the hammer.' (Dogen)

Many blessings to all beings in all worlds."

I hope this is helpful.

David,
Thanks for your answers to the four questions. (I shall not pass over them. The real question is: where is the wise son?)

Some of the statements you quote are very open; I imagine they might be of more use to the initiate than the novice. Some appear inaccurate or at least inscrutable: "...*all phenomena are... just perfect*" – what does this mean? An evil act (certainly a phenomenon) is surely not "just perfect" (even if the onlooker or victim has risen above the act's potential to cause suffering by virtue of a clear mind). If a Buddhist must "refrain from all evil and practise all that is good," there are obviously evil and good phenomena; if all is already "just perfect" the moral distinction could never be made.

But I am going to refrain from analyzing more of what you say in keeping with our goal of avoiding frank debate; my purpose in probing these issues was only to bring out a few more fundamental Jewish ideas.

Elephants

Akiva,
There is an elephant in the room.

We have not discussed this elephant yet. We've discussed almost everything else.

The elephant I refer to is not my learning from Buddhism. It is the fact that I am now exploring new avenues in Judaism, guided by you, an Orthodox rabbi.

If you "succeed" in turning me away from Zen back toward the riches of the religion of my birth and I become a happy, well-adjusted Reform Jew, will you consider yourself to have failed? Or if I join the Renewal movement, will you think I have simply changed costumes? If I go to one of the institutes now teaching Jewish meditation techniques, or trendy seminars on the Kabbala, will you find this mission worthwhile or a failure, a waste of your time or a learning experience for us both?

I found an essential connection to the Divine as I sat in meditation. I don't think any course of Jewish study could have opened the door as widely, shone the light as brightly on my Jewish foundations, as Zen did. There I encountered what Judaism had never managed to show me. You say that it is all there in Judaism; I have read your letters, I have seen the tip of the iceberg of your knowledge, and I believe you. You have shown me a lot. There is beauty and symmetry in so much of what you say. But what happens now? Now that you have shown me these riches, how might I continue to study and understand them? How do I fashion a life around these ideas whose density and richness I can barely fathom?

I study with two Orthodox rabbis whom you know, and they are among my favorite people. They love to teach and to learn. They are not judgmental and they don't presume (or appear) to judge those of us who are not Orthodox. But some of my friends mistrust these gentle guides, thinking that there must be some undetectable proselytizing brainwave they're sending out. Look out! these friends seem to be saying, they're only using you to create a race of Orthodox zombies. Some of these friends, resentful of what they presume to be a persistent condescension on the part of the Orthodox, defend themselves by attacking Orthodoxy. I wonder what good this could possibly do.

I am curious to know how you will determine whether you have succeeded or failed in bringing me more fully into the orbit which you may believe God designed for me. By what yardstick will you measure my Judaism, and your teaching, now that we have taken this journey?

And I want to know, in concrete terms, how I could live my life and bring along the spiritual resonance and sense of purpose I began to find in silent meditation.

I thank you for all you've taught me to this moment.

David,
You know, elephants come in two kinds – African and Indian, and three colors – grey, pink and white.

As far as the colors go, I am afraid this one is the drab grey variety – we are both far too sober to see the pink ones, and alert enough to know that our subject is anything but useless.

The other question is a little harder to decide. With my African background and your Indian experience, we shall have to look more closely.

In South Africa, where I come from, Judaism looks very different than it does in your part of the world. When you ask what my attitude would be if you became committed to one of the newer brands of Judaism, it is hard for me to convey to you how I see that question. Where I grew up there is really only one kind of Judaism, and that is the original, Torah-from-Sinai version, what you call "Orthodox." There is no significant presence of any other kind. I do not mean that all South African Jews are observant; the point I mean to bring out is that they know where the real thing is. They may live up to that standard to a greater or lesser degree, but they have not redefined the standard. They have not changed the rules. There is a certain intellectual honesty in that, and for many of my South African contemporaries any other brand of Judaism is nothing but a sell-out.

It is difficult to show you how deep this goes. We were brought up with a strong awareness of the European and particularly Lithuanian Torah world. Our communities always subscribed to that model; there was never a defection. Learning and observance diminished over the decades of the past century, even drastically, but a certain connection, a clear awareness of Torah, was preserved. There, virtually all agree on what Judaism is; you may identify with it on a personal level to your own degree or you may reject it personally, but even in your rejection you agree on what it is that you are rejecting.

The standard does not inhere in a brand name; the Judaism I mean to discuss with you is the one that is true to its origin at Sinai, the one that has kept us alive through the centuries, the one that predicates its understanding and practice on what it hears from its Source, the one that understands that commandments mean obligations. Any version that bases itself on modernity, convenience, popularity or accessibility at all costs is not what I mean.

You inhabit an environment in which Jewish consciousness is often far removed from its original point of attachment; in your immediate vicinity you can probably find any shade of Judaism you care to seek, and for all I know each claims to be the authentic one. My task is not to unravel that confusion; it is to share Torah with you as deeply as I can. That is all I can do, and that is all that is needed; if it is genuine

Torah it will speak for itself and you will be able to unravel the real from the mistaken without me.

Your destiny placed you where you began, largely detached from the chain of Jewish history among compatriots whose self-awareness is often more American than Jewish, if it is Jewish at all. Your path took you eastwards to discover more of your Jewishness, and you are now following a new turn in that path. My trek out in the African savannah never wandered as far as yours; I never needed to look elsewhere, only to look more deeply.

You came of age in a society that has lost virtually all knowledge of what Judaism is, whose children would not know the genuine article even if they were shown it clearly; among all the options they would probably identify it as the *least* likely to be correct, and that is probably the only thing they would feel certain about. They have been stripped of their language and their very *names*. In South Africa virtually every Jewish child is given a Hebrew name; often his English name is chosen only because it is the closest equivalent – I was called Kevin only because that is close to my real name of Akiva; that English name was given secondarily in deference to a non-Jewish society in which I would have to move. But in America a Jew may ask in all sincerity: "Rabbi, what is the Hebrew for Nicholas?" This Jew thinks he is Nicholas! Do you know that even in the depth of Egyptian exile the Jews never changed their names or their language? Even in Egypt, and *before* they received the Torah. These are basic expressions of Jewishness, a beaten-down persecuted slave people knew that, and this fellow thinks he is Nicholas! And if I should try to explain his tragedy to him, he could not hear me. Of course not; it is Nicholas who is listening, and anyway he has lost his language.

You ask me what my aim is in this attempt to communicate. It is simply to learn Torah and to share that learning with anyone who is ready to hear. It is not formally to prove Judaism (or to disprove Buddhism, for that matter) in the sense of a derived mathematical proof. It is not to attack anyone else's ideas either, no matter how I may feel about them. But I shall tell you this: where there are wrong ideas, the right ones will displace them.

I learned that in Africa too: on the far-flung farms of the bushveld, rainwater is collected in large cisterns or barrels. After a long dry season, the water in these barrels may be turbid and useless. But it is not poured out to make place for the clear water of the next rain; the barrel is too fixed and heavy for that. Rather, when the season's rain comes its fresh water is channelled into the barrel and it simply displaces the old. Enough fresh water will displace all the lifeless liquid until the barrel is filled with pure water as surely as if it had been emptied first.

Who has the strength to empty the heavy barrels? The best I can do is try to fashion a conduit for the rain; to become a channel for that rain to run into any barrel that has not yet rusted shut.

What should you do in practice? I would not have presumed to tell you had you not asked directly. Learn Torah assiduously with full concentration, full-blooded Torah with no "ism" appended. Fulfill the mitzvot as best you can, grow gradually in their understanding and practice. Attach yourself to a teacher who is beyond reproach and will not hesitate to tell you the truth, even and especially about yourself; require that of him. What else is there?

As for speaking about the non-Torah Judaisms that abound in your country – that is called political and I decline. I am going to remain impervious to your probing on that subject. What is not clear by now will not become clearer.

I do not know too much about Indian elephants, but I know the African ones quite well. Many trips into the African bush and hours spent watching them have taught me that they are regal creatures who live in the pristine wild, far from human society and unmodified by human husbandry. They are gentle by nature although they may be dangerous when aroused, and despite their mass they can move surprisingly fast. And they are thick-skinned.

Akiva,

I have not come all this way with you to engage you in a political debate. What concerns me, though, is that while I have been trying to form a dynamic and vibrant Jewish practice, you might consider my efforts misguided or worse.

To put it another way, my journey through Buddhism back to Judaism – and all the struggles of my ancestors that predated it – was a path to Jewish practice and worship that confounded the odds, defied centuries of persecution, survived thirty years of indifference to my Jewish origins. I would hate to have come all this way only to be told that I had taken a wrong turn many miles back, that my cause was lost, that my spiritual pocket had been picked by knaves claiming to be my guides and companions.

I know Jews of all stripes who consider themselves active, committed and literate. They attend every kind of shul *and their means of Jewish observance vary widely. It goes far deeper than the political, for me, to ask what would constitute a Jewish practice to you.*

David,

Let me try to make it clearer. Start with a community where Torah is learned and kept for its own sake, not for the sake of its adherents; where the people live up to it, not where they make it serve them. You have the sensitivity to discern that; look carefully: do they start by asking what Torah requires of them, or do they start with preconceptions built on Western cultural notions, modern humanistic attitudes, post-modern permissive visions or *any other agenda* than God and His Torah? What are they sure of: that God knows what He is doing, that our great sages throughout history have always been our eyes to objectivity, that Torah emanates from its infinite source through Sinai – or their own personal views?

Anyone whose Judaism is based on the premise of his own comfort, who requires that Judaism accord with his own notions of value or convenience, who is sure that God could not ask anything of him that is difficult or requires courage, is not expressing authentic Judaism *even where his practice happens to accord with normative Torah practice* – his actions may be correct, but his values are not. What did Abraham teach us if not this, that what God asks of us is what we strive to fulfill? Abraham was not afraid to argue with God; his was not a passive, mindless acceptance. Nevertheless, when he was asked to act, the Divine standard is the one he bore, not his own, and even when what was asked of him was an act of sacrifice.

And do not judge the product by its label or the card it carries. To be sure, seek a kosher label, that should be obvious; but it is not enough. Distressing though it may be, many who wear the best of labels are not *spiritual* enough to inspire you.

Make your teachers those who are beyond reproach, unquestionably refined and objective, spiritually dedicated beyond compromise. Would you have settled for less in Buddhism?

Last Letters

Akiva,
It strikes me that much of what you say, as eloquent and layered as it is, can be reduced to this: no matter how fine, how true, how recognizable Zen practice is, it is not Jewish practice. It is not Jewish, and you are.

David,
I think that is well summed up. A Jew does not need anything outside of Judaism, just as a man does not need any woman other than his wife.

"The Torah was commanded to us by Moses, an inheritance of the community of Jacob." In Hebrew the word for inheritance, *morasha,* is close to the word for betrothed, *m'orasa.* The Sages make this play on words: do not say inheritance, say betrothed. The Torah is given to us as a betrothed – we are married to it. Picture the insult to a wife who is told that her charms must be complemented by another woman's; her husband needs that. What kind of marriage is that? Now if the woman is deficient, that is one sort of problem; but if she is absolutely perfect, loyal and beautiful in every way, possessing indescribable depth and refinement of character, and her husband is looking elsewhere, there is something lacking in *him.*

This Jewish husband needs to reveal his wife's beauty. He has been so busy looking around he has failed to see her. He has been struck by an Eastern woman, shall we say, but she is not his. The last place he may think of looking is to the woman by his side, but that is whom he must learn to see.

David, I will admit that my initial prejudice when I entered this correspondence with you was that I would discover in Buddhism that which led a certain sharp Jewish academic, when asked to review the central dogmatic text of a popular "new" form of Judaism and compare it with the age-old Torah-from-Sinai version, to express as: "What's good isn't new, and what's new isn't good."

But from the insight you have presented into Zen Buddhism, at least as practised in the West, it seems that virtually everything you have demonstrated is there in Judaism, as I have tried to show in some detail. Failure to study Torah and keep its commandments, believing these to be unnecessary because Buddhism provides all the teaching and practice that is true and necessary while Judaism does not, is an error so deep that it clearly reflects how distant one who takes that step must be from his Torah roots.

Such a Jew has never realized the depth and beauty of his own; his sterile relationship at a distance has left him unfulfilled. Our generation is the victim of an unusually deep deficiency of genuine Torah education.

You found your way back to the beginnings of Jewish investigation through your Buddhist experience; you doubt that you would have rediscovered your Judaism without it. You have pointed out that in our disaffected age Buddhism appears to be a better preparation for Judaism than Judaism is; in your case that irony is reality. That is your story, and you must live it; in an unconventional way you have come to discover some of the conventions you were never given.

But let us not see that as ideal; we are not going to suggest that route in general. We need to be careful here. If I told you of a person suffering from amnesia who was cured by a severe blow to the head, would you begin recommending blows to the head for amnesiacs? I think you would agree that we should respond to that sort of cure with mixed feelings – we would have to acknowledge that it worked, but we would have serious reservations about prescribing it' as standard therapy.

But there is an issue that bothers me more: what do you do for those who choose amnesia?

Akiva,
In any exploration there is a hint of rebellion.

And in any rebellion, even if it is steeped in pride, there is always a hint of shame. In rebelling, aren't we pushing away that which nourished us?

Even so, the urgency of my spiritual search meant that I would not permit myself to be limited by what others thought was proper. That Zen awakened me to my Jewish neshama *may be sad commentary on the depth of our exile, but it's also something of a new beginning and a happy ending.*

If it truly can be said that many contemporary Jews have "chosen amnesia," then you must begin your outreach by trying to understand the bittersweet freedom of forgetting. You must understand that life, the delicious lightness of its burdens, the sweet simplicity of belonging only to independence and to seeking.

We're reminded each Passover of the child who does not even know what to ask, where to begin. Our wandering is at the very core of who we are, and teachers like you will, I hope, remember that in the grand scheme of things there is only the slightest of differences between us.

With your help and the help of others, I have just barely begun to understand what Judaism is, and what it is to me. I have taken the first steps toward knowledge.

In so doing, I have started over. What Zen has taught me and awakened in me is real and ancient. If what I have found is a precursor to Torah, then I have to take that shard of knowledge and remake from it the vessel of my own Jewish identity. I have to learn Hebrew and study hard, but I must also live in the world. Perhaps this is the greatest truth: each day, in our commitment and our study, in our love of God and our fight against sameness, we have to begin again.

Though I do not understand or unquestioningly accept everything you say, I see the work and the wisdom in it.

We must all begin again, all the time. That is what amnesiacs do, isn't it?

Regards,

David.

Glossary

amida: lit. "standing;" central section of prayer service
Amshenover Rebbe: Rabbi Shimon Shalom Kalish of Amshenov (1883–1954)

Beis Halevi: Rabbi Yosef Dov (Yosha Ber) Soloveitchik of Brisk (1820–1892)
brit: covenant; circumcision

Chafetz Chaim: Rabbi Yisrael Meir Hacohen Kagan of Radin (1840–1933)
chavruta: study partner
Chazon Ish: Rabbi Avraham Yeshaya Karelitz (Lithuania and Bnei Brak, 1878–1953)
chok (pl. chukkim): commandment(s) the reasons for which entirely transcend human understanding

d'veykut: cleaving; intense bonding
da'at: knowledge; deep understanding
derech eretz: correct behavior reflecting good character
Derech Hashem: classic work by Rabbi Moshe Chaim Luzzatto (1707–1746)
din: strict justice

Ethics of the Fathers: Section of Mishna dealing mainly with ethical teachings
etrog: citron; one of the four species held during the festival of Succot

Gaon of Vilna: (gaon: lit. "genius") Rabbi Eliyahu ben Shlomo Zalman of Vilna (1720–1797)
gemara: Talmud, the Oral Law

halacha: Torah law
Hashem: lit. "the Name" of God
havdalah: ceremony marking transition from Sabbath to weekday

kabbala: esoteric Torah wisdom
kashrut: laws of permitted and forbidden foods
kedusha: holiness
Kuzari: Classic debate and argument for Judaism by Rabbi Yehuda Halevi (Spain, c.1080–1145)

lulav: willow branch; one of the four species held during the festival of Succot

Maharal of Prague: Rabbi Yehuda Loewe ben Bezalel of Prague (c.1512–1609)
Maharsha: Rabbi Shmuel Eliezer Eidels (Poland, 1555–1631)
Maimonides: Rabbi Moshe ben Maimon (Rambam) (1135–1204)
matza: unleavened bread
mazal: zodiac element
mechitza: partition between men's and women's sections in synagogue
Midrash: Torah sources which delve deeper than the plain meaning of the Scriptural text
minyan: quorum of ten required for communal prayer
Mishna: the definitive statements of the Oral Law
mitzva (pl. mitzvot): commandment
mussar: the study and practice of Torah character building

nazirite: *(nazir)* one who adopts temporary ascetic status, abstaining from grapes and wine
Nefesh Hachaim: classic work by Rabbi Chaim of Volozhin (1749–1821), disciple of the Vilna Gaon
neshama: soul

Path of the Just *(Mesillat Yesharim):* classic *mussar* work by Rabbi Moshe Chaim Luzzatto (Ramchal) (Italy, 1707–1746)
pidyon ha'ben: mitzva of redemption of firstborn son

Rabbi Chaim Shmulevitz: Rosh Yeshiva of the Mir yeshiva; Mir and Jerusalem (1901–1979)
Rabbi Eliyahu Eliezer Dessler: author of Michtav M'Eliyahu (Russia, London and Ponovez Yeshiva in Bnei Brak; 1891–1954)
Rabbi Elchanan Wasserman: Rosh Yeshiva and Torah leader, Baranowitch (1875–1941); disciple of the Chafetz Chaim
Rabbi Moshe Chaim Luzzatto (Ramchal) author of The Path of the Just *(Mesillat Yesharim)* classic *mussar* work (Italy, 1707–1746)
Rabbi Moshe Feinstein: Rosh Yeshiva and halachic authority (Russia, USA,1895–1986)
Rabbi Samson Raphael Hirsch: Torah leader, Germany (1808–1888)
Rabbi Elazar Menachem Man Shach: Rosh Yeshiva and Torah leader (1894–2001)
Rabbi Simcha Wasserman: (1901–1992) son of Rabbi Elchanan Wasserman
Rabbenu Yona: Rabbi Yona of Gerona, author of Shaarei Teshuva (The Gates of Repentance) (c.1180 – 1263)
Rabbi Simcha Zissel Ziv: the "Alter of Kelm" (1824–1898), leading exponent of *mussar,* disciple of Rabbi Yisrael Salanter
Rabbi Tzadok Ha'Cohen: Rabbi Tzadok Ha'Cohen Rabinowitz (Lublin, 1823–1900)
rachamim: kindness, mercy
Ramban: Rabbi Moshe ben Nachman (1194–1270); Nachmanides
Ramchal: See Rabbi Moshe Chaim Luzzatto
ratzon: desire, will, volition
Rosh Hashana: New Year
Rosh Yeshiva: dean of a Talmudic academy

sefer Torah: Torah scroll
Sfat Emet: Rabbi Yehuda Aryeh Leib Alter of Ger (1847–1903)
Shma Yisrael: statement of God's unity
shofar: ram's horn; sounded on Rosh Hashana
simcha: joy
succah: booth; temporary dwelling used during Succot

Succot: Festival of Tabernacles

Talmud: the Oral Law
tefilla: prayer
tikkun: spiritual "correction," bringing to perfection
Tisha B'Av: ninth of the month of Av; anniversary of the destruction
   of the Temple and other tragedies
Turei Zahav: commentary on the Code of Jewish Law by Rabbi David
   Halevi (1586–1667)
tzaddik (pl. tzaddikim): righteous individual
tzitzit: fringes worn on corners of four-cornered garment

Vilna Gaon: see Gaon of Vilna

yeshiva (pl. yeshivot): academy of Talmudic learning
Yom Kippur: Day of Atonement